Probate Causes and Related Matters

Albert Keating

B.C.L., LL.B., LL.M., B.L.

DUBLIN
ROUND HALL SWEET & MAXWELL
2000

Published in 2000 by
Round Hall Ltd
43 Fitzwilliam Place
Dublin 2, Ireland.

Typeset by
Gilbert Gough Typesetting, Dublin.

Printed by
MPG Books, Cornwall

ISBN 1–85800–190–0

A catalogue record for this book
is available from the British Library.

Preface

The present book, *Probate Causes and Related Matters*, arose out of the alliance formed by the author's two books, *Probate Law and Practice* and *Probate Law and Practice Case Book*. It might very well be called the offspring of the two. *Probate Law and Practice*, being a textbook, had to range over all the material necessary for a textbook and proportionate treatment to each of the areas covered by it. The extent of the treatment given was determined by the degree of judicial attention given to a particular area and by the frequency such area was encountered in practice but controlled by the need to be proportionate. *Probate Law and Practice Case Book* switched the spotlight to the authorities which lay undercover of footnotes, or at most referred to by citing passages, in the textbook. As a companion to the textbook it dealt with the authorities referred to in areas covered by the textbook and the same approach was taken to it by giving greater representation to areas of more frequent judicial activity and as such of more immediate and continuing concern to practitioners and academics alike. The objective of the present book is to provide a selective and in-depth treatment of the causes which give rise to probate actions challenging the validity of a will and of related matters which may arise following upon the making of a grant of probate. The depth of treatment accorded to such causes and matters would be disproportionate in a textbook consisting of so many other areas. The amount of case material necessary for a case book would be too extensive and disproportionate if the whole material of a case were presented in a book of this nature. Thus, the offspring book while bearing certain genetic traits of the parent books has its own individual characteristics as well. Its most distinctive characteristic is the selective and in-depth treatment it accords to a cause or matter complemented by a selective and in-depth treatment of the case law dealing with the cause or matter. Similar to *Probate Law and Practice* and *Probate Law and Practice Case Book*, the present book is about Irish law and the rich underlay of Irish authorities.

The book is divided into two parts, Part One deals with probate causes which may result in the making or breaking of a will and pleaded as such in a probate action. The Part also deals with section 27(4) applications, the admissibility of extrinsic evidence and the issue of costs. Part Two deals with such related matters as the quality or the legal right of a spouse, section 117 applications by children, appropriations, assents, the construction of words and phrases used in a will, the limitation of actions relevant to succession matters and the introduction of a foreign element. The main reason for including a chapter on the introduction of a foreign element is that it was felt that this will become of increasing importance owing to Ireland's membership of the E.U. and the policy of free movement of E.U. citizens.

As the author exhales a sigh of relief over the last pages of this he realises that the task of publishing it must begin for others. As in the case of his last two books he knows that this task will be undertaken with the usual professionalism and panache by the staff of Round Hall Ltd. As the author completes this his third book on probate, and as the horizon dims as regards any more on the subject, he remembers with affection and gratitude the various people who shared his venture from the first book. The first person who comes to mind is Mr Justice Morris, President of the High Court, who has honoured the author on three occasions with glowing and learned forewords. The author remains permanently in his debt. The author also recalls with affection and gratitude the various professionals in Round Hall Ltd. who were involved in the venture from the start. The first book was put through its paces by Thérèse Carrick, Catherine Dolan, Commissioning Editor and Selga Medenieks, Managing Editor. Selga has since gone to pastures new. The second book was seen through again by Catherine Dolan and by Kieran Lyons, Editor (as he then was). The third book again involved the most efficient and courteous Catherine Dolan and the ever polite and competent Kieran Lyons, Editorial Manager (as he now is) with the help of his new and able assistant, Orla Fee.

The author also remembers with affection the kind and humorous support he received in dark moments from his colleagues A.W. Scott (Tony), Grainne Callanan-Weston and Dr Shane Kilcommins when the thread snapped in the labyrinth and he thought himself adrift, Tony has since retired and has donned the mantle of *Il Penseroso. Esto perpetua*. A new man, Jason O'Riordan, has now arrived on the scene. A sincere thanks to all of them.

As an author may also be a family man and cannot claim time as his own, any given is by leave. Such leave was not only granted but lavished on the author by Ruth, Grattan, Sarah, Eddie and Giorgio. A heartfelt thanks to all.

It is the author's sincere hope that the present and past books are worthy of all these magnificent people.

Finally, the author wishes to make the appropriate acknowledgments to the Incorporated Council of Law Reporting for Ireland, the Incorporated Council of Law Reporting for Northern Ireland and Butterworths, for certain passages extracted from judgments in The Irish Reports, Northern Ireland Reports and All England Reports, respectively.

Albert Keating
May 2000
College Street Campus
Waterford Institute of Technology

Foreword

It has been a great pleasure for me to write forewords to Mr Albert Keating's first two works on probate related matters. In the foreword to his *Probate Law and Practice*, I said "the book will undoubtedly be of great assistance to members of the legal profession concerned with probate in its many dimensions" and in the foreword to his *Probate Law and Practice Case Book* I said that the work would "prove to be both an indispensable tool for the practitioner and a trustworthy guide for the student".
I believe that time has shown that in each of these statements I was correct.

In the preface to his present work, *Probate Causes and Related Matters*, Mr Keating says that the book might well be called the offspring of his two earlier works. Indeed, who would know better than he if this is the case. However, to so describe his present work creates the danger that it might be regarded as being of less importance than its forebears. This would indeed be a grave mistake because *Probate Causes and Related Matters* is an important and significant work in which Mr Keating identifies and confronts a variety of fundamental elements which may be potential problems encountered in a probate-related practice and litigation. Perhaps of more importance is that the work gives clear sign posts to anyone seeking them, of a means of avoiding or solving such problems. Any practitioner in probate-related matters will benefit from consulting this work. If the mark of a true expert in his subject is his ability to generate confidence and trust in the reader, then in my view, Mr Keating fits that description. The manner and assurance with which he throws light on to the infinite variety of problems which can arise due to the idiosyncrasies of human nature (or simply Murphy's law), in, for instance, the execution of wills in accordance with section 78 of the Succession Act or the strange twilight world of testamentary capacity, leaves you in no doubt that you are in safe hands by referring to *Probate Causes and Related Matters*. The light continues to shine throughout the work.

Mr Keating has succeeded in making a very valuable comparison between the law in this jurisdiction and other jurisdictions which I have no doubt will be of benefit and advantage to both practitioners and students. He has demonstrated again his ability to mark out the essence of any judgment and to relate it to existing jurisprudence. Once again I unreservedly and wholeheartedly give Mr Keating's latest book my recommendation.

The Hon. Mr Justice Frederick Morris
President of the High Court

To my mother, Maureen

Table of Contents

PROBATE CAUSES AND RELATED MATTERS

AUSTRALIA

LBC Information Services
Sydney

CANADA AND the USA

Carswell

NEW ZEALAND

Brooker's
Auckland

SINGAPORE AND MALAYSIA

Thomson Information (S.E. Asia)
Singapore

Abbreviations

Ad. & E.	Adolphus & Ellis's Reports (1834–1841)
Add.	Addams' Ecclesiastical Reports (1822–1826)
All E.R.	All England Law Reports
A.C./App. Cas.	Appeal Cases (A.C. – 1891 to date)
Atk.	Atkyns (1736–1755)
B. & A.	Barnewell & Adolphus' King's Bench Reports (1830–1834)
B. & Ald.	Barnewall & Alderson (1817–1822)
B. & S.	Best & Smith (1861–1870)
Beav.	Beavan's Rolls Court Reports (1838–1866)
Bing.	Bingham's Common Pleas Reports (1822–1840)
Bro. Ch. C.	Brown's Chancery Cases (1778–1794)
Carth.	Carthew's King's Bench Reports (1668–1701)
C.B.N.S.	Common Bench Reports (New Series) (1856–1865)
Ch./Ch. D.	Chancery (1891 to date) (1875–1890)
Ch. App.	Chancery Appeals (1865–1875)
Cl. & F.	Clark & Finnelly's House of Lords Cases (1831–1846)
C.L.Y.B.	Current Law Year Book
Co./Co. Rep.	Coke's King's Bench Reports (Eliz. I–James I)
Cox Eq.	Cox's Equity Cases (1745–1797)
Cowp.	Cowper's King's Bench Reports (1774–1778)
Cr.M. & R.	Crompton, Meeson & Roscoe's Exchequer Reports (1834–1835)
Cr. & M.	Crompton & Meeson's Exchequer Reports (1832–1834)
Cr. & Ph.	Craig & Phillips' Chancery Reports (1840–1841)
Curt.	Curteis' Ecclesiastical Reports (1834–1844)
D. & War.	Drury & Warren's Irish Chancery Reports (1841–1843)
Dea. & Sw.	Deane & Swabey's Ecclesiastical Reports (1855–1857)
De G. & J.	De Gex & Jones' Chancery Reports (1856–1859)
De G. & Sm.	De Gex & Smale's Vice-Chancellor's Reports (1846–1852)
De G.F. & J.	De Gex, Fisher & Jones' Chancery Reports (1831–1846)
De G.J. & S.	De Gex, Jones & Smith's Chancery Reports (1831–1846)
De G.M. & G.	De Gex, Macnaghten & Gordon's Chancery Reports (1851–1857)
Dick.	Dicken's Chancery Reports (1559–1792)

Dr. & Sm.	Drewry & Smale's Vice Chancellor's Reports (1859–1865)
Dr. & War.	Drury & Warren's Irish Chancery Reports (1841–1843)
Drew.	Drewry's Vice Chancellor's Reports (1852–1859)
E. & B.	Ellis & Blackburn's Queen's Bench Reports (1852–1858)
E. & E.	Ellis & Ellis' Queen's Bench Reports (1858–1861)
Eq.	Equity Cases (1866–1875)
Esp. N.P.	Espinasse's Nisi Prius Reports (1793–1810)
Fam.	Family Division (1972 to date)
Fam. L.J.	Family Law Journal
H. & C.	Hurlstone & Coltman (1862–1866)
Hag. Ecc.	Haggard's Ecclesiastical Reports (1827–1833)
Hare	Hare's Chancery Reports (1841–1853)
H.L.C./H.L. Cas.	House of Lords Cases (1847–1866)
Hurl. & C.	Hurlstone & Coltman's Exchequer Reports (1862–1866)
I.C.L.M.D.	Irish Current Law Monthly Digest
I.L.T.	Irish Law Times
Ir. Eq.	Irish Equity Reports (1838–1850)
Ir. Jur. Rep.	Irish Jurist Reports (1935 to date)
Ir. R. C.L.	Irish Reports, Common Law
I.L.R.M.	Irish Law Reports Monthly
I.L.T.R.	Irish Law Times Reports
I.R.	Irish Reports (1833–1893) (1893 with date to date)
John. & H.	Johnson & Hemming's Vice-Chancellor's Reports (1859–1862)
Jur.	Jurist (1837–1854)
K. & J.	Kay & Johnson's Vice Chancellor's Reports (1854–1958)
K.B.	King's Bench Division (1901–1952)
Keen	Keen's Rolls Court Reports (1836–1838)
Lee	Lee's Ecclesiastical Judgements (1752–1758)
L.J.C.P.	Law Journal Reports, New Series, Common Pleas
L.J. Ch.	Law Journal Reports, Chancery (1831–1946)
L.J.Ir.	Law Journal, Irish
L.J.P.D. & A.	Law Journal Reports, New Series, Probate, Divorce, Admiralty (1876–1946)
L.J.P.M. & A.	Law Journal Reports, Probate, Matrimonial & Admiralty (1860–1865)
L.J.P. & M.	Law Journal Reports, New Series, Probate & Matrimonial (1858–1875)
L.R. H.L.	Law Reports, House of Lords (1866–1875)
L.R. Ir.	Law Reports, Ireland (1878–1893)
L.R.P. & D.	Law Reports, Probate & Divorce Cases (1865–1875)
L.T./L.T.R.	Law Times Reports (1859–1947)

Lutw.	Lutwyche's Common Pleas Reports
M. & Gr.	Manning & Granger (1840–1844)
M. & K.	Mylne & Keen (1832–1835)
M. & W.	Meeson & Welsby's Exchequer Reports (1836–1847)
Mac. & G.	Macnaghten & Gordon's Chancery Reports (1849–1852)
Madd.	Maddock's Reports (1815–1822)
McCl. & Y.	McCleland & Younge's Exchequer Reports (1824–1825)
Mer.	Merivale's Chancery Reports (1815–1817)
Milw.	Milward's Irish Ecclesiastical Reports
Mod. Rep.	Modern Reports (1669–1732)
Moo. P.C./Moore P.C.	Moore's Privy Council Cases (1836–1862)
My. & Cr.	Mylne & Craig's Chancery Reports (1835–1841)
N.C.	Notes of Cases (1841–1850)
N.I.	Northern Ireland Law Reports (1925 to date)
N.I.Y.B.	Northern Ireland Year Book
N.Z.L.R.	New Zealand Law Reports (1883 to date)
O.R.	Ontario Reports (1823 to date)
P.	Law Reports, Probate (1890 to date)
P. & D.	Law Reports, Probate & Divorce (1865–1875)
P. & M.	Probate & Matrimonial (1858–1875)
P.D.	Law Reports, Probate, Divorce and Admiralty Division (1875–1890)
P. Wms.	Peere Williams' Chancery Reports (1695–1735)
Ph.	Phillips' Chancery Reports
Phill. Ecc. Judg.	Phillimore's Ecclesiastical Judgments (1809–1821)
Phill. Ecc. R.	Phillimore's Ecclesiastical Reports (1809–1821)
Prec. Ch.	Precedents in Chancery (1689–1722)
Q.B./Q.B.D.	Queen's Bench Division (1841 to date) (1875–1890)
Rob./Rob. Eccl.	Robertson's Ecclesiastical Reports (1844–1853)
Rus.	Russell's Chancery Reports (1823–1829)
Russ. & M.	Russell & Mylne's Chancery Reports (1829–1833)
Salk.	Salkeld's King's Bench Reports (1689–1712)
Sch. & Lef.	Schoales & Lefroy (1802–1807)
Sim.	Simons' Vice Chancellor's Reports (1826–1852)
S.J.	Solicitors' Journal (1857 to date)
Sw. & Tr.	Swabey & Tristram's Ecclesiastical Reports (1858–1865)
Taunt.	Taunton's Common Pleas Reports (1807–1819)
T.L.R.	Times Law Reports (1884–1950) (1951 to date)
Turn. & R.	Turner & Russell's Chancery Reports (1822–1825)
Vern.	Vernon's Chancery Reports (1681–1719)
Ves. Jun.	Vesey Junior's Chancery Reports (1754–1817)
Ves. Sen.	Vesey Senior's Chancery Reports (1746–1755)
Wightw.	Wightwick's Exchequer Reports (1810–1811)

W.L.R.	Weekly Law Reports (1953 to date)
W.N.	Weekly Notes (1866–1952)
Y. & C.	Younge & Collyer's Exchequer Reports (1834–1842)
You.	Younge's Exchequer Reports (1830–1832)

Table of Cases

Table of Statutes

Table of Rules of Court

CONSTITUTIONS – IRISH

STATUTES OF THE UNITED KINGDOM

PART ONE

Probate Causes

CHAPTER 1

Execution by section 78

INTRODUCTION

1–01 As the existence of a valid will is fundamental to the creation of testamentary rights it is essential that the will giving rise to those rights is executed in compliance with the rules contained in section 78 of the Succession Act. Consequently, if there is any flaw in the due execution of the will by virtue of non-compliance with section 78, probate of the will may not be granted and testamentary rights created by it will cease to exist. In any probate cause or action, an allegation of non-compliance with section 78 may therefore form the first ground where there is a challenge to the validity of the will. Related matters, such as the legal right of a spouse and applications by children under section 117, are also dependent upon the existence of a valid will. Therefore, it is of fundamental importance that the provisions of section 78 be complied with when a will is being executed. However, there are also matters on which section 78 is silent and which have been left to the court to decide. For instance, the basic question of what constitutes a valid signing by a testator is a matter which has always been left to the court to decide in a particular case and as a result there is a fairly substantial body of case law dealing with the matter.[1] It will be seen from the case law that the court will endeavour to save a will if at all possible, but it will not go so far as to break the law so as to fix a testator's blunder.

1–02 The rules for the due execution of a will are themselves simplicity incarnate. A will must be signed by a testator in the presence of two witnesses who must be jointly present when the testator subscribes his name. However this simple procedure may be complicated by the fact that a testator owing to illness or injury may be unable to make his normal signature and is capable only of writing his initials or making a mark.[2] Where initials are used or a mark is made the court may be asked to rule on the sufficiency of the signing although this could be avoided by a testator using the alternative procedure allowed by the rules which provides that a testator may direct another person to sign the will on his behalf.[3]

---

[1] *Bennett v. Brumitt* L.R. 3 C.P. 28; *Addy v. Grix* 3 Ves. 504; *Baker v. Dening* 8 Ad. & E. 94; *In the Goods of Bryce* 2 Curt. 325; *Hindmarsh v. Charlton* 8 H.L. 160; *In the Goods of Emerson* 9 L.R. Ir. 443; *In the Goods of Kieran* [1933] I.R. 222.
[2] *In the Goods of Kieran*, above, n.1.
[3] Succession Act 1965, s. 78, r.1; see *Parker v. Parker* Milw. 541; *Fulton v. Kee* [1961] 1.

1–03   However, where a testator does not wish to use this alternative procedure he may seek the assistance of another in signing his name. Where he
insists on signing the will himself in such circumstances a question may arise
as to the degree of physical contribution a testator must make to an assisted
signature for it to be valid.[4] The provisions of section 78 are clear in that a
testator must sign his will or alternatively he may direct another to sign on his
behalf, thus where a testator finds it difficult to sign his will by making his
usual signature, and in order to fend off a future challenge, the more prudent
course would be to direct another person to sign on his behalf. It may also
happen that a testator may have signed his name before the arrival of the witnesses and if such is the case a question may then arise not only as to the
sufficiency of the signature appearing in the will but also as to whether the
testator had made a sufficient acknowledgment of the signature in the presence of the witnesses.[5]

1–04   Two witnesses are required by section 78 to be present when the testator makes his signature. Again the requirement is simple but may be complicated by the fact that one of the witnesses may not have been in the immediate
presence of a testator when he subscribed his name. A question may arise as to
what constitutes 'presence' for the purposes of a valid attestation, for instance,
would the witnesses be deemed sufficiently present where one, or indeed both,
of the witnesses were not in the immediate presence of the testator when he
made his signature but were in such a position that they were capable of seeing the testator sign had they cared to look?[6] The witnesses are also required
to attest by their signatures the signature of a testator and just as in the case of
a testator a question may arise as to what constitutes a valid signature by a
witness.[7]

1–05   Where the will itself consists of several sheets of paper it must also be
shown that all the sheets were under the 'control' of the testator at the time of
execution. Where the sheets are pinned together the element of control will be
evident from this fact, however, any misplacement of the executed sheet if it
does not appear as the last sheet in the will may have to be explained in evidence. Where the sheets of paper are separate and unconnected they may still

---

[4]   *Fulton v. Kee*, above, n.3.
[5]   Succession Act, s. 78, r.2; *Hudson v. Parker* 1 Rob. 14; see *In the Goods of Gunstan* 7
P.D. 102; *In the Goods of Thomson* 4 N.C. 653; *Kavanagh v. Fegan* [1932] I.R. 566;
Inglesant v. Inglesant L.R. 3 P. & D. 172; *Dubourdieu v. Patterson* 54 I.L.T.R. 23; see
also *Burke v. Moore* I.R. 9 Eq. 609; *Fulton v. Kee*, above, n.3; *In the Goods of McDonald*
[1942] I.R. 201.
[6]   *Mulhall v. Mulhall* [1936] I.R. 712.
[7]   Succession Act 1965, s. 78; *Mulhall v. Mulhall*, above, n.6; *In the Estate of Bulloch*
[1968] N.I. 96; *Bell v. Hughes* 56 L.R. Ir. 407; *In the Goods of Ellison (No. 1)* [1907] 2
I.R. 480; *Roberts v. Phillips* 4 E. & B. 450.

be presumed to be under the control of the testator if the last sheet of the will is duly attested.[8]

1–06 It may appear from the fabric of the will that certain alterations have been made to it. If such is the case it must be established that the alterations were in existence before the will was executed, or alternatively, that they were executed separately by the testator and witnesses in accordance with section 86 of the Succession Act. Where it appears that alterations are not executed then the court must determine their validity from the evidence adduced by the party relying on the alterations. However, reliance on section 86 may be completely obviated by the preparation of a fresh will incorporating the changes which a testator may wish to make to his will and thereby avoiding any costly proceedings for the purposes of determining the validity of alterations which appear in the will.[9]

1–07 Certain documents may also be 'adopted' by a will. A testator may, for instance, have prepared an inventory of articles which is to form the subject matter of a bequest in his will and for this purpose he may incorporate the inventory by reference to it in the bequest and thus allowing such document to be admitted to probate with the will. However, to do so he must comply with the rules relating to the incorporation of documents.[10]

1–08 It may happen that although a will was validly executed by a testator it is nowhere to be found after his death. If such is the situation and there is evidence of due execution and contents, an affidavit of contents exhibiting any draft, if any, may be admitted to probate by the court.[11]

1–09 A great deal of time may have elapsed between the making of a will and a testator's death as a result of which at the time when probate is sought neither draughtsman nor witnesses may be still alive or cannot be traced thus leaving no immediate party to the execution of the will available. Does this dearth of evidence preclude a will from being admitted to probate? Where

---

[8] *In the Goods of Madden* [1905] 2 I.R. 612; *In the Goods of Tiernan* [1942] I.R. 572; *In re Rice* I.R. 5 Eq. 176; *Marsh v. Marsh* 1 Sw. & Tr. 528.

[9] *In the Goods of Rudd* [1944] I.R. 180; *In the Goods of Benn* [1938] I.R. 313; *Grenville v. Tylee* 7 Moo. P.C.C. 320; *William v. Ashton* 1 John. & H. 115; *Duffy v. Duffy* 11 I.L.T.R. 126; *In the Goods of Duffy* I.R. 5 Eq. 506; *Moore v. Moore* I.R. 6 Eq. 166.

[10] See Rules of the Superior Courts, Ord. 79, r.14; *Haberghan v. Vincent* 2 Ves. Jun. 228; *Sheldon v. Sheldon* 1 Rob. 81; *Woodroofe v. Creed* [1894] 1 I.R. 508; *In the Goods of Spotten* 5 L.R. Ir. 403; *Newton v. Newton* 7 Ir. Jur. (n.s.) 129; *In re Mitchell* 100 I.L.T.R. 185; *In the Goods of M'Kenna* 42 I.L.T.R. 50; *In the Goods of Kehoe* 4 L.R. Ir. 343.

[11] *Patten v. Poulton* 1 Sw. & Tr. 55; *Finch v. Finch* L.R. 1 P. 371; see *Miller's Irish Probate Practice* (Dublin 1900) p. 72; see Chap. 4.

such is the case and a will is challenged, the court may rely on such evidence as is still available and apply presumption of due execution.[12]

1–10   A question of liability may also arise out of the preparation and execution of a will and the extent of the duty of care owed by a solicitor. Where a will is prepared by a solicitor the duty of care which he owes to the testator to ensure that the will is duly executed also extends to any beneficiary in the will, and if the rules relating to due execution are not complied with and a beneficiary loses the gift left to him in the will as a result, the solicitor may be liable in damages to the extent of the loss incurred by the beneficiary.[13]

THE SIGNING BY THE TESTATOR

1–11   While section 78 provides that a will must be signed by the testator it does not specify what will constitute a valid signature. One has to turn for guidance to the decisions of the court to see what has been acceptable as a valid signature in former times. Where a testator has signed his will other than by way of his full signature a question may arise touching upon the validity of the signature made by him. The signing by a testator with his mark or by his initials has received early approval by the court as a valid substitute for a signature. A mark when used as a substitute for a signature is usually made in the form of a cross. The origin of a cross as a valid mark was traced by the court in *Bennett v. Brumfitt*[14] to the practice of the Anglo-Saxons:

> "in attesting their charters, was to prefix the sign of the cross to their names. Hence it came to pass, that, when a person who cannot write is to make his mark, he usually makes a cross. And I apprehend that such Saxons as could not write made their crosses, and the scribe wrote their names."

A mark was accepted as a sufficient signature by Sir William Grant in *Addy v. Grix*[15] and this was so even though there was no proof that the testator could not write.[16] Where initials are used by a testator it was held in *In the Goods of Savory*[17] that this form of signing was also sufficient. In that case the testatrix's solicitor had prepared the attestation clause reciting that the testatrix had made her will by executing her mark. When he observed that she had put her initials instead of a mark he returned the will to her to make her mark in the

[12] *In the Goods of Peverett* [1902] P. 205; *In the Estate of Denning* [1958] 1 W.L.R. 462; *In the Goods of Uniacke* [1964] I.R. 166; *In the Estate of Early* [1980 I.R. 223.
[13] *Wall v. Hegarty and Callanan* [1988] I.L.R.M. 124; *Ross v. Caunters* [1980] Ch. 297; see also *Finlay v. Murtagh* [1979] I.R. 249.
[14] *Bennett v. Brumfitt*, above, n.1.
[15] 3 Ves. 504; *Baker v. Dening*, above, n.1.
[16] *In the Goods of Bryce*, above, n.1.
[17] 15 Jur. 1042.

presence of witnesses. She made her mark above her initials but the witnesses did not re-attest adequately as the pen they were using ran out of ink and one witness merely traced over his original signature with a dry pen. It was held that, although the second execution failed, the first signing, where initials were used, was sufficient. In *In the Goods of Blewitt*[18] Sir James Hannen relied on the dicta in *Hindmarsh v. Charlton*[19] and he went on to say that:

> "A mark is sufficient though the testator can write: *Baker v. Dening*.[20] Initials, if intended to represent the name, must be equally good. . . . The language of the Lord Chancellor in *Hindmarsh v. Charlton*[21] seems equally applicable to the testator's signature as to the witnesses' subscription: 'I will lay down this as to my notion of the law that to make a valid subscription as a witness there must either be the name or some mark which is intended to represent the name'; and Lord Chelmsford said: 'the subscription must mean such a signature as is descriptive of the witnesses, whether by mark or initials, or by writing a name in full'."

Sir James Hannen further stated that the initials of the testatrix were sufficient. The same principle was applied by Warren J. in *In the Goods of Emerson*.[22] In that case the testator in the presence of two attesting witnesses affixed a seal stamped with his initials to his will which was handwritten by himself and placed his finger on the seal saying: "This is my hand and seal." Although it was held by Warren J. that the will was sufficiently signed he cautioned: "a seal, qua seal, is not sufficient." However, he went on to hold that the testator by touching the seal with his finger when using the expression "This is my hand and seal" intended the seal to be a signature as well as a seal and was therefore sufficient.

1–12 An attempt by a testator to sign his will by using his initials may instead be treated as his mark where the initials appear to be indecipherable scrawls on the face of the will. This type of signing occurred in *In the Goods of Kieran*.[23] In that case the will was drawn up by the testator's solicitor in accordance with his instructions. The testator, having first read the will, and having expressed satisfaction with it, signed it. However, as he was so debilitated because of an illness he was unable to subscribe his usual signature. He finally only managed to make two indecipherable scrawls. In a grounding affidavit by his solicitor supporting a motion to have the will admitted to probate, he deposed that the two scrawls were the result of the testator's attempt to write his initials "E" and "K". Because of the failed attempt to make a

---

[18] L.R. 5 P.D. 116.
[19] 8 H.L. 160 at 167.
[20] 8 Ad. & E. 94.
[21] Above, n.19.
[22] Above, n.1.
[23] Above, n.1.

signature the solicitor added the words "his" before the "E" and "mark" after the letter "K". The solicitor also amended the text of the attestation clause by adding the words: "The testator made his mark being unable to write owing to physical debility." The will was subsequently attested by the solicitor and the testator's nurse as witnesses. A question arose as to the sufficiency of the testator's mark as a signature. Hanna J. considered it as settled law that the signing may be satisfied by a name, by initials or by a mark. However, he thought the case under consideration was different in fact. The testator started to sign his name, and in that effort he succeeded only in making two scrawls that were indecipherable, and then consented to these being treated as a mark. What the testator put on paper was neither a signature nor initials nor the usual cross. He came to the conclusion that the two scrawls were placed by the testator "as a personal act or acknowledged as such by him, animo testandi, to verify the making of the will as his own act..... I am satisfied on the evidence here that not only did the testator commence to make his signature animo testandi but continued in the same state of mind until the termination of the execution of his will, and accordingly, I admit this will to probate."[24]

1–13 Rather than sign the will himself a testator may direct some other person present at the execution to sign on his behalf.[25] However, the testator's direction to another to sign on his behalf need not be expressly made or even voiced; it is enough that the testator manifests the direction by his conduct.[26] Where the testator insists on signing the will himself but needs assistance in doing so, one of the issues which the court will have to consider is the amount of physical contribution he made to his signature in order for it to be a sufficient signing of his will. It is accepted that a testator wishing to execute his own will need not depend solely on his own efforts; he may be assisted in making his signature by name or even his mark.[27] However, the sufficiency of the act is not a matter of "efficiency or degree" and in itself the act may be inadequate to accomplish the signing; but considered in relation to the surrounding circumstances, it must suffice to indicate, on the part of the testator, an intention to execute his will. A voluntary holding of a pen while the signature is made, for instance, would be an act capable of manifesting such an intention and of constituting a personal signing by the testator, or a touching rather than a holding of the pen provided the touching is deliberate and involves some physical act sufficient to show the animus testandi. In *Fulton v. Kee*[28] the testator was suffering from disseminated sclerosis which made any movement of his hands extremely difficult. One of the witnesses guided the

---

[24] *ibid.* at 229
[25] Succession Act, s. 78, r.1.
[26] See *Parker v. Parker*, above, n.3; *Fulton v. Kee*, above, n.3.
[27] Above, n.3 at 13.
[28] Above, n.3.

testator's hand in making a mark. It was argued in that case that if a testator allowed a passive contact to continue, when able to break it if he so desired, there would be a sufficient participation on his part in the signing to make the signature his own. However, Lord MacDermott L.C.J. could not accede to this submission. Something positive and discernible was required of the testator and not just a matter of abstention. Although having regard to the all the circumstances of a case, conduct on the part of a testator, which would not justify a finding that he himself had executed his will personally, might well be capable of implying a direction to someone else to sign on his behalf. For instance, a testator who is incapable of using his hands for any purpose may direct another person to have his limp writing hand placed on that person's hand and the person so directed then writes the testator's name while the testator's hand rests on his may be regarded as a signing by direction, but not as a personal execution by the testator.

1–14 Where a testator makes his signature in the absence of the witnesses he may later acknowledge the signature made by him in their presence, and such acknowledgment will have the same effect as if he had actually originally signed in the joint presence of the witnesses.[29] The acknowledgment must however be made before the witnesses sign their names otherwise it will be invalid. A testator should inform the witnesses before they sign their names that he is acknowledging his signature. A testator may do this by indicating that the signature is his.[30] It was said by Dr. Lushington that:

> "Acknowledgment may be expressed in words that will adequately convey the idea, if the signature be proved to have been then existent; no particular form of expression is required either by the word 'acknowledge' or by the exigency of the act to be done. It would be quite sufficient to say 'that is my will', the signing being there and seen at the time, for such words do import an owning thereof; indeed, it may be done by any other words which naturally include within their true meaning acknowledgment and approbation."[31]

The testator is not required to state that the document he had already signed is his will since it is the signature, and not the will, which is being acknowledged. The witnesses must however actually see the signature, or had the opportunity of seeing it had they cared to look. Sir F.H. Fust remarked that:

> "When a paper is produced by a testator to the witnesses, with the name signed thereto, and they have the opportunity of seeing his name, and they attest the same by subscribing the paper, they being present at the same time, this is a sufficient acknowledgment of his signature by the testator."[32]

---

[29] Succession Act, s. 78, r.2.
[30] *Hudson v. Parker*, above, n.5; *In the Goods of Gunstan*, above, n.5.
[31] *Hudson v. Parker*, above, n.5 at 25.
[32] *In the Goods of Thomson*, above, n.5 at 644.

However, where a testator remains silent or is unable to speak, a request by one witness to another to attest a will which has already been signed by the testator and within the hearing of the testator may be a sufficient acknowledgment. This was considered by Hanna J. in *Kavanagh v. Fegan*.[33] In that case one of the witnesses who gave evidence at the trial had only a vague memory of the circumstances surrounding the execution of the testatrix's will. The other witness was too ill to attend the trial. The witness who gave evidence was party to what must have been the swiftest execution of a will ever carried out! She "ran into the room, signed the paper, and then ran out again." However, she was told that she was wanted for the purpose of witnessing the will of the testatrix. When she arrived she saw the will either on the testatrix's bed or in the other witness's hand. She was definite that the testatrix could see her when she signed her name as witness, the will at the time was on a table at the foot of the bed. She also stated that the signature was the "very image" of the testatrix's signature and that she had no doubt that it was hers and that she saw the other witness put her name to the will. The testatrix was very ill at the time and was unable to speak. Hanna J. was of the opinion that he was entitled to infer as a matter of fact that a request made by one witness to another in the presence and hearing of the testatrix to sign the will as witness was an acknowledgment by the testatrix of her signature in the presence of the witness. He cited the judgment of Sir J. Hannen in *Inglesant v. Inglesant*[34] which dealt with the legal position where a witness signs the will in the presence of a silent testator at the request of another witness. Sir J. Hannen in support of his judgment quoted Lord Brougham as stating:

> "Their Lordships therefore consider it is quite clear that Rowley was called upon to witness the signature, and that this was an acknowledgment to Rowley by the testator that this was his signature. This is still further proved, because it is sworn by Caukwell that he (Caukwell) said to Rowley (in all probability in the hearing of the testator), 'It is Mr. Jackson's signature, or Mr. Jackson's instrument, you are to witness'."[35]

He also cited a passage from the judgment of Gibson J. in *Dubourdieu v. Patterson*:[36]

> "There is no doubt as to the law : a will must be signed, or the signature as a visible fact acknowledged, in the presence of two witnesses. It has been argued in this case that an opportunity of seeing is sufficient, and that Lowry could have turned the leaf and looked at the signature if he had chosen. But if, for example, a book had been placed over the signature which the witnesses could have moved if they had chosen, the will would not have been properly attested. If the signature is visibly apparent on the face to the witnesses of the document,

---

[33] Above, n.5.
[34] Above, n.5.
[35] *Faulds v. Jackson* 6 No. of Ca. Suppl., 1.
[36] Above, n.5.

they are supposed to have seen it, and the Court considers that they did see it; but it is otherwise if it is not visibly apparent. The testatrix in this case was a capable woman, she was informed how the will should be executed, the witnesses signed in the belief that the will was duly made, the will was kept by the testatrix among her papers, and there is a good attestation clause signed by the two witnesses. The evidence afforded by that, that the will was duly executed signed and acknowledged, is only got rid of by clear evidence to the contrary."

Thus vague and uncertain evidence will not have the effect of rebutting the presumption of due execution. It was said by Hanna J. that evidence in rebuttal must be "cogent and reliable" in order to displace the presumption in favour of the due execution of the will. Moreover, where the alternative mode of signing by directing another person to sign on behalf of a testator is used and the direction to sign by the testator is not given in the presence of the witnesses the testator may be required to acknowledge that the signature is his in the presence of the witnesses.[37] Otherwise the witnesses would have no certain means of identifying the testator with the signature unless he acknowledges it. However, where they witness both the signature and the direction, a further acknowledgment by the testator is not necessary.

1–15 While it is clear that a testator is required only to acknowledge his signature in the presence of the witnesses, it may also become necessary, where the attestation clause makes no reference to the testator signing his will, to establish that the document on which the testator's signature was already made was in fact his will. In *In the Goods of McDonald*[38] the attestation clause in the will was drafted in such a way that it made no reference to the testator signing his will. The will was in the handwriting of the testator and was signed by him and two witnesses. Neither of the witnesses to the will could remember whether the testator was the first to sign the will. Nor could they remember whether the testator had acknowledged his signature. One of the witnesses was unsure whether the testator's signature was on the will before he signed his name as witness, but was sure, however, that the testator did not sign after he and the other witness had signed the will. The authorities cited by Maguire P. in his judgment were supportive of the view that where a testator produces a paper and gives the witnesses to understand it is his will, it is not necessary to have direct evidence that his name was on the paper when he asked the witnesses to sign.[39] One of the authorities he cited was *Beckett v. Howe*[40] and the facts of that case were that a few days before the will was executed the testator invited one of the intended witnesses to his home to witness his will;

---

[37] See *Burke v. Moore*, above, n.5; *Fulton v. Kee*, above, n.3 at 10.
[38] Above, n.5.
[39] *Gwillim v. Gwillim* 3 Sw. & Tr. 200; *Beckett v. Howe* 2 P. & D. 1; *Pearson v. Pearson* 2 P. & D. 1.
[40] Above, n.39.

to the other he said that he wished him to witness a paper but did not state the nature of the paper to be witnessed by him. At the arranged time the witnesses arrived and the testator produced a paper carefully folded up so that the witnesses could not see what was written on it. The testator made the remark in the presence of both witnesses that the death of his wife necessitated an alteration in his affairs, and then asked the witnesses to sign, which they did. There was, therefore, no direct evidence that the signature was there at the time when the testator acknowledged the paper as his will. Lord Penzance stated however that:

> "The Court may judge, from the appearance of the paper, and the circumstances of the case generally."

Lord Penzance then went on to refer to the case of *Gwillim v. Gwillim*[41] where it was said by Sir C. Cresswell that:

> "If it were necessary to have direct evidence that the name of the testator was on the will when he acknowledged it by asking them to witness his will, the proof of the executor would fail; but the certainty is not necessary. . . . I am, therefore, at liberty to judge from the circumstances of this case whether the name of the testator was on the will at the time of attestation or not."

Maguire P. observed that the case before him differed in some slight respects from the facts in *Beckett v. Howe*. There was a clear acknowledgment by the testator that the paper was his will. The document was not folded up and the two witnesses were able to see the signature. From the position of the testator's signature and the circumstances of the case Maguire P. was able to conclude that the name of the testator was written at the time the witnesses signed the will, and based on the authorities referred to, he was satisfied that the testator acknowledged the paper as his will and that the will was validly executed.

THE PRESENCE AND SIGNING BY THE WITNESSES

1–16   Section 78 also requires that a testator must make or acknowledge his signature in the presence of two or more witnesses and each of the witnesses must attest by his signature the signature of the testator in the presence of the testator, but no form of attestation is necessary nor will it be necessary for the witnesses to sign in the presence of each other. The 'presence' of witnesses has been given a very liberal interpretation by the court as a result of which it will not be fatal to the execution of a will if the witnesses are not in the immediate presence of a testator so long as they are in a position to have an unimpeded view of his signing the will regardless of the distance from him. In *Mulhall v.*

---

[41] Above, n.39.

Mulhall[42] the will was signed in the presence of one witness only. The second witness was in another room. The testator then brought the will into the room where the second witness was present and asked him to witness his will. Based on these facts alone the execution of the testator's will would have failed because both witnesses were not present at the time when he signed his will. However, the facts also disclosed that when the testator signed his will in the presence of one witness the door of the room was open allowing the other witness to see the testator sign. Maguire J. held that he had enough evidence to entitle him to hold that the will was duly executed in the joint presence of the two witnesses in accordance with the statute. The witnesses are also required to sign their names in the same way as a testator is required to sign his name, and the same questions may arise in relation to the sufficiency of their signatures as in the case of the testator's. Although a handwritten signature is preferable because it is more easily authenticated, it has long been established that witnesses, as in the case of testators, need not sign by name and that the signing by initials or a description or mark will suffice. Although a valid subscription may be made by a mark or by initials the witness must subscribe himself, another person cannot do it for him.[43] Lord MacDermott L.C.J. in *In the Estate of Bulloch*[44] was also of the opinion that a witness may properly subscribe his name by using a stamp which puts his name on the will. However, a witness must make some physical contribution to the signing himself even though the effort is made with the assistance of another. "An acknowledgment of his own signature by a witness is not sufficient. The result of the cases is that there must be some physical act done by the witness in connexion with the transfer of the ink to the paper, and done with the intention to attest the paper; these three things are requisite. It is not important what the physical act done by the witness may be; nor is it necessary that the witness should afterwards be able to recognise his mark."[45] In *In the Estate of Bulloch*[46] one of the witnesses used a rubber stamp bearing his name which was affixed to the will on his behalf by his wife. Applying the dicta of Warren J. where a rubber stamp is used, Lord MacDermott L.C.J. stated that this meant:

> "that the attesting witness must do some physical act, as, for example, by touching the stamp or holding the hand or arm of the person applying it to the paper, with the intention of attesting. In the circumstances the will was not properly attested."

Although it would seem by section 78 that a testator may write his signature on any part of the will so long as it was intended to give effect to the writing

---

[42] Above, n.6.

[43] *In bonis Amiss* 2 Rob. Ecc. 116; 163 E.R. 1262; see *In bonis Hannah Cope* 2 Rob. Ecc. 335; 163 E.R. 1337.

[44] Above, n.7.

[45] *Bell v. Hughes*, above, n.7 at 408 *per* Warren J.

[46] Above, n.7.

signed as his will, the section is silent as regards the position of the witnesses'
signatures.

However, turning to a leading case on the matter, *Roberts v. Phillips*,[47]
and which was referred to by Andrews J. in *In the Goods of Ellison (No. 1)*,[48]
Lord Campbell C.J. said that:

> "The mere requisition that the will shall be *subscribed* by the witnesses we
> think is complied with by the witnesses who saw it executed by the testator
> immediately signing their names on any part of it at his request with the inten-
> tion of attesting it."[49]

In *In the Goods of Ellison (No. 1)*[50] the two witnesses to the will signed their
names in the blank spaces left for the names of the executors. The testator
directed them to sign in this way having first acknowledged his signature in
their presence. Andrews J. citing *Roberts v. Phillips*[51] as an authority held that
the will was duly attested as there was satisfactory evidence that the testator
produced the will to the witnesses, acknowledged his signature in their presence, and indicated where they should sign their names.

1–17   Where a will consists of several sheets of paper not only must the will
be signed and attested, all of the sheets of paper must also be under the 'control' of the testator when the will was executed. This situation may become
less of a problem if all of the sheets of paper are pinned together which may be
sufficient to show the requisite control, but where they are unconnected the
element of control may have to be established although it may be assisted by
the fact that the last sheet of paper was attested and therefore raising the presumption that the whole will was also present at the place of execution.[52]
However, even where the sheets of paper are pinned together a problem may
arise where the attested sheet appears otherwise than at the end of the will. In
In the Goods of Madden[53] the testatrix's will consisted of four sheets of paper
pinned together. Her signature and the attestation clause under which the witnesses signed their names appeared on the first page of her will. According to
the evidence the first page was the last page of her will which was mistakenly
attached to the beginning of the will. Andrews J., after careful consideration
of the evidence which had been adduced, came to the conclusion that what the
testatrix wrote on the sheets of paper was all written at the same time, and that
the sheet pinned on front was written last, and that when the will was signed
the four sheets were all together in the same place. He found that the hand-

---

[47]   Above, n.7 at 459.
[48]   Above, n.7.
[49]   See also *The Goods of Streatley* [1891] P. 172.
[50]   Above, n.7.
[51]   Above, n.7.
[52]   *In the Goods of Madden*, above, n.8; *In the Goods of Tiernan*, above, n.8.
[53]   Above, n.8.

writing was the same, and was all uniform, and it appeared to have all been written with the same ink. The four sheets of paper were manifestly written to constitute a will, and if the sheet pinned on front was placed at the end, the four sheets would read consecutively as constituting a perfectly formal will, ready for execution. He regarded the attestation clause as referring to what she had already written. However, where several sheets are not pinned together and are separate and unconnected all may still constitute the last will if the last sheet is attested, and, although no part of the will may have been seen by the witnesses, may be admitted to probate on the presumption that the whole will was under the control of the testator. This presumption may, however, be rebutted by the circumstances of the case or by the evidence. In *In the Goods of Tiernan*[54] the will was written by the testator on three separate sheets of notepaper. They were not fastened together. There was no catchword from one sheet to the next. They were also unnumbered. The will was enclosed in an envelope and the three sheets bore the appearance of having been folded together with corresponding creases in each before being placed in the envelope. The presiding judge was not satisfied with the affidavit evidence surrounding the execution of the will and directed that the attesting witnesses appear at the hearing and give evidence. One of the witnesses was unsure of the position of the three sheets containing the will which were placed on a table at the time of execution. Hanna J. was satisfied that the other sheets of paper containing the dispositions of the will, while not under the attestation sheet, were on the table and, as a matter of inference, under the control of the testator. The matter for decision, however, was whether on the facts found he could admit to probate, a will the execution of which was on a separate sheet of paper and at the time was unattached to the will and not in any way physically associated with it. He referred to a number of past decisions for support. One such authority was *Bond v. Seawell*[55] in which the witnesses never saw the first sheet of the will but they were shown the last sheet of the will which they attested. The headnote of the case stated that it may be presumed that when the witnesses only saw the last sheet of the will that the whole will was in the room and Lord Mansfield indicated that that it was not necessary that each sheet or page should be shown to the witnesses. Although the facts differed from the case under consideration Hanna J. thought the principle established by that case should apply.[56] He found that the authorities established that:

> "if a will be written on several and disconnected sheets of paper and the last only be attested, although no part of the will may have been seen by the witnesses, it should be admitted to probate on the presumption that the whole will

---

[54] Above, n.8.

[55] 3 Burr. 1773; 97 E.R. 1092.

[56] See also *In re Rice*, above, n.8; *In the Goods of Madden*, above, n.8; *Lewis v. Lewis* [1908] P. 1; *Gregory v. The Queen's Proctor* 4 N.C. 620; *Marsh v. Marsh*, above, n.8.

was in the room and under the control of the testator at the time of execution. The presumption may, however, be rebutted by the circumstances of the case, or by evidence, which would be a question for the Court or the jury."[57]

Therefore, in his opinion the will of the testator fell within this principle and ought to be admitted to probate.

THE EXECUTION OF ALTERATIONS

1–18   Although section 86 of the Succession Act specifically deals with the question of alterations of wills, they are also required to be executed in the same way required for a will under section 78. However, section 86 further elaborates on the mode of execution of alterations by providing that if the signature of the testator and the signature of each witness is made in the margin or on some other part of the will opposite or near the alteration or at the foot or end of or opposite to a memorandum referring to such alteration, and written at the end of some other part of the will, this will be sufficient to execute the alteration. Order 79 rule 10 of the Rules of the Superior Courts also provides that interlineations and alterations appearing in a will are invalid unless they existed prior to its execution, or, if made afterwards, unless they were executed and attested in the mode required by law, or unless they were made valid by the re-execution of the will, or by a subsequent codicil to the will. Where alterations or interlineations are not duly executed, or cited or identified in the attestation clause, an affidavit in proof of their having existed in the will prior to its execution must be filed, except when the alterations are but of small importance, and are evidenced by the initials of the attesting witnesses.[58] As Order 79 is silent on the question of what constitutes an alteration of small importance the facts of a particular case may require the court to decide the matter. Order 79 rule 12 goes on to provide that alterations in the nature of erasures and obliterations are not to prevail unless proved to have existed in the will prior to its execution, or unless they were rendered valid by the re-execution of the will, or by the subsequent execution of a codicil. If no satisfactory evidence can be adduced as to the time when such erasures and obliterations were made, and the words erased or obliterated are not entirely effaced and can be ascertained by an inspection of the paper, they must form part of the probate.

1–19   Where unexecuted alterations appear in the will and there is some doubt whether they were made prior to the execution of it, it is well settled, "that whoever alleges such alteration to have been done before the execution of the

---

[57] *In the Goods of Tiernan*, above, n.8 at 580.
[58] Rules of the Superior Courts, Ord. 79, r.11.

will is bound to take upon himself the *onus probandi*."[59] In *In the Goods of Rudd*[60] the testator, by his will, bequeathed the residue of his estate to his brothers and sisters. He subsequently made a codicil which was expressed to be further and in addition to his will. The codicil was in his own handwriting and after making various changes to the bequests in his will included the words "My brother Wm. in South Africa is not to benefit by my decease." These words were written in an ink different from that used in the rest of the codicil. It appeared that before they were written the testator went over the last letter of the word immediately preceding them and added a full stop. The writing of the words themselves was more cramped than was the writing of the rest of the document, and the words appeared to have been squeezed into a space less than they would normally require. The codicil concluded with the words: "these alterations and additions I now make, being of sound mind and condition, as witness my hand this in the presence of witnesses." One of the executors named in the codicil made an affidavit in which he stated that he was well acquainted with the handwriting of the testator and was of opinion that the will and codicil were written by the testator. The witnesses to the codicil deposed in their affidavits that at the time of execution of the codicil they were not aware of the contents of the codicil and were not able to say definitely whether the words "My brother Wm. In South Africa is not to benefit by my decease" appeared in it at the time of execution. The first question which Maguire P. had to decide was whether the words "my brother Wm. In South Africa is not to benefit by my decease" in the codicil of January 26, 1931, were an alteration within the meaning of the words in Section 21 of the Wills Act 1837. He was satisfied that they were in the handwriting of the testator as was the rest of the document. They were, however, written in ink different to that used by the testator in the rest of the codicil. The writing of the words in the sentence with which he was concerned was more cramped than was the writing in the rest of the document. In view of all the facts and circumstances he concluded that these words were not written as part of the same continuous act which the writing of the rest of the codicil appeared to have been and that they were inserted after the rest of the document was completed. The next question was whether these words were inserted before the will was executed. Towards the solution of this question there was nothing to assist him in the evidence before him. Having referred to the rule stated in *Grenville v. Tylee*[61] he held that the onus had not been discharged, and accordingly, he granted liberty to apply for probate of the will and codicil excluding the words referred to in the codicil.

1–20 The court may also place reliance on the internal evidence furnished

---

[59] *Greville v. Tylee*, above, n.9; *Cooper v. Bockett* 4 Moo. P.C.C. 419; *In the Goods of Rudd*, above, n.9 at 182.

[60] Above, n.9.

[61] Above, n.9.

by the will. In *In the Goods of Benn*[62] two lines of the will of the deceased testatrix were completely obliterated with a blue copying pencil and adhesive stamp paper leaving the underlying words indecipherable. There was also an interlineation in blue pencil noting a change of address of one of the legatees. The main question arose in respect of an interlineation in the principal disposition of the testatrix's property which appeared as follows:

> and poperty [*sic*]
> "The rest of my money/ I die seized or possessed of, to my sister Georgina, to be divided with her daughter as she thinks best."

A question arose as to whether the underlying words "and poperty" were to be included in the grant of probate and whether the effect of their inclusion would also cover property owned by the testatrix other than her money. Hanna J. was of the opinion that, having regard to the internal evidence and the opinion of a handwriting expert, the words "and poperty" were inserted before execution. There was no direct evidence of any kind as to the time when the interlineation was made and there was no declaration of the testatrix before the execution of the will as to its contents or her interlineations. Therefore the question arose – how far was he entitled in law to rely on internal evidence and whether it was sufficient to draw an inference that the words "and poperty" were inserted before the execution of the will. He referred to *Williams v. Ashton*[63] and thought that the correct view of the law was that as expressed by Lord Hatherley[64] in that case:

> "I do not think that it is quite a correct mode of stating the rule of law, to say that alterations in a will are presumed to have been made at one time or another. The correct view, as enunciated in the case of *Doe v. Palmer*[65] is that the onus is cast upon the party who seeks to derive an advantage from an alteration in a will, to adduce some evidence from which a jury may infer that the alteration was made before the will was executed. I do not consider that the Court is bound to say that it will presume such alterations to have been made either before or after execution. With regard to a will, I do not see any necessary presumption of the kind."

This view was approved of in *Duffy v. Duffy*[66] as was also the view expressed in *Williams v. Ashton*[67] that the burden of proof in this respect rested on the person claiming the benefit of such alterations and that very slight evidence will suffice to supply the want of any presumption that they were made before

---

[62] Above, n.9.

[63] Above, n.9.

[64] *ibid.* at 118.

[65] 16 Q.B. 747.

[66] Above, n.9.

[67] Above, n.9; see also *Simmons v. Rudall* 1 Sim. N.S. 115.

the execution of the will. On the question of character or weight of evidence to be acted upon it was said by Warren J. in *In the Goods of Duffy*[68] that:

> "The result of these cases, especially of *In the Goods of Hindmarch*,[69] appears to be that the presumption that alterations were made after the execution only exists in the absence of all evidence to the contrary, and that very slight affirmative evidence is sufficient to rebut the presumption, and sustain the alterations as made before execution, and therefore, valid."

On the question as to whether the interlineations or alterations were made before the execution, Warren J. in *Moore v. Moore*[70] said that:

> ". . . the Court is not confined to any species of evidence, but may act upon any evidence which, having regard to all the circumstances, reasonably leads the judgment to the conclusion that the alterations were made before execution."

Hanna J. relying on the authority of the foregoing cases held that the court could rely on its own judgment of the internal evidence as presented by the fabric of the will, and also on the evidence of handwriting experts on the appearance of the writing in the documents. Accordingly, he ordered that the words "and poperty" be admitted to probate and inserted in the grant.

INCORPORATION OF DOCUMENTS

1–21 A testator may refer to a document *de hors* in his will for the purpose of incorporating it into his will. Two conditions however must be satisfied for the procedure to work: first, the document to be incorporated must be in existence at the time of execution, and secondly, the testator must clearly identify the document by the words used by him in the will.[71] Documents may be incorporated in a similar way by codicils.[72] The document which a testator wishes to incorporate need not itself be executed, in fact, if the document is unexecuted, the process of incorporating it may result in its execution indirectly as it will also form part of the eventual probate of the will.[73] Examples of incorporated unexecuted documents include a schedule of silver plate[74] and a list of goods referred to in the will.[75] Where the document to be incorporated is an executed one the same rules must be observed for it to be effec-

---

[68] Above, n.9.
[69] L.R. 1 P. & D. 307.
[70] Above, n.9.
[71] Rules of the Superior Courts, Ord. 79, r.14; *Haberghan v. Vincent*, above, n.10.
[72] *Woodroofe v. Creed*, above, n.10; *In the Goods of Wilmot* 1 Sw. & Tr. 36; *In the Goods of Spotten*, above, n.10; *In the Goods of Pearse* L.R. 1 P. 382; *Newton v. Newton*, above, n.10.
[73] See *Sheldon v. Sheldon* 1 Rob. 81 *per* Dr. Lushington.
[74] *In the Goods of Ashe* 2 Jur. (n.s.) 526.
[75] *In re Mitchell* 100 I.L.T.R. 185.

tively incorporated.[76] Examples of incorporated executed documents include parts of a revoked will[77] and a codicil partially restoring a revoked codicil.[78]

OMNIA PRAESUMUNTUR RITE ET SOLEMNITER ESSE ACTA

1–22   In an action challenging the due execution of a will, the will may still be upheld notwithstanding the paucity of direct evidence surrounding the due execution of it. In such a case the court may presume that a will was validly signed and attested, *omnia praesumuntur rite et solemniter acta*. However, there are limits placed on the presumption. In *In the Goods of Peverett*[79] Sir Francis Jeune stated that:

> "Two things may be laid down as general principles. The first is, that the Court is always extremely anxious to give effect to the wishes of persons if satisfied that they really are their testamentary wishes; and, secondly, the Court will not allow a matter of form to stand in the way if essential elements of execution have been fulfilled."

In that case the will in question was a holograph will. There was no attestation clause. Both witnesses were dead; but the signature of one of them was proved, and it was also established that the other was not an unlikely witness. There was also no doubt that the will was in the handwriting of the testatrix and bore her signature. While applying the two principles to the case Sir Francis Jeune was conscious of the fact that he was going to the farthest limit.

1–23   However, Sachs J. in *In the Estate of Denning*[80] although he referred to the general principles laid down by Sir Francis Jeune in *In the Goods of Peverett*[81] was prepared to go a step further: "Having taken into account all factors, I think it proper to take that step further because it seems to me that there is no other practical reason why those names should be on the back of the document unless it was for the purposes of attesting the will." In that case the document concerned consisted of a small sheet of paper, one side of which contained the date and dispositive words followed by a word intended to read, "signed" and the signature, "Alice Mary Denning, Spinster." On the reverse side, turning the sheet upside down, appeared the names, "Edith Freeman" and "Dorothy Edwards," in different handwritings. These handwritings on the back corresponded with that on the front. No persons of the names Edith Freeman or Dorothy Edwards, could be traced. The only beneficiaries were John

---

[76] *In the Goods of the Countess of Durham* 3 Curt. 57; *In the Goods of Darby* 4 N.C. 427.
[77] See *In the Goods of M'Kenna*, above, n.10; *Jorden v. Jorden* 2 N.C. 388.
[78] *In the Goods of Kehoe*, above, n.10.
[79] Above, n.12.
[80] Above, n.12.
[81] Above, n.12.

Harnett and his sister, Mary Jane Harnett. The testatrix told John Harnett that she had made a will and that he and his sister were the beneficiaries. It did not appear that the testatrix's signature was verified, nor was it known when or where the will was discovered. However, the testatrix had in her lifetime declared that she had made a will of the exact nature of the document in question. Sachs J. was satisfied that the document was the last will of the testatrix.

1–24   Davitt P. in *In the Goods of Uniacke*[82] when considering the limit which the court will go to in applying the presumption thought that Sachs J. in *In the Estate of Denning*[83] had "expressly and deliberately" exceeded it. In *Uniacke* a grandson of the deceased sought liberty to apply for a grant of letters of administration with the purported will annexed. The document in question was in will form and was purported to have been executed by the deceased. There was no evidence as to where it was originally discovered but it appeared to have been kept by the deceased's son in a box in his house for a long time. The deceased's son was her principal beneficiary under the will. The document was not a holograph as the deceased signed by a mark which suggested that she was unable to write. There was no attestation clause. There was no evidence as to the identity of the person who drew up the document. The persons who subscribed their names as witnesses were long dead and from a comparison between the handwriting of the witnesses and the handwriting in which the will was written it was evident that the document was not written by either of them. There was also no evidence to identify the handwriting of the witnesses. Davitt P., refusing probate, held that Sachs J. went to the utmost in *In the Estate of Denning*[84] and that he was not prepared to go any further, in fact he doubted if he would have gone as far.

1–25   The Supreme Court considered the application of the presumption in *In the Estate of Early*.[85] In that case the deceased was an elderly man. He died in the house of a distant relative who had cared for him during his last years. His only assets consisted of a farm. Nearly two years after his death this distant relative produced a document purporting to be the will of the deceased leaving his farm to her. The document although signed by the deceased and two witnesses contained no attestation clause. The two witnesses were dead when the document was produced. The signature of one of the witnesses who was a friend of the deceased was identified by his widow. There was no evidence, however, verifying the signature of the deceased. The court was asked to apply the maxim *omnia praesumuntur rite et solemniter esse acta* to the circumstances surrounding the execution of the document. O'Higgins C.J. in

---

[82]   Above, n.12.
[83]   Above, n.12.
[84]   Above, n.12.
[85]   Above, n.12.

his judgment thought that it was asking too much of the court to apply the presumption to the circumstances of the case. It was essential that evidence be adduced to show that the will was actually signed by the deceased. The evidence in support of the application established that the document was signed by one of the witnesses. Although the application of the presumption was also capable of carrying the apparent attestation of the second witness, since a person bearing that name and address existed and was a friend of the decease, there was, however, a complete absence of any evidence to verify the signature "Hugh Early" as being that of the deceased. In fact, not only was there an absence of supportive evidence, there was also an allegation, though of doubtful authenticity, that the signature was not that of the deceased. Applying the presumption to the facts of the case, O'Higgins C.J., was of the view that two conditions must be observed:

> "In the first place an intention to do some formal act must be established. In the second place there must be an absence of credible evidence that due formality was not observed. Here it can be said that the second condition is established. But what of the first ? While the document has a testamentary flavour, it is established that it is not a holograph. In the absence of any evidence that it was signed by the deceased, there is no evidence of an intention on his part to enter into the formality of making a will."[86]

The evidence was insufficient to justify the making of a grant.

1–26　　Where a will cannot be found after the death of the testator the court may also apply the presumption of due execution. However, in the case of lost wills, for the presumption to apply, another presumption has to be rebutted, for if a will is last known to have been in the possession of a testator there is a prima facie presumption that the testator destroyed it animo revocandi. The evidence required to rebut this presumption must be "clear and strong",[87] and although it is not necessary to show how the will was lost, the court must be satisfied that it was not found after a diligent search has been conducted.[88] Once the presumption is rebutted the court may then admit evidence of its contents.

THE LIABILITY OF A SOLICITOR

1–27　　Generally, a solicitor has a contractual duty to carry out the terms of his retainer and a tortious duty to exercise reasonable care and skill in attending to his client's affairs. The question of liability will not be affected by the

---

[86] *ibid.* at 226–227.
[87] See *Miller's Irish Probate Practice* (Dublin 1900) p. 72.
[88] See *Patten v. Poulton*, above, n.11; *Finch v. Finch*, above, n.11.

nature of the consideration provided by the client as it makes no difference whether a solicitor provides his professional services on a voluntary basis or for reward.[89] The whole question of a solicitor's contractual and tortious liability in relation to the preparation and execution of wills was considered by Sir Robert Megarry in *Ross v. Caunters*.[90] In that case it was held that if a solicitor is retained by a testator to draft and execute a will and the will confers a benefit on a named legatee, the solicitor must know that if he fails in his professional duty to draft and execute the will properly a beneficiary will suffer loss. Therefore, a solicitor owes a duty of care in preparing and executing a will not only to the testator but also to a beneficiary. Barrington J. in *Wall v. Hegarty and Callanan*[91] approved and adopted the judgment of Sir Robert Megarry in *Ross v. Caunters*, and having also taken into account the Supreme Court decision in *Finlay v. Murtagh*,[92] stated that "a solicitor does owe a duty to a legatee named in a draft will, to draft the will with such reasonable care and skill as to ensure that the wishes of the testator are not frustrated and the expediency of the legatee defeated through lack of considerable care and skill on the part of the solicitor." The circumstances of that case were that the plaintiff was the executor and legatee in a will which was not attested in accordance with section 78 of the Succession Act. As a result of the will being condemned the plaintiff lost his legacy of £15,000. He sued the firm of solicitors retained by the testator for breach of duty of care which he alleged was owing to him as legatee to ensure that the will was properly drafted in accordance with the testator's instructions and executed and attested in accordance with section 78, and he further sought to recover damages for his loss of legacy and for the expenses he had incurred in attempting to establish the will. The firm of solicitors admitted that the signature of one of the witnesses was later added to the will in their offices. Barrington J. held that if a solicitor owes any duty to a named legatee then it is quite clear that the solicitor in the present case had failed to show the appropriate care and skill. As regards the plaintiff's loss, had the will been validly executed, the plaintiff would have received his legacy of £15,000, and he was entitled to recover the value of that legacy. However, when assessing the value of a legacy other circumstances had to be taken into account, like, for instance, whether the testator's estate was insolvent which might result in a legatee receiving nothing at all notwithstanding the validity of the will, or indeed, that the will might be invalid on some other ground in respect of which the solicitor had no responsibility. But none of these latter circumstances was applicable to the present case. There were sufficient funds in the testator's estate to meet the payment of the legacy

---

[89] See *Finlay v. Murtagh*, above, n.13; *Midland Bank Trust Co. Ltd. v. Hetts, Stubbs & Kemp* [1979] Ch. 384 *per* Oliver J.

[90] Above, n.13.

[91] Above, n.13.

[92] Above, n.13.

of £15,000. In addition to the loss of the £15,000 legacy, the plaintiff had sustained loss in getting involved in legal proceedings to uphold the will. It appeared to Barrington J. that a solicitor who drafts a will in which an executor is named must foresee that the executor will eventually seek the admission of the will to probate. It therefore followed that the ordinary costs incurred by the executor in having the will admitted to probate flowed naturally from the solicitor's lack of care and were recoverable against him. Even if the plaintiff's loss in getting involved in legal proceedings to have the will admitted to probate did not flow directly from the original lack of care, Barrington J., was of the opinion, that based on the principles laid down in *Donoghue v. Stevenson*[93] and *Hedley Byrne*[94] the loss would still be recoverable because of the circumstances surrounding the sending of a copy of the will to the plaintiff. The defendants sent a copy of the will without drawing the plaintiff's attention to the fact that it had not been validly executed. Barrington J. also identified another heading under which the plaintiff was entitled to recover damages:

> "Had the will been valid, the plaintiff would, in the normal course, have been entitled to interest on his legacy at the conclusion of the executor's year at a rate which the law allowed, there being no express provision for the payment of interest on legacies in the will."

However, in the present case, as the plaintiff was also the executor, he reserved for further argument the question of the plaintiff's entitlement to recover interest on the legacy.

SUMMARY

1–28 It can be seen from the foregoing that any departure from the norm as expressed in section 78 regarding the signing by a testator and the attesting by witnesses may result in a challenge to the will, and if such is the case the vitiating element introduced by such a departure will be considered by the court in determining whether the presence of such an element invalidates the will. The court will be assisted in this exercise by the abundance of past decisions dealing with the sufficiency of a testator's and witnesses' signatures and the requirement that two witnesses be present at the execution. One must also be mindful of the fact that where a will consists of several sheets of paper the testator must have control over the whole will and this may be evident by the prior fastening of the sheets together and the execution taking place and appearing on the last sheet of the will. Where a will contains alterations which are not executed in the manner prescribed by section 86 of the Succession

---

[93] [1932] A.C. 562.
[94] [1964] A.C. 465.

Act, then it is essential that evidence be adduced of their existence prior to the execution of the will. However, any question of alterations and the requirement to adduce evidence of them may be eliminated by the simple expediency of reprinting the entire will incorporating the alterations.

1–29 Documents referred to by a will may also be admitted to probate as forming part of the will. The document to be incorporated must, however, be in existence at the time of execution, and must be sufficiently identifiable by the will for the incorporation to take effect. The document may be executed or unexecuted, and where unexecuted, may be viewed as being vicariously 'executed' by virtue of the incorporation.

1–30 It may happen that there is a considerable lapse of time between the execution of the will and the death of the testator as a result of which there may be little or no direct evidence of due execution because the witnesses may also have died or cannot be traced. This fact alone will not prevent the will from being admitted to probate as the court may presume that the will was validly executed. However, where the presumption of due execution is resorted to it may be rebutted by the evidence adduced at the trial: the evidence in favour of applying the presumption may be outweighed by the evidence in rebuttal. The presumption may also be applied even though a will is lost or cannot be found. However, where a will is last known to have been in the possession of a testator, although it may be presumed to have been validly executed it may also be presumed to have been destroyed *animo revocandi*. Thus a will, although presumed to have been duly executed, may yet not be admitted to probate where the evidence is insufficient to rebut the presumption of revocation.

1–31 Where a will is professionally drafted either on a voluntary basis or for reward, a duty of care is owed not only to the testator but also to the beneficiaries that the will was properly executed. Any loss sustained as a result of an invalid execution may be recovered by the beneficiaries, though the amount recoverable may depend, however, on the state of solvency of the testator's estate. Furthermore, any costs incurred by an executor having to get involved in legal proceedings because of professional negligence may also be recoverable.

1–32 In the final analysis, the metamorphosis of a document or documents into a testamentary instrument can only take place when executed in compliance with section 78.

CHAPTER 2

The Principle of Knowledge and Approval

INTRODUCTION

2–01   A will, in order to be valid, must not only be duly executed by a testator who has a sound disposing mind, it must also be executed by a testator who at the time knew and approved of the contents of the will. If a testator was not given an opportunity to know and approve of the contents of his will it may be invalidated. The requirement that a testator must know and approve of the contents may on its own form the basis of a challenge to the validity of a will, although it is usually pleaded with two or three other grounds, *viz.* that the will was not duly executed, that the testator lacked testamentary capacity and that the testator was unduly influenced. When the principle becomes an issue it must be shown that the testator knew and approved of the contents either at the time of giving instructions or at the time of execution of the will. On either of these two dates a testator must know and approve of the contents of his will and this may be established where it is shown that a testator had read the will himself or that it was read over to him by another perhaps by the person who prepared the will so as to afford him the opportunity of confirming that the will truly reflects his wishes or of having certain matters arising out of the will explained to him more clearly, and apparently, where this has been done at the instructions stage it need not be repeated at the date of execution provided it is further established that he knew that he was executing a will. Order 79 rule 62 of the Rules of the Superior Courts must also be mentioned in this regard as it specifically requires that in the case of a blind and illiterate testator a grant of probate or letters of administration with the will annexed will not be allowed to issue by the probate officer unless he is satisfied by affidavit evidence that the will was read over to the testator before its execution, or that the testator had at such time knowledge of its contents.

2–02   However, where the principle is raised as an issue the circumstances surrounding a case will determine the approach to be adopted by the courts. Where it is shown that a will was procured and prepared by a person who was also a beneficiary or who had a benefit increased by a subsequent codicil, the vigilance of the court will be awakened and it will view such circumstances as suspicious and the onus of proof will rest on such person to satisfy the court of the righteousness of the transaction.[1] This onus may be discharged by adducing evidence which establishes that the testator knew and approved of the contents of the will at the time of execution. Where no such circumstances exist but yet there is some doubt as to whether a testator knew and approved of the contents owing to his state of health or age the issue of whether he knew and approved may involve an evaluation of his intellectual capacity by the court.[2] The evidence adduced will determine whether he had sufficient intellectual capacity to know and approve of the contents of his will although in this instance where such evidence is not forthcoming, the court may apply the presumption of testamentary capacity where a will has been duly executed.[3] Also in such a case where there is evidence forthcoming that a testator knew and approved of the *instructions* given for his will this may be sufficient to satisfy the court that he knew and approved of the contents of his will "provided that the circumstances were such as would enable the Court to say that he knew the will had been drawn according to his instructions."[4] Where a testator is merely confirming instructions already given with knowledge and approval it may not be necessary to show that he knew and approved of contents at the time of execution provided that he understood that he was executing a will.[5] Furthermore, although section 77 (1) of the Succession Act is expressed in the margin to deal with capacity to make a will the expression "sound disposing mind" used in the section was held by McCarthy J. in *In the Goods of Glynn, Deceased: Glynn v. Glynn*[6] to be "a legislative adoption of a judicial term of art requiring that a testator should know and approve of the contents of the will and, at the time of execution of the will, be of sound mind, memory and understanding." Lynch J. *In the Estate of Blackhall*[7] shared the same view.

2–03   As a result of recent Supreme Court decisions[8] where there are no suspicious circumstances surrounding the knowledge and approval by a testator of the contents of his will it seems that the main issue for the court to determine where the principle is raised is whether the testator had sufficient intellectual appreciation of the contents of his will either at the time he gave the instructions for it or at the date of execution especially where ill-health or old age is introduced as a vitiating element. A failure by a testator to have a

---

[1]   *In Re Begley, Deceased: Begley v. McHugh* [1939] I.R. 479; *In the Goods of Corboy, Deceased: Leahy and Corboy v. Corboy and Leahy* [1969] I.R. 148.

[2]   *In the Goods of Glynn, Deceased: Glynn v. Glynn* [1990] 2 I.R. 326; *In the Estate of Blackhall*, unreported, Supreme Court, April 1, 1998.

[3]   *In the Goods of Glynn, Deceased: Glynn v. Glynn*, above, n.2; *In the Estate of Blackhall*, above, n.2.

[4]   *In Re Wallace; Solicitor for the Duchy of Cornwall v. Batten* [1952] 2 T.L.R. 925 cited in I*n the Goods of Glynn, Deceased: Glynn v. Glynn*, above, n.2.

[5]   *In the Goods of Glynn, Deceased: Glynn v. Glynn*, above, n.2; *Parker v. Felgate* 8 P.D. 171.

[6]   Above, n.2.

[7]   Above, n.2.

[8]   *In the Goods of Glynn, Deceased: Glynn v. Glynn*, above, n.2; *In the Estate of Blackhall*, above, n.2.

sufficient intellectual appreciation to know and approve of the contents of his will may also result in a lack of testamentary capacity as the expression "sound disposing mind" has been held to encapsulate the two.

PROPOSITIONS OF KNOWLEDGE AND APPROVAL

The principle of knowledge and approval was discussed at great length in *Beamish v. Beamish*[9] and the following helpful propositions in relation to the principle were laid down by the President in the course of his judgment:

1. Knowledge and approval of a will is necessary and must be proved.

2. The execution of a will by a competent testator is presumptive and prima facie proof of the fact.

3. If the competent testator has read the will, or heard it read, the presumption is strong and conclusive, unless there are special circumstances attending the execution of the will.[10]

4. Among such special circumstances are fraud, as explained in *Fulton v. Andrew*,[11] and which so explained includes dereliction of duty, as illustrated in that case and *Hegarty v. King*.[12]

5. Whether read or not, if in any way the contents of the will have been brought to the notice of the testator, the effect is the same.[13]

6. Even when there has been a reading of the will, but the state of the testator was such that he could not have an intelligent appreciation of the words, he must be taken to have known and approved of the will if the words were bona fide used by a person whom he trusts to draw it up for him.[14] In *Rhodes v. Rhodes*[15] it was said by Lord Blackburn in relation to this proposition that: "Their Lordships think that there is no difference between the words which a testator himself uses in drawing up his will, and the words which are bona fide used by one whom he trusts to draw it up for him. In either case there is a great risk that words may be used which do not express the intention. There are probably very few wills in which it might not be contended that words have been so used. However this may be, the Court which has to construe the will must take the words as they find them."[16]

---

[9] [1894] 1 I.R. 7.

[10] See *Hastilow v. Stobie* L.R. 1 P. & M. 64; *Atter v. Atkinson* L.R. 1 P. & M. 665.

[11] L.R. 7 H.L. 448.

[12] 7 L.R. 3 P. & M. 11; see also *Donnelly v. Broughton* [1891] A.C. 435.

[13] *Guarghouse v. Blackburn* L.R. 1 P. & M. 116; *Harter v. Harter* L.R. 3 P. & M. 11.

[14] *Rhodes v. Rhodes* 7 App. Cas. 192; *Morrell v. Morrell* 7 P.D. 70.

[15] Above, n.14.

[16] See *Collins v. Elstone* [1893] P. 1.

2–05 In *Beamish v. Beamish*[17] the plaintiff was named as a legatee by the testator in his will dated June 3, 1887. The will contained the following clause:

> "But should he (that is to say), the testator's son (the defendant), William Beamish, die unmarried, or having no male heir to possess and inherit the estate, subject to the annuities, charges, and conditions mentioned in this my will, then and in that case I leave and bequeath the estate, subject to the annuities, charges, and conditions aforesaid, to Marmion Beamish (the plaintiff), the eldest son of my son Richard Beamish, M.D."

The testator subsequently made two wills dated October 24 and November 3, 1891, respectively, each of which contained a revocation clause and each of which omitted by mistake the clause mentioned above. The will of October 24 was copied out by the testator's daughter and under his directions; the will of November 3 was drawn up by a relative of the testator also under his directions. The plaintiff claimed that the above clause in the will of 1887 had not been revoked by the two subsequent wills as the testator neither knew nor approved of the revocation clauses contained in them and that all three wills should be admitted to probate as together constituting the last will of the deceased. However, it was held by the President, citing Lord Hannen in *Harter v. Harter*,[18] that it was beyond the jurisdiction of the court to correct the mistake, and accordingly, he admitted to probate the will of November 3, 1891 as the last will of the testator.

THE APPLICABILITY OF THE PRINCIPLE IN SUSPICIOUS CIRCUMSTANCES

2–06 Generally, the principle is that where a testator has had a will read over to him and he subsequently executes it, a presumption arises that he knew and approved of it. However, for the principle to be applied it must be shown to the satisfaction of the court, or a jury in the case of a jury trial, that the will was read over to the testator in such a way as to make plain its contents.[19] The principle is more rigorous in its application where the will of the deceased was prepared by a person who takes a benefit under it especially where the circumstances surrounding it arouse the suspicion of the court and thus making it necessary for the propounding party in such circumstances to adduce evidence not only to remove the suspicion but also to satisfy the court that the testator knew and approved of the contents of the will.[20] In *Re Begley, Deceased:*

---

[17] Above, n.9.

[18] Above, n.13 at 20.

[19] *In Re Begley, Deceased: Begley v. McHugh*, above, n.1; *Beamish v. Beamish*, above, n.9.

[20] *In the Goods of Corboy, Deceased*: Leahy and *Corboy v. Corboy and Leahy*, above, n.1; *Tyrrell v. Painton* [1894] P. 151; *Barry v. Butlin* 2 Moo. P.C. 480; *Fulton v. Andrew*, above, n.11; *Brown v. Fisher* 63 L.T. 465; *In Re Begley, Deceased: Begley v. McHugh*, above, n.1.

Begley v. McHugh[21] Sullivan C.J. stated that they were circumstances in connection with the preparation and execution of the will which should have aroused the suspicion of the jury, but did not. In that case the deceased made her will on March 29, 1934 and died on December 16, 1937 at the age of 81 years. The value of her assets was approximately £21,000 of which £13,915 represented the value of shares owned by her. She died unmarried and was survived by a number of relatives. By her will she left pecuniary legacies to the value of £4,500 for charitable purposes and also left the residue of her estate to be divided among two named charities. Her will was made three years prior to her death. At the time of making her will it was established in evidence that she did not appreciate the true value of her shares and consequently did not appreciate the value of the estate left by the residuary clause in her will. The will was prepared by her solicitor and he also read it out to her. However, there was some doubt as to whether the testatrix understood the true value of the shares in the residuary clause. The grounds of appeal relied on were that the findings of the jury in favour of the will were contrary to the weight of the evidence adduced at the trial.

2–07   There was evidence that one of the executors had considerable influence over the testatrix. The evidence also established that he induced the deceased to make a will; that he suggested that she should give instructions for her will to a particular solicitor; that the solicitor to whom she gave instructions had never acted as solicitor for the deceased and was unknown to her; that he had acted as solicitor for the executor; that the executor had interviewed the solicitor before he attended the deceased and took her instructions; that he did not inform any of the next-of-kin some of whom lived on the same street that the deceased intended to make a will, and that he did everything he could to keep her intention secret; that the value of the property disposed of by the will was approximately £21,000 of which £18,500 was bequeathed for charitable purposes with which the executor sympathised. The solicitor also admitted in evidence that in preparing the draft will he omitted six legacies amounting to £1,450 which he had been instructed to include in the will and had altered other legacies without any authority from the deceased to do so.

2–08   Sullivan C.J. in the course of his judgment stated that: "There is clear authority for the proposition that, where a competent testator has had a will read over to him and subsequently executes it, a presumption arises that he knew and approved of its contents, and that proposition has not been challenged by the respondents in this case. But in order that that proposition should apply in any case it must be established to the satisfaction of the Court, or of the jury if the case is tried with a jury, that the will was read over and that it

---

[21] Above, n.1.

was read over in such a way as to make plain its contents to the testator."[22] He referred to the speech of Lord Cairns L.C. in *Fulton v. Andrews*[23] for the statement that: "The jury must be satisfied that the will was read over, and, in the second place, must also be satisfied that there was no fraud in the case." He also referred to *Garnett-Botfield v. Garnett-Botfield*[24] and considered that the view expressed by Sir F.H. Jeune in that case was similar in tenor and effect to that of Lord Cairns in *Fulton v. Andrews*.[25]

2–09 On reviewing the evidence adduced Sullivan C.J. stated that although it was for the jury to decide on the truth and accuracy of it he did not know to what extent they accepted the evidence of the solicitor who drafted the will. It was therefore impossible for him to say that the presumption which the appellants relied on ever arose in the case and that the argument based on its existence must fail. He could not interfere with the verdict of the jury.

THE ONUS OF PROOF IN SUSPICIOUS CIRCUMSTANCES

2–10 The onus of proof in suspicious circumstances is relative to the propounding party's involvement in the preparation of the will and to the extent he benefits by it. Where the propounding party prepares the will the *onus probandi* lies on him and he must satisfy the conscience of the court that the will was executed by a free and competent testator.[26] Where the propounding party not only prepares the will but also takes a benefit under it, this circumstance will generally excite the suspicion of the court and will thus cause it to be vigilant and jealous in examining the evidence adduced in support of the will and places a further onus on the propounding party to remove such suspicion to the satisfaction of the court.[27] Lord Hatherley in *Fulton v. Andrew*[28] was of the view that where beneficiaries in a will were instrumental in its preparation: "There is a farther onus upon those who take for their own benefit, after having been instrumental in preparing or obtaining a will. They have thrown upon them the onus of shewing the righteousness of the transaction." The onus of proof in such circumstances will be the same for strangers as well

---

[22] Above, n.1 at 491-492.

[23] Above, n.11 at 463.

[24] [1901] P. 335.

[25] Above, n.11 at 463.

[26] *Barry v. Butlin*, above, n.20; *Fulton v. Andrew*, above, n.11; *In the Goods of Corboy, Deceased: Leahy and Corboy v. Corboy and Leahy*, above, n.1.

[27] *Paske v. Ollatt* 1 Phillim. 323; *Wyatt v. Ingram* 3 Hagg. Ecc. 466; *Billinghurst v. Vickers* 1 Phillim. 187 at 199; *Barry v. Butler*, above, n.20; *Fulton v. Andrew*, above, n.11; *In Re Begley, Deceased: Begley v. McHugh*, above, n.1; *In the Goods of Corboy, Deceased: Leahy and Corboy v. Corboy and Leahy*, above, n.1.

[28] Above, n.11 at 471.

as for near relatives of the testator.[29] In *In the Goods of Corboy, Deceased: Leahy and Corboy v. Corboy and Leahy*[30] the foregoing principles regarding the onus of proof were referred to by Budd J. in the course of his judgment for the Supreme Court. The facts of *Corboy* involved a testator who was in very frail health and a legatee who prepared a codicil to his will which increased her share in the estate. When the codicil was read over to the testator he nodded his approval and signed it by making a mark. Prior to his illness the testator was an astute businessman but because of his state of health – which was diagnosed as artio-sclerosis – it was difficult to evaluate his degree of understanding. The situation was further exacerbated by the fact that the testator found it difficult to speak and was unable to express his wishes clearly. The case mainly turned on the question of the onus of proof placed on a person in the legatee's position. Budd J. also referred to the House of Lords decision in *Wintle v. Nye*,[31] and in particular to the speech of Viscount Simonds[32] where he said:

> "It is not the law that in no circumstances can a solicitor or other person who has prepared a will for a testator take a benefit under it. But that fact creates a suspicion that must be removed by the person propounding the will. In all cases the court must be vigilant and jealous. The degree of suspicion will vary with the circumstances of the case. It may be slight and easily dispelled. It may, on the other hand, be so grave that it can hardly be removed."

The quantum of proof required was considered by Sellers L.J. when *Wintle v. Nye* was before the Court of Appeal[33] and whose judgment was approved of by Viscount Simonds in the House of Lords. Sellers L.J. was of the opinion that where the evidence of any witness is challenged on vital matters and is the only evidence forthcoming the court is under a duty to scrutinise it carefully and to balance the probabilities of its accuracy and reliability. The court has an "extraordinary burden of investigation" and the approach to the evidence should be suspicious and critical. The approach "should be an unreadiness, but not an unwillingness, to believe it after close scrutiny and careful consideration." Applying the principles to the case before him, Budd J. was of the view that as the legatee was directly involved in the preparation of the will and the procurement of its execution they were circumstances that ought to excite the vigilance of the court and that the court should be vigilant and jealous in examining the evidence in support of the codicil. No pronouncement in favour of the codicil should be made by the court until the suspicions were removed to the satisfaction of the court and that the codicil was what the tes-

---

[29] *Hegarty v. King*, above, n.12 at 22 *per* Deasy L.J.
[30] Above, n.1.
[31] [1959] 1 W.L.R. 284.
[32] Above, n.31 at 291.
[33] [1959] 1 All E.R. 564.

tator wished. The legatee was not in the position of other ordinary legatees who had only to establish that the codicil was read over to a testator of sound mind and memory and who was capable of understanding it. As she had been instrumental in procuring the codicil benefiting her she had also to show the righteousness of the transaction. It was incumbent upon the court to be vigilant and jealous in assessing the evidence which had been called with the object of dispelling the suspicion. He saw no room for indulgence in reviewing and weighing up the evidence. The evidence could only be assessed in the light of the well-established requirements as to the discharge of the onus of proof which rested on the legatee.

2–11 Budd J. having considered the evidence relied on by the legatee to prove the testator had knowledge and approval of the contents of the codicil found that there was a lack of "positive testimony." It was mainly based on deductions. Knowledge and approval was deduced from the fact that the testator nodded his head when the codicil was read out to him. One of the witnesses was not in a position to evaluate his power of comprehension, nor did he question the testator to assure himself of what the testator really intended to convey by his nod. He thought that a skilled lawyer would have found great difficulty in assessing the testator's real attitude of mind, considering the difficulties of communication that existed. The legatee was the only person to give evidence in point but as she benefited from the will procured by her the onus of proof rested on her to remove the suspicions surrounding the execution of the codicil. She did not say in evidence that she had explained the codicil and its effect in detail, and there was no other witness who did so. The suspicions surrounding the execution of the codicil were not removed and the evidence fell short of discharging the onus resting on the legatee of proving that the testator knew and approved of the contents of the codicil. He went on to pronounce against the codicil and declared it invalid.

2–12 It would appear however that the codicil was doomed even before Budd J. considered whether the testator had knowledge and approval of it because before he went on to consider the applicability of the principle of knowledge and approval he was of the view that the evidence adduced fell short of proving the testamentary capacity of the testator on the date in question. He was of the opinion that the evidence disclosed that the testator's illness had affected his mental powers. He had admitted difficulties of communication. He took little interest in everyday affairs. His condition had worsened on the date he executed the codicil. It became vitally important that the testator's capacity be firmly established on the date in question. Nothing short of firm medical evidence by a doctor who was in a position to assess the testator's mental capacity was required and as no such evidence was forthcoming the onus of proof regarding the testator's capacity had not been sufficiently discharged.

WHERE THERE ARE NO SUSPICIOUS CIRCUMSTANCES

2–13　Where there are no suspicious circumstances surrounding the execution of a will and a question of knowledge and approval by the testator is raised, it appears that the only matter which must be established is that the testator gave instructions for the preparation of his will and that he knew he was executing a will. Even a failure to remember the nature of these instructions will not invalidate the will embodying them once there is an appreciation of the act of execution. It was said by Sir J. Hannen in *Parker v. Felgate*[34] that:

> "A person might no longer have capacity to go over the whole transaction, and take up the thread of business from the beginning to the end, and think it over again, but if he is able to say to himself, 'I have settled up that business with my solicitor. I rely upon his having embodied it in proper words, and I accept the paper which is put before me as embodying it'; it is not, of course, necessary that he should use those words, but if he is capable of that train of thought in my judgment that is sufficient."

The reasoning of Sir J. Hannen was later followed by Devlin J. in *In Re Wallace; Solicitor for the Duchy of Cornwall v. Batten*[35] when he said that:

> "The defendants therefore rely on the principle, which according to the authorities has been well established, that if a testator gives instructions for a will to be drawn, and if the Court is satisfied that he knew and approved the contents of those instructions, it is not necessary that the Court should also be satisfied that he approved of the contents of the will, provided that the circumstances were such as would enable the Court to say that he knew the will had been drawn according to his instructions."

In *Perera v. Perera*[36] Lord MacNaghten, while approving the rules laid down by Sir J. Hannen in *Parker v. Felgate*, went on to state: "If a person has given instructions to prepare a will making a certain disposition of my property; I have no doubt that he has given effect to my intention, and I accept the document which put before me as carrying it out." McCarthy J. in his majority judgment for the Supreme Court in *In the Goods of Glynn, Deceased: Glynn v. Glynn*[37] thought that the view of Lord MacNagthen expressed the law of England and that he was unable "to identify any weakness in the conclusion as expressed by Lord MacNaghten." He went on to say that:

> "Further it seems to me to be supported by common sense and, indeed, by public policy. A duly attested will carries a presumption of due execution and testamentary capacity."

---

[34]　Above, n.5 at 174.
[35]　Above, n.4 at 930.
[36]　[1901] A.C. 354.
[37]　Above, n.2.

He thought that it was a fundamental matter of public policy that a testator's wishes should be carried out no matter how bizarre, eccentric or whimsical they may appear to be. "One man's whimsy is another man's logic." In *In the Goods of Glynn, Deceased: Glynn v. Glynn* the testator died on February 14, 1982 at the age of 77. He suffered a massive stroke on October 5, 1981 and was thereafter confined to hospital. He executed his will on October 20 of the same year. On that day, without obtaining any medical advice, the witnesses concluded that the testator knew what he was doing and was capable of making a will. One of the witnesses drew up the will in accordance with the deceased's instructions. He left all his property to a second cousin with whom he had no connection other than that they both shared the same family name, and excluded his elder sister who was unmarried and who lived all her life with him on the family farm. Neither of the witnesses who gave evidence at the trial was a beneficiary in the will. The testator's doctor, however, was of the opinion that the testator was disorientated on the day he executed the will. He also concluded that the testator's level of consciousness was such that he was unable to communicate any of his own ideas and that some method would first have to be devised for him, "some code whereby he understood and agreed that the ideas that were being communicated to him coincided with his own ideas." Another doctor was of the same opinion. Although the case involved the knowledge and approval by the testator of the contents of the will McCarthy J. was of the view that "the nub" of the matter was the testator's capacity on the date he executed his will. However, the testator was not giving instructions for his will on that date, he was confirming instructions already given and on being told that the document presented to him was his will he placed his mark on it and that he fully appreciated what he was doing. McCarthy J. was also of the view that if on that date he gave instructions for a will, even a simple one, "it may be that the validity of its execution could be challenged." At the very beginning of his judgment McCarthy J. set the scene for a debate by stating that expression "sound disposing mind" in section 77 of the Succession Act was "a legislative adoption of a judicial term of art requiring that a testator should know and approve of the contents of the will and, at the time of execution of the will, be of sound mind, memory and understanding."[38] Lynch J. in *In the Estate of Blackhall*[39] was also of the view that the expression "encapsulates two distinct requirements which are neatly expressed in the usual form of questions submitted (as in this case) for determination by the court of trial namely: 1. Was the testatrix of sound disposing mind, memory and understanding? and 2. Did the testatrix know and approve of the contents of the will in dispute?" Thus it would seem that whenever the principle of knowledge and approval of contents is raised it may also raise a question of the soundness

---

[38] Above, n.2 at 337.
[39] Above, n.2.

of mind of the testator. In *In the Estate of Blackhall* the testatrix was the tenant for life of a leasehold interest by virtue of a marriage settlement. The settlement also gave the testatrix a power of appointment over the property among her children and in default of appointment the property passed to her children equally. She had three daughters and one son. By her will of 1966 she exercised the power in favour of her three daughters only. She made another will in 1976 revoking her 1966 will, and by the will of 1976 she exercised the power of appointment in favour of all of her four children equally. The testatrix was almost one hundred years old when she died in March 1977. A question arose as to whether the testatrix knew and approved of the contents of her will and whether she was of sound disposing mind when she made it. Lynch J. stated that, in relation to the question of knowledge and approval, he had no doubt that the onus of proving the validity of the will is on the person who propounds it, "but where there is a challenge to a will based on the state of knowledge or state of health of a testator, the onus is on the person who challenges the will." He also stated that it is well-established that where a will is formally valid there is also a presumption of testamentary capacity and he cited the Supreme Court decision of *In the Goods of Glynn, Deceased: Glynn v. Glynn*[40] in support of this. The evidence showed that the will was read over to the testatrix and Lynch J. was quite satisfied that she understood the contents of the will. As there were no suspicious circumstances regarding the preparation of the will *In Re Begley and In the Goods of Corboy* were not relevant to the case. In those cases the changes in the deceased's will favoured those who procured them. By contrast there was no procurement of the will by the son of the testatrix and the change made to the will was a simple one. While he placed less reliance than the trial judge on the presumption of knowledge and approval arising from proof of execution and a prior reading over of the will before execution, he was of the view that the evidence was such that the trial judge was entitled to come to the same conclusion without reliance on the prima facie presumption that the testatrix knew and approved of the contents of the 1976 will and was of sound disposing mind. In relation to the question as to whether the testatrix had a sound disposing mind which was also raised in the case, Lynch J. accepted the evidence of her general practitioner and solicitor that the testatrix was capable of making a will and that there was no evidence before him which rebutted the presumption of testamentary capacity. The fact that the testatrix was almost a centenarian when she executed the 1976 will did not of itself disqualify her from making a valid will. He cited the following passages from the case of In *the Estate of Beliss: Polson v. Parrott*:[41]

"The Court of King's Bench in *Banks v. Goodfellow* dealt both with cases of

---

[40] Above, n.2.
[41] 45 T.L.R. 452 at 454-455.

exclusion and of defective memory, and laid down the principle in the form in which it has since been applied. These are two passages from the judgment: 'Though the mental power may be reduced below the ordinary standard yet if there be sufficient intelligence to understand and appreciate the testamentary act in its different bearings, the power to make a will remains. The standard of capacity is the capacity on the part of the testator to comprehend the extent of the property to be disposed of and the nature of the claims of those he is excluding'. Citing with approval an American authority, the court adopted these additional illustrative statements: 'By the terms a sound and disposing mind and memory it has not been understood that a testator must possess these qualities of the mind to the highest degree neither has it been understood that he must possess them as great a degree as he may formerly have done: the mind may have been in some degree debilitated, the memory may have become in some degree enfeebled, and yet there may be enough left clearly to discern and discreetly judge of all those things and all those circumstances which enter into the nature of a rational, fair and just testament."

O'Flaherty J. concurred, and having observed that the will was a simple one, went on to say that the essential duty of the court is to make sure that the deceased was of sound disposing mind, memory and understanding and knew and approved of the contents of her will and was satisfied that the evidence was sufficient to establish such matters, and once there was such evidence then the question of presumptions was not a significant factor. When considering old age *per se* he referred to the statement made by Harman J. in *Re Shaw Deceased*[42] in relation to the will of George Bernard Shaw: "it is rather youthful exuberance than the circumspection of old age that mars its symmetry." As a result of *In the Goods of Glynn* and *In the Estate of Blackhall* the principle of knowledge and approval may also be used to determine whether a testator had a "sound disposing mind" therefore equating a testator's lack of intellectual appreciation of the contents of a will with capacity to make a will although a person may have the capacity to make a will but yet not have sufficient expertise to know and approve of the contents of his will, for instance, like the testatrix in *In Re Begley* who did not appreciate the value of a residuary clause in her will.

2–14   Thus it would seem that where there are no suspicious circumstances surrounding the preparation and execution of a will any question involving knowledge and approval by the testator of the contents of his will may include an evaluation of his capacity to make a will. As a result of the Supreme Court decision in *In the Goods of Glynn* a testator will be deemed to have a sound disposing mind if he was capable of giving instructions for his will even though at the time of execution he did not know and approve of the contents of the will provided he was aware that he was executing a will. Where a will on its

---

[42] [1957] 1 W.L.R. 729 at 732.

face appears to be valid it will be presumed that not only was it duly executed but also that the testator had the necessary capacity to make it. However, such presumptions may not be relied on by the court if the evidence is sufficient to show that the will was duly executed and that the testator had testamentary capacity.[43] While old age may be a factor taken into account by the court when evaluating a testator's capacity, it will not by itself invalidate a will, if it is established in *evidence* that a testator knew and approved of the contents of his will either by reading it himself or by having it read over to him by another person, and that he understood that he was executing a will.

SUMMARY

2–15   Where the question of knowledge and approval is raised and there are suspicious circumstances and some benefit is derived from it by the person who prepared it and who is also propounding it, the onus of proof rests on that person to show that the testator knew and approved of the contents, which may necessarily involve an appraisal of the testator's intellectual capacity for the court to ascertain whether he had the requisite sound disposing mind at the time. Where there are no suspicious circumstances it would appear that the question of knowledge and approval by a testator of the contents of his will would seem to depend on whether or not he had a sound disposing mind either at the time he executed the will or at the time he gave instructions for the preparation of it, provided he understood that he was executing a will when it came to that stage. If the contents were read over to him at the time of execution and the evidence sufficiently establishes that he had a sound disposing mind at that time the court may rely on that evidence only without resorting to the presumptions of due execution and of testamentary capacity.[44]

2–16   As a result of the judgments of McCarthy J. in *In the Goods of Glynn* and Lynch J. in *In the Estate of Blackhall* the expression 'sound disposing mind' used in section 77(1) of the Succession Act "encapsulates" not only questions of testamentary capacity to make a will but also questions of knowledge and approval by a testator of the contents. It is interesting to note that it is stated in the margin of section 77 that it is a provision dealing with "capacity to make a will." Therefore, it may be asked whether the principle of knowledge and approval only becomes relevant where suspicious circumstances surround the making of a will because it seems that where there are no such circumstances the only matter which remains to be determined by the court is whether or not the testator had a sound disposing mind, either at the instruc-

---

[43] *In the Estate of Blackhall*, above, n.2.
[44] *In the Estate of Blackhall*, above, n.2.

tions' stage or at the time of execution. However, a situation can be envisaged where it may not be a question of a testator having a sound disposing mind but rather whether a testator had failed to appreciate a major provision in his will because its legal repercussions were not explained to him with sufficient clarity by the draughtsman of the will. As the lack of knowledge and approval is a ground for invalidating a will the draughtsman of a will should ensure that the will is read by a testator before execution or, preferably, that the will be should read over to him accompanied by an explanation of the legal effect of the provisions so as to make assurances doubly sure that the principle has been complied with bearing in mind such matters as the age, state of health and understanding of a particular testator.

CHAPTER 3

Testamentary Capacity and Undue Influence

INTRODUCTION

3–01 For a will to be valid it must not only be executed in compliance with section 78 of the Succession Act,[1] it must also be made by a person who has the legal capacity to do so. Capacity basically involves two matters: age and mental condition of the testator. Section 77 of the Succession Act provides that for a person to make a valid will he must be at least eighteen years and of sound disposing mind. Insofar as age is concerned, although there is a specified minimum age, there is no maximum age. Once eighteen is attained a will cannot be invalidated on the grounds of age only. The other requirement that a person must have 'a sound disposing mind' may prove to be a difficult matter because the vagaries of the human mind are not subject to precise definition. A testator's mental condition may of course be impugned on the grounds of mental ill-health, but other factors, like the effects of old age and physical ill-health, may also introduce some doubt regarding the mental condition of a particular testator. While old age and ill-health alone will not deprive a person of capacity, the effect of such on a person's mental well-being may result in the loss of capacity. However, the statutory expression is that a testator must have 'a sound disposing mind' and this has been held by McCarthy J. in *In the Goods of Glynn, Deceased: Glynn v. Glynn* [2] to be "a legislative adoption of a judicial term of art requiring that the testator should know and approve of the contents of the will and, at the time of execution of the will, be of sound mind, memory and understanding." It is all a question of degree and will depend on the evidence adduced at a trial of the issues. Where a testator's mental condition is impugned there are also certain presumptions which may be applied by the court: one, a duly executed will carries with it a presumption of testamentary capacity,[3] and two, there is a general presumption against insanity which is common to all areas of law, although this presumption may be reversed where a person is already diagnosed as suffering from mental illness. The onus of proof rests on the party who alleges incapacity.[4] However, where the barometer dips below the requisite degree of capacity this will result in the invalidation of a will.

---

[1] See Chap. 1.
[2] [1990] 2 I.R. 326 at 337.
[3] *In the Goods of Glynn, Deceased: Glynn v. Glynn*, above, n. 2.
[4] *In the Estate of Blackhall*, unreported, Supreme Court, April 1, 1998.

3–02 The way in which a testator disposes of his property may be of little or no assistance when the question of testamentary capacity is raised, as a testator is free to dispose of his property as he wishes subject to law,[5] although his estate may later be accountable for any statutory rights or claims ignored by him in the will.[6] When it comes to the disposition of property: "One man's whimsy is another man's logic."[7] Where mental incapacity is alleged it is the condition of mind of the testator which will be in question and not the way he disposes of his property.

3–03 A word on the evidence entertained by the court where incapacity is alleged. No legal practitioner in his right mind would prepare a will for a person who was certified as suffering from mental illness unless there is sufficient medical evidence to show that he has recovered from his illness or that he had entered a period of what is known as a 'lucid interval.' In such a case the medical evidence will be of paramount importance in establishing capacity. Where there is no diagnosis of mental ill-health, and where it is alleged that old age or physical ill-health had deprived the testator of capacity, the evidence adduced must establish that such factors had depreciated the testator's mind so much that he could not possibly have a sound mind, memory and understanding. In such a case, while medical evidence will be of importance, more weight may be given to the evidence of the testator's family or those who knew him well, and to the evidence of the legal practitioner who attended him and took his instructions for the will subsequently executed by him.[8]

3–04 The plea of undue influence may be raised in the alternative to lack of capacity in the pleadings. The allegation in this instance is not that a testator lacked the capacity to make a will, but rather that it was not "the offspring of his own volition" as a result of pressure exerted by another person.[9] Pressure which goes beyond the bounds of persuasion may amount to undue influence and thereby impugn the whole will or such parts of it as were affected by it.[10] The party who alleges undue influence must prove it without benefit of presumption, as in probate law, the nature of the relationship between testator and the person alleged to have exerted undue influence will not, unlike in contract law and in equity, give rise to a presumption of undue influence. The evidence must establish not only that influence was exerted but also that it was undue and affected the testator's will.

---

[5] See *In the Goods of Glynn, Deceased: Glynn v. Glynn*, above, n. 2.

[6] See Succession Act 1965. Part IX.

[7] *In the Goods of Glynn, Deceased: Glynn v. Glynn*, above, n. 2 at 340-341.

[8] See *Duffy v. Kearney and Duffy*, unreported, High Court, August 10, 1994, O'Hanlon J.

[9] *Hall v. Hall* L.R. 1 P. & D. 481; *Wingrove v. Wingrove* 11 P.D. 81.

[10] *Hall v. Hall*, above, n. 9 at 482; *Wingrove v. Wingrove*, above, n. 9 at 82; *Re Kavanagh: Healy v. MacGillycuddy and Lyons* [1978] I.L.R.M. 175.

THE EFFECT OF ILL-HEALTH AND OLD AGE ON CAPACITY

3–05 The effect of ill-health on a testator's capacity was considered by McCarthy J. in *In the Goods of Glynn, Deceased: Glynn v. Glynn.*[11] The facts of that case were that the testator died on February 14, 1982, at the age of 77. He suffered a massive stroke on October 5, 1981, and was thereafter confined to hospital. He executed his will on October 20. On that day, without obtaining any medical advice, the witnesses concluded that the testator knew what he was doing and was capable of making a will. One of the witnesses drew up the will in accordance with the deceased's instructions. He left all his property to a second cousin with whom he had no connection other than that they both shared the same family name, and excluded his elder sister who was unmarried and who lived all her life with him on the family farm. Neither of the witnesses was a beneficiary in the will. The testator's doctor, however, was of the opinion that the testator was "disorientated" on the day he executed the will. He also concluded that the testator's level of consciousness was such that he was unable to communicate any of his own ideas and that some method of communication would first have to be devised for him, "some code whereby he understood and agreed that the ideas that were being communicated to him coincided with his own ideas." Another doctor was of the same opinion. The question was whether his state of ill-health deprived him of testamentary capacity. McCarthy J. held that the deceased in the present case was merely confirming instructions already given and he was told truthfully that the document represented what he had expressed to be his testamentary wishes, and as the two witnesses were quite satisfied that he knew what he was doing, the will was a valid one. McCarthy J. thought that the principle involved was summarised by Lord MacNagthen in *Perera v. Perera*[12] who in turn approved the rules laid down by Sir James Hannen in *Parker v. Felgate*[13] in the following terms:

> "If a person has given instructions to a solicitor to make a will, and the solicitor prepares it in accordance with those instructions, all that is necessary to make it a good will, if executed by the testator, is that he would be able to think thus far: 'I gave my solicitor instructions to prepare a will making a certain disposition of my property; I have no doubt that he has given effect to my intention, and I accept the document which put before me as carrying it out'."

3–06 The decision in *Duffy v. Kearney and Duffy*[14] is a good example of the approach taken by the court to the evidence given at a trial involving testamentary capacity. In that case the testator was a bachelor who lived alone on a

---

[11] Above, n. 2.

[12] [1901] A.C. 354.

[13] 8 P.D. 171.

[14] Above, n. 8.

farm in close proximity to his brother, Vincent Duffy, the plaintiff, who also farmed in the same locality. The defendants were a sister and brother of the deceased who had left Ireland and went to live in the United States many years before the death of the deceased and who made only occasional visits to Ireland prior to his death. The testator left his farm to the plaintiff. At the time of making his will, however, he was extremely ill in hospital which caused the defendants to have doubts about his capacity to make a will. As a result of such doubts they entered a caveat which eventually led to a full probate action challenging the validity of the will made by the deceased. O'Hanlon J. in the course of his judgment considered the evidence given by a medical expert and the solicitor who prepared the deceased's will regarding the mental capacity of the deceased at the date of execution of the will. Although he stated that the evidence of the medical expert had to be treated with respect, he nevertheless went on to say that "what he had to say about the general effect of the human intellect and perception of personal relationships and affairs of administration of drugs of the type which were administered to the deceased during his last illness . . . was not, in my opinion, sufficient to dislodge the very comprehensive evidence given by Mr. O'Carroll, Solicitor, and by the other witnesses who visited and conversed" with the deceased. The solicitor knew the deceased and had acted for the deceased's family for a long period before the will was made. The evidence of the deceased's solicitor as to the general physical and mental state of the deceased was strongly supported by the evidence of the other witnesses who visited him in hospital around the time of execution of the will and the general conclusions of another medical practitioner about the capacity of the deceased. O'Hanlon J. had no difficulty in declaring in favour of the will and finding that the deceased testator was of sound disposing mind.

3–07 While the Succession Act specifies that a testator must be at least eighteen years to make a valid will, it does not specify an upper age limit.[15] Thus, once a testator attains the age of eighteen years a will cannot be invalidated on the grounds of age only. However, age may impinge on the second prerequisite for making a valid will, *viz.* that a testator must be of "sound disposing mind."[16] As no two persons are alike so also the debilitating effects of old age may affect persons in different ways, and where the question of age is raised as a vitiating factor concerning capacity, the mental condition of the particular testator existing at the time he executed the will will be considered by the court. One would hardly expect a forty year old testator to lack capacity due to the debilitating effects of old age, but should he, unfortunately, exhibit symptoms of what is known as premature senility it will not be age, but rather the attendant effects of such a condition on his mind, which will deprive him of

---

[15] s.77.
[16] *ibid.*

capacity. In the case of a testator of advanced years one might expect a diminution of mental powers, however, in a particular case it may be shown that the testator exhibited no signs of declining mental powers. In fact in certain famous instances it was quite evident that advanced years had a rejuvenating, and not a debilitating, effect. It is generally agreed that W. B. Yeats wrote his best work towards the end of his life.[17] Among his last poems was one entitled 'Politics', but apparently politics were the last thing on the poet's mind as his attention was fixed on "that girl standing there" and wished "that I were young again/ And held her in my arms." George Bernard Shaw is another case in point. He was ninety-four when he made his will and it was said by Harman J. in *Re Shaw Deceased*[18] that "it is rather youthful exuberance than the circumspection of old age that mars its symmetry." Therefore, the question whether the debilitating effects of old age affected the capacity of a testator to make a valid will will depend on the mental condition of a particular testator at the time he executed the will. The question of old age and capacity to make a will was raised in the Supreme Court decision in *In the Estate of Blackhall.*[19] In that case the testatrix was the tenant for life of a leasehold interest by virtue of a marriage settlement. The settlement also gave the testatrix power of appointment over the property among her children and in default of appointment the property passed to her children equally. She had three daughters and one son. By her will of 1966 she exercised the power of appointment in favour of her three daughters only. She made another will in 1976 revoking her 1966 will and by the will of 1976 she exercised the power of appointment in favour of all of her four children equally. The testatrix was almost one hundred years old when she died in March 1977. One of the questions which arose was whether she was of sound disposing mind when she made her will in 1976. The court heard the appeal in July 1997 and reserved judgment. However, the court decided to re-list the case and furnished the parties in writing with four questions on which it wished to hear further argument, namely:

1.   Whether the learned trial judge was correct in relying for his decision partly upon a presumption of validity.

2.   Whether the learned trial judge should have regarded the onus of proof of a sound disposing mind as being on the plaintiff.

3.   If so, would the evidence of the solicitor upon whose evidence the learned trial judge partly relied have been sufficient to discharge that onus of proof.

4.   If not, was there other evidence which would have discharged that onus

---

[17] *The Tower*, 1928, aged 63; *The Winding Stair and Other Poems*, 1933, aged 68; *New Poems*, 1938, aged 73. He died in 1939.
[18] [1957] 1 W.L.R. 729 at 731.
[19] Unreported, Supreme Court, April 1, 1998.

had the learned trial judge to look beyond the evidence of the solicitor and the presumption upon which the learned trial judge acted.

3–08 Lynch J. during the course of his judgment noted that while section 77(1) of the Succession Act provided for a minimum age there was no maximum age above which a person was precluded from making a valid will. Therefore, the fact that the testatrix was nearly one hundred years old when she executed the 1976 will did not disqualify her from making a valid will. As to her intellectual capacity to make a valid will, Lynch J. referred to *In the Estate of Beliss: Polson v. Polson* [20] and cited the following passages from the judgment in that case for a statement of the principle to be applied in cases where the intellectual capacity of a testator is called in question:

> "The Court of King's Bench in *Banks v. Goodfellow* dealt both with cases of exclusion and of defective memory, and laid down the principle in the form in which it has since been applied. These are two passages from the judgment. 'Though the mental power may be reduced below the ordinary standard yet if there be sufficient intelligence to understand and appreciate the testamentary act in its different bearings, the power to make a will remains. The standard of capacity is the capacity on the part of the testator to comprehend the extent of the property disposed of and the nature of the claims of those he is excluding.' Citing with approval an American authority, the court adopted these additional illustrative statements: 'By the terms a sound and disposing mind and memory it has not been understood that a testator must possess these qualities of the mind in the highest degree neither has it been understood that he must possess them as great a degree as he may formerly have done: the mind may have been in some degree debilitated, the memory may have become in some degree enfeebled, and yet there may be enough left clearly to discern and discreetly judge of those things and all those circumstances which enter into the nature of a rational, fair and just testament'."

He went on to say that the real issue before the court was whether the trial judge was entitled to find as he did on the evidence before him that the testatrix was of a sound disposing mind within the meaning of section 77(1)(b) of the Succession Act.

> "This concept encapsulates two distinct requirements which are neatly expressed in the usual form of questions submitted (as in this case) for determination of the court of trial:
>
> 1. Was the testatrix of sound mind, memory and understanding? and
> 2. Did the testatrix know and approve of the contents of the will in dispute?"

3–09 In the light of the evidence Lynch J. was of the opinion that the trial judge was entitled to find that the testatrix had the capacity to make a valid will even if she required matters of a complex nature explained to her.

---

[20] 45 T.L.R. 452 at 454-455.

WHERE MENTAL ILL-HEALTH IS ALLEGED

3–10 Whenever mental ill-health is alleged to invalidate a will the onus of proof lies on the party making the allegation to establish that the testator's mind was so affected by it that he was incapable of making a valid will. It is not so much that a testator suffered from mental ill-health at the time of execution of the will but rather that it was so severe as to deprive him of testamentary capacity over a period of time. "It is absolutely and essentially necessary to look to the peculiar circumstances of each individual case; and to judge the whole character of the person whose mental capacity is the subject of enquiry, what was the state and condition of mind of that individual; not only with respect to the immediate times at which a will is executed, but at the intermediate states of his life."[21] The nature of the illness may be so obvious that the court may have no difficulty in finding that a testator lacked capacity or it may be of a nature which may become evident only over a period of time thus making it more difficult for the court to determine the precise moment that a testator began to lose the capacity to make a will. It was said by Lord Cranwoth in *Boyse v. Rossborough* that:

> "There is no difficulty in the case of a raving madman or a drivelling idiot, in saying that he is not a person capable of disposing of property; but between such an extreme case, and that of a man of perfectly vigorous understanding, there is every shade of intellect, every degree of mental capacity. There is no possibility of mistaking midnight for noon. but at what precise moment twilight becomes darkness is hard to determine."[22]

However, where a person is diagnosed as suffering from a particular mental illness and as a result of which his mind cannot be said to be sound, testamentary incapacity will be the inevitable consequence.[23] Certain types of mental illness have been given more sympathetic consideration by the court than others and the existence of such may not be found to have deprived a person of testamentary capacity. For instance, where it shown that the testator was subject to an insane delusion the first approach of the court is to treat it with great distrust and every presumption should be made against it.[24] One of the factors which the court will take into account when deciding whether the insane delusion deprived a testator of capacity will be the terms of the will itself and the way in which the testator disposed of his property, and if ties of natural affection and the claims of near relatives are ignored this may be viewed as a manifestation of the delusive state of mind of the testator and influenced the testator when he made his will. It was said by Cockburn C.J. in *Banks v. Goodfellow* that:

---

[21] *Mudway v. Croft* 3 Curt. 671 at 676 *per* Sir H.J. Fust.

[22] 6 H.L.C. 2 at 45.

[23] See *Banks v. Goodfellow* L.R. 5 Q.B. 549 at 559.

[24] Above, n. 23 at 570.

"Where insane delusion has once been shown to have existed, it may be difficult to say whether the mental disorder may not possibly have extended beyond
the particular form or instance in which it manifested itself. It may be difficult
to vary how far the delusion may not have influenced the testator in the particular disposition of his property. And the presumption becomes additionally strong
where the will is . . . one on which the natural affection and the claims of near
relationship have been disregarded."[25]

It may also be shown that the delusive state of mind did not extend to the
whole will and was confined to a part of the will only and if such is the case
the will may be admitted to probate with the impugned part excluded.[26] An
insane delusion is the existence of such a false image in the mind of a testator
which persists notwithstanding the production of evidence showing that it is
false and cannot by reasoning with him remove it from his mind.[27] When determining the existence of such a delusion "you must of necessity put to yourself this question and answer it, 'can I understand how any man in possession
of his senses could have believed such and such a thing?' And if the answer
you give is, 'I cannot understand it', then it is of the necessity of the case that
you should say that the man is not sane."[28] An insane delusion must be distinguished from an unreasonable fear, belief or suspicion, eccentricity or caprice
and although some of these states may later develop into something irrational
they will not by themselves invalidate a will.[29] The insane delusion must be
proved to have existed at the time of execution of the will.[30]

3–11   Although the general presumption of sanity will be applied by the court
this may be reversed where it is established that a testator has been diagnosed
as being mentally ill and is undergoing treatment for it.[31] For instance, where
a person has been diagnosed as a paranoid schizophrenic and even though
such a mental condition is incurable, he may still have capacity to make a will,
where it is established that the condition can be effectively controlled by the
use of medication. Such was the case in *O'Donnell v. O'Donnell* [32] but the
evidence showed that the negative elements of such a condition were not apparent to the testator's solicitor or to those who knew him and who had dealings with him. No such elements were present when he executed his will and
when the tests laid down in *Banks v. Goodfellow* [33] were applied by the court
the testator was not found wanting in capacity to make a valid will. Where it is

---

[25] Above, n. 23 at 570.
[26] Above, n. 23 at 570; *In the Estate of Bohrmann* [1938] 1 All E.R. 271.
[27] *Walcot v. Alleynn* Milw. 76; *Dew v. Clark* 3 Add. 79; *Re Bliss* 141 L.T. 245; *Battan Singh v. Amirchand* [1948] A.C. 161.
[28] *Boughton v. Knight* L.R. 3 P. & D. 64 at 68 *per* Sir J. Hannen.
[29] *Austen v. Graham* 8 Moo. P.C. 341; *Boughton v. Knight*, above, n. 28.
[30] *Wheller v. Alderson* 3 Hag. Ecc. 598.
[31] *Bannatyne v. Bannatyne* 2 Rob. 472 at 501.
[32] Unreported, High Court, March 24, 1999, Kelly J.
[33] Above, n. 23.

alleged that the testator made his will during the course of a a lucid interval the presumption that he lacked capacity may first have to be rebutted.[34] Where it is established that a person suffered from an insane delusion evidence of his recovery may be gathered from admissions by him of the imaginary nature of his delusion and where he recommences to behave in a rational manner.[35] The onus of proof lies on the party alleging that the will was executed during a lucid interval and the standard of proof required for proving the existence of a lucid interval will be the same as that required for proving that a person lacked capacity to make a will [36] Once a person has been diagnosed as suffering from a mental illness, and where it is alleged that the testator made his will during a lucid interval, medical evidence of its existence will become of vital importance as the evidence of relatives and friends alone will not suffice. As regards the evidence of the testator's family and friends where a lucid interval is alleged it was cautioned by Sir J. Nichol in *Groom v. Thomas* that:

> "Where there is calmness, when there is rationality on ordinary subjects, those who see the party usually conclude that his recovery is perfect, and family and those around the unfortunate person, partly from ignorance of the disorder, partly from delicacy in interfering, partly from their own wishes to believe him well again, form incorrect opinions on the subject."[37]

3–12   The mental condition of senile dementia is a condition associated with old age, although there is the rather rare condition of premature senility which may affect a person who is not elderly. It is manifested mainly by a testator being unable to remember recent events in his life. As one of the prerequisites of a sound disposing mind includes that of memory it is the memory of the testator which will be in question where senility is alleged. While the ravages of age may be visited upon the entire mind of a person, senility leads to a particular disintegration of the memory. The degree of capacity required by a person who is diagnosed as suffering from senility was considered by Cockburn C.J. in *Banks v. Goodfellow* where he said, *inter alia*, that:

> "the memory may have become in some degree enfeebled, and yet there may be enough left clearly to discern and discreetly judge, of all those things and all those circumstances which enter into the nature of a rational, fair and just testament. But if they so far failed as that these cannot be discerned and judged of, then he cannot be said to be of sound disposing mind and memory."[38]

The onus of proof lies on the party who alleges that a testator did not possess a sound disposing mind on the grounds of senility. In the absence of a medical

---

[34] *Nichols v. Binns* Sw. & Tr. 239.
[35] *Waring v. Waring* 6 Moo. P.C. 354; *Bannatyne v. Bannatyne*, above, n. 31.
[36] *Smith v. Tebbitt* L.R. 1 P. & D. 354 at 398.
[37] 2 Hagg. Ecc. 433 at 442.
[38] Above, n. 23 at 567.

history of the testator's senility by his regular medical practitioner, more weight will be given to the evidence of the testator's legal practitioner and to that of those who were close to him and in a position to form common sense judgements in relation to his behaviour, rather than to medical evidence given by a medical practitioner who was not personally acquainted with the testator's medical history.[39] A legal practitioner who entertains some doubt regarding the capacity of an elderly person to make a will should first seek medical opinion preferably from that person's regular medical practitioner regarding his capacity to make a will and keep it on file with the will as such may be required in the event of a future challenge.[40]

UNDUE INFLUENCE

3–13 The parties and circumstances surrounding the making of a will may also become the subject of the court's scrutiny where it is alleged that the testator was unduly influenced when making his will. In other words, the allegation in this instance is that the will made by the testator was not freely made by him. Where the volition of a testator is alleged to have been suppressed the degree of pressure exerted by the person alleged to have applied it will be considered by the court to see the effect it had on the testator. Was the testator in question influenced by the kind of pressure exerted? The leading authorities on the matter[41] have set down the parameters at persuasion only and anything beyond that would be considered pressure, the essential ingredient of undue influence. Even persuasion must be limited to that which "appeals to the affection or ties of kindred, to sentiment of gratitude for past service, or pity for future destitution, or the like – these are all legitimate, and may fairly be pressed on a testator. Even where a testator has been 'persuaded or induced by considerations' in favour of a particular person 'which you may condemn, really and truly to intend to give his property to another, though you may disapprove of the act, yet it is legitimate in the sense of its being legal."[42] Pressure of whatever character, "whether acting on the fears or the hopes, if so exerted as to overpower the volition without convincing the judgement, is a species of restraining under which no valid will can be made."[43] The character of the testator may also be taken into account and where pressure takes the form of importunity or threats, which the testator has not the moral courage to resist, or complies with for the sake of peace and quiet, and if the pressure

---

[39] Above, n. 28.
[40] *Clery v. Barry* 21 L.R. Ir. 152.
[41] *Hall v. Hall*, above, n. 9; *Wingrove v. Wingrove*, above, n. 9.
[42] *Hall v. Hall*, above, n. 9 at 482 *per* Sir J.P. Wilde; See also *Wingrove v. Wingrove*, above, n. 9 at 82 *per* Sir J. Hannen.
[43] *Hall v. Hall*, above, n. 9 at 482.

used "is carried to a degree in which the free play of the testator's judgement, discretion or wishes is overborne, [it] will constitute undue influence, though no force is either used or threatened."[44]

3–14   The onus of proof lies on the party who alleges the existence of undue influence and the evidence adduced must establish that not only was influence exerted by a particular party but that it was undue and that it affected the testator's will. In probate law, the nature of relationship that existed between the testator and the person alleged to have exerted undue influence will not give rise to any presumption of its existence. In contract law and in equity certain fiduciary relationships will raise a presumption of undue influence requiring evidence in rebuttal, but probate law is exceptional in this respect. Although there is no such presumption in probate law, the circumstances of a case may nevertheless excite the vigilance of the court and where such is the case the righteousness of the transaction may have to be proved to the satisfaction of the court. For instance, where the solicitor who prepared the deceased's will was left a legacy it may be incumbent on him to establish the righteousness of the transaction to the satisfaction of the court.[45] The righteousness of the transaction may be established by showing that the testator knew and approved of the contents either by reading the will himself or by having it read over to him by another.[46]

3–15   The party who alleges undue influence must prove it to the satisfaction of the court. The evidence adduced at the trial must also be material to the issues alleged.[47] The existence of undue influence in prior dealings with the same person may allow the court to conclude that such influence was also exerted on the testator when he made his will.[48] In *In the Goods of Breen: Breen and Kennedy v. Breen and Others* [49] one of the issues raised was that the testatrix was unduly influenced when she made her will. The deceased made her will on June 22, 1991, leaving the family home and contents to one of her daughters. The deceased was also the owner of certain lands which were not disposed of by her will owing to pressure exerted by members of her family at the time. As she was seriously ill at the time the defendants claimed, *inter alia,* that the plaintiffs exerted undue influence on her, and if they were successful a previous will made by the deceased which disposed of all of her assets would become her last will. Barr J. having stated that the onus of proof was on the

---

[44] *ibid.*

[45] *Hegarty v. King* 5 L.R. Ir. 299.

[46] *In re Begley, Deceased: Begley v. McHugh* [1939] I.R. 479.

[47] *Boyse v. Rossborough*, above, n. 22 at 48; *Baudins v. Richardson* [1906] A.C. 169; *Craig v. Lamourex* [1920] A.C. 349.

[48] *Boyse v. Rossborough*, above, n. 22; *Craig v. Lamourex*, above, n. 46.

[49] Unreported, High Court, May 5, 1995, Barr J.

defendants to establish the alleged undue influence on their mother, went on to say that the greatest difficulty facing them was the contents of the will itself. It contained only one bequest, a bequest of her house to one of her daughters, which caused no contention among the family. Therefore, Barr J. held that the defendants had failed to establish that the will of 1991 was brought about by undue influence on her by anyone. If it transpires that the influence was not exerted over the whole will, but was confined to part only, the impugned part will be excluded from the probate.[50] Finally, there was a time when particulars of undue influence in probate were not required to be furnished save only the name of the party alleging that it was exerted,[51] but now particulars of undue influence in probate must be furnished in the same way as in other cases where undue influence is alleged.[52]

SUMMARY

3–16 All persons who have attained the age of eighteen years are entitled to make a will. Once a will is executed in compliance with the statutory rules not only will there be a presumption of due execution but also it will be presumed that the testator had the capacity to make it. Where a will is challenged on the grounds of lack of capacity a testator's mental condition will become the focus of the court's attention as will all such factors which may have affected his mental condition. The onus of proof to show that a testator lacked capacity will rest on the party who so alleges. The weight given to the evidence will depend on its source: in the absence of a medical history of a testator's state of health by his regular medical practitioner, greater weight may be given to the evidence of those who were acquainted with the testator during his lifetime rather than medical evidence not based on the medical history of the testator. Even a diagnosed state of mental ill-health may still not deprive a testator of capacity if it can be shown that such a condition is controllable by administering medication coupled with evidence of normal behaviour by those who knew him and had dealings with him. As well as the entitlement of all persons aged eighteen years and upwards to make a will, they have also the right to dispose of their property by will in the way they wish to dispose of it within the parameters of the law, and although a disposition of their property may not follow the norm by benefiting their family or those close to them, the will will not be impugned on that ground only and may be of little or no assistance in establishing lack of capacity. Besides, those who would naturally expect to benefit by a will, for instance, a testator's spouse and children, may have recourse to

---

[50] *Allen v. M'Pherson* 1 H.L.C. 191 at 209; *Fulton v. Andrew* L.R. 7 H.L. 448; *Farrelly v. Corrigan* [1899] A.C. 563.
[51] See *Wallace v. McDowell* [1920] 2 I.R. 194.
[52] *In the Goods of Rutledge* [1981] I.L.R.M. 198.

the respective provisions of the Succession Act for the purpose of establishing legal rights or instituting proceedings.

3–17   Where undue influence is alleged it must be shown to be of a kind which goes beyond the bounds of persuasion and that it affected the testator's free volition. If it is established in evidence that the testator was subject to undue influence the whole will may be impugned or such parts as were affected by it, and where it was affected in part only the remainder of the will will be admitted to probate.

CHAPTER 4

Animus Revocandi

INTRODUCTION

4–01   The probate jurisdiction of the court as regards wills may be summarised by saying that it consists in determining which document or documents should be admitted to probate as constituting the last will of a testator. Although Swinburne says that 'no man can die with two testaments' yet any number of testamentary documents may be admitted to probate together constituting the last will of a testator. The mere fact that one will follows another does not by that fact alone mean that the prior will is entirely revoked unless it is expressly or by implication revoked by the later will, or that the two are incapable of standing together. A prior will may be expressly revoked by a later will or codicil containing a suitable revocation clause, or it may be revoked by 'some writing' declaring an intention to revoke and executed in the same manner as a will, or by destroying it animo revocandi.[1] But where two wills exist and the later does not revoke the prior one the court may consider the language of the two documents to ascertain the intention of the testator, and where there is doubt whether the later will was intended to be a total or partial substitution of the prior one extrinsic evidence of the testator's intention may be admitted by the court, but only to ascertain whether the testator intended "to substitute or supplement, to revoke or to retain, the dispositions in the earlier will."[2]

4–02   Where there are two documents the court will determine the extent of the revocation intended by the testator by a form of comparative analysis between the documents. Where there are inconsistencies evident in two documents the analysis may go so far as even comparing disposition for disposition in each of the documents and having done so may admit to probate either the two documents or one document in its entirety and partly the other, as comprising the last will of the testator.[3] On the other hand, the later of two wills may, by virtue of the dispositions contained in it, impliedly revoke the earlier will in its entirety, and be admitted to probate as the last will.[4] However, where an analysis reveals that two testamentary documents are materially inconsist-

---

[1] Succession Act 1965, s. 85 (2).
[2] *Reeves v. Reeves* [1909] 2 I.R. 521 at 535-536.
[3] *Reeves v. Reeves*, above, n.2.
[4] *In the Goods of Martin* [1968] I.R. 1.

ent and irreconcilable and that they both contain revocation clauses and bear the same date neither document may be admitted to probate and thus resulting in an intestacy.[5] Where one testamentary document is in existence only and it is alleged that that document was revoked by subsequent testamentary documents which are not forthcoming at the trial, nothing less than clear and satisfactory evidence of the subsequent documents will be required to revoke the testamentary document propounded by the plaintiff.[6] Moreover, a later executed document, though not formally prepared, may revoke and replace an earlier will, for instance, a duly executed instructions' sheet may revoke a prior will.[7] Even 'some writing' which expresses simply an intention only to revoke a prior will may be sufficient to revoke a prior will provided that it was signed and witnessed.[8]

4–03 Section 85(2) of the Succession Act also allows for the destruction of a will to be used as a means of revocation provided that the act of destruction is carried out animo revocandi. However, for destruction to be an effective means of revocation the act of destruction and the *animus revocandi* must be coexistent to complete the revocation: one without the other will not suffice. Therefore any mistaken destruction of a will will not revoke it because the intention is lacking and proof of its contents may subsequently be admitted to probate. There are many ways by which a will may be destroyed but if the chosen form of destruction does not succeed in destroying the will the attempted revocation will fail notwithstanding the existence of the *animus revocandi*.[9] Just as a prior will may be partially revoked by a subsequent one, a will may also be partially revoked by destruction and the parts remaining intact admitted to probate.[10]

4–04 However, whatever form of revocation is used it will not be absolute if it is dependent upon and relative to another event occurring at the time of the purported revocation, for instance, a testator may revoke a current will in the mistaken belief that an earlier will made by him would be revived,[11] or he may destroy an earlier will with the intention of making a fresh will which fails to materialise.[12] This is where the doctrine of dependent relative revocation may be applied by the court, and although the evidence (internal and extrinsic) adduced showing the *animus revocandi*,[13] or indeed, lack of it, will be central

---

[5] *In the Goods of Millar* [1931] I.R. 364.
[6] *In the Goods of Miller* [1940] I.R. 456.
[7] *In the Goods of Brennan* [1976] I.R. 633.
[8] Succession Act 1965, s. 85(2); *In the Goods of Eyre* [1905] 2 I.R. 540.
[9] *Cheese v. Lovejoy* 2 P.D. 251.
[10] *In the Goods of Bentley* [1930] I.R. 455.
[11] *In the Goods of Hogan* [1980] I.L.R.M. 24.
[12] *West v. West* [1921] 2 I.R. 34; *In the Goods of Irvine* [1919] 2 I.R. 485.
[13] *Reeves v. Reeves*, above, n.2.

to the application of the doctrine, the circumstances surrounding the case will also be taken into account by the court.[14]

4–05 Thus in the absence of an express revocation, the *animus revocandi* will become the focus of the court's attention to ascertain whether a testamentary document was indeed revoked *animo revocandi*.

EVIDENCE OF THE *ANIMUS REVOCANDI*

4–06 The court will begin its search for the *animus revocandi* among the documents executed by the testator. In doing so it will also be guided by Swinburne's maxim which states 'no man can die with two testaments.' Yet Swinburne's maxim mentions 'testaments' and not 'documents' thus any number of documents may together comprise a testator's last testament and be admitted to probate as such. Where there is some doubt however as to whether a testator intended a later testamentary document to be a complete substitution for a prior document or that he intended merely to revise a prior document, extrinsic evidence may be adduced for the purpose of showing an intention "to substitute or supplement, to revoke or to retain, the dispositions in the earlier will."[15] It may be remarked in passing however that the rules regarding the admissibility of extrinsic evidence of a testator's *animus revocandi* in probate actions are not as rigorous as those applied in construction suits where extrinsic evidence of the testator's intention is sought to be admitted.[16] In probate actions the main function of the court is to discover what document or documents the testator intended to be his last will; in construction suits this function will be to ascertain the testator's intention from the language used by him in his will which has already passed probate and subject to the provisions contained in section 90 of the Succession Act regarding the admission of extrinsic evidence.[17]

4–07 Where there is some confusion then surrounding the documents which are meant to constitute the last will of a testator, the court will search among the documents to ascertain what document or documents the testator intended to constitute his will. It may happen that where two testamentary documents are produced neither may be treated as representing the last will because of

---

[14] *In the Goods of Hogan*, above, n.11.

[15] *Reeves v. Reeves*, above, n.2 at 535-536; See also *Methuen v. Metheun* 2 Phill. 416; *Jenner v. Ffinch* L.R. 5 P.D. 106; *Townsend v. Moore* [1903] P. 66; *In the Estate of Bryan* [1907] P. 125.

[16] See Chap. 6.

[17] See *Rowe v. Law* [1978] I.R. 55; *In Re Collins: O'Connell v. Bank of Ireland*, unreported, Supreme Court, May 19, 1998.

the inconsistencies that exist in them. Such was the case in *Reeves v. Reeves*.[18] In that case proceedings were instituted to ascertain which of two testamentary documents constituted the last will of the testatrix, Mary Reeves. She left two wills dated April 24, 1903 and August 28, 1905, respectively. The plaintiffs and defendant, Thomas Somerville Reeves, were named as executors in the former document, though notwithstanding this letters of administration with the will of August 28, 1905 annexed was granted to Thomas Somerville Reeves alone. The other defendants, were his sister, Mrs Fleming, and her daughter, who were appointees named in each document. In addition, an argument with reference to the construction and effect of the document of August 28, 1905 was put forward on behalf of the defendant, Mrs Fleming, which, if sustained, would have effectively excluded the earlier will from recognition. Furthermore, the defendants, Thomas Somerville Reeves and Mrs Fleming, were objects of the power of appointment which the testatrix purported to exercise, and were members of the class who would take in default of appointment. The plaintiffs sought the recall of the grant of letters of administration with the will of August 28, 1905 annexed, and a grant of probate of the two testamentary documents, while the defendants Mrs Fleming and a Mrs Large claimed that the later of the two documents alone should be admitted to probate. The question for determination by the court was whether the will of April 24, 1903 was revoked, wholly or partially, by the will of August 28, 1905, or was so inconsistent with it that the two documents could not stand together. Kenny J. considered the authorities on the subject of the revocation of one testamentary document by another of a later date. He found that the governing principle was accurately stated in *Williams on Executors* (6th ed. at p. 156; 9th ed., p. 138) as follows:

> "The mere fact of making a subsequent testamentary paper does not work a total revocation of a prior one, unless the latter expressly, or in effect, revoke the former, or the two are incapable of standing together; for though it be a maxim, as Swinburne says above, that 'no man can die with two testaments,' yet any number of instruments, whatever their relative date, or whatever form they may be (so as they be clearly testamentary) may be admitted to probate as together containing the last will of the deceased. And if a subsequent testamentary paper, whether in form of will or a codicil, be partially inconsistent with one of earlier date, then such latter instrument will revoke the former as to those parts only where they are inconsistent."[19]

When applying this principle the language of the two documents may be examined to see whether the later will was intended to be a complete substitution for the earlier one, or an addition in whole or in part, and extrinsic evidence of the testator's intention may be admitted "but only as to the intention to

---

[18] Above, n.2.
[19] *ibid.* at 535-536; See also *Lemage v. Goodban* L.R. 1 P. & D. 57 at 62; *Cadell v. Wilcocks* [1898] P. 21; *Kent v. Kent* [1902] P. 110; *Leslie v. Leslie* I.R. 6 Eq. 332 at 334.

substitute or supplement, to revoke or to retain, the dispositions in the earlier will" and not for the purpose of filling in blanks or supplying deficiencies.[20]

4–08 When undertaking such a comparative analysis between two testamentary documents the use of the words 'this is my last will' will by no means be conclusive when revocation is being considered. In fact, the analysis conducted by the court may even be as particular and in-depth as comparing disposition for disposition in each document: "if there be clear words of gift in an earlier will that disposition ought not to be regarded as revoked, unless by equally clear language; the onus of showing revocation rests on the party alleging it."[21]

4–09 In *Reeves v. Reeves*[22] Kenny J., although satisfied that when the testatrix made the will of 1905 she meant to supersede the will of 1903, found that the execution of the intention fell somewhat short of complete accomplishment, and even though, as a result of his analysis, it was apparent that only parts of the 1903 will were unrevoked, he considered it advisable to admit the whole will to probate together with the will of 1905.

4–10 In the case of two existing wills the later one may be held to revoke by implication the earlier one in its entirety even in the absence of a revocation clause in the later will. This matter was considered by O'Keeffe P. in *In the Goods of Martin*.[23] In that case the testatrix was a widow who died without issue having made two wills. The second will contained no revocation clause and consisted of a legacy of 'all my money' and a bequest of personal belongings. The estate of the testatrix consisted of stocks and shares, monies in deposit and current accounts in two banks, and monies in Irish and English Post Office Savings Banks. An application was made for a grant of letters of administration with the second will annexed, or with both the first and second will annexed. O'Keeffe P. considered it well-settled that the meaning of the word 'money' may cover much more then the primary meaning of the word so that a gift in a will of "all my money" may be equivalent to "all my personal estate."[24] However, he was not inclined to broaden the meaning to include a gift of the testatrix's personal belongings. He thought that one must consider the consequences of a more restrictive meaning in order to arrive at an opinion as to what the deceased meant to include. There was a valid residuary clause in the earlier will and if the deceased did not intend to revoke that will by the

---

[20] *ibid.*

[21] *Townsend v. Moore*, above, n.15 at 77 *per* Vaughan Williams L.J.

[22] Above, n.2.

[23] Above, n.4.

[24] *Caldeck v. Stafford and Lindemere* [1930] I.R. 196; *Perrin v. Morgan* [1943] A.C. 399; See Chap. 14.

later one the residuary clause still stood. However, the residuary legatee was seven years dead at the date of the second will and influenced by this consideration O'Keeffe P. came to the conclusion that the words "all my money" in the later will covered the entire personal estate of the deceased other than the personal belongings and that the earlier will was impliedly revoked.

4–11   However, where two existing wills bear the same date and contain a revocation clause and are found to be materially inconsistent and irreconcilable the result may be an intestacy. In *In the Goods of Millar*[25] two wills of the same date were executed by the testatrix. Each will contained a revocation clause. There was no evidence to establish the order of execution. They were also inconsistent. As a result it was held by Hanna J. that the court could not construct a will by selecting and omitting parts of two inconsistent testamentary documents so as to make a consistent whole. He cited *Phipps v. Earl of Anglesley*[26] which he thought clearly stated the law on the matter: "If there are two inconsistent wills of the same date, neither of which can be proved to be the last executed, they are both void at common law for uncertainty so far as they are inconsistent and will let in the heir." However, the court given the opportunity will construe matters in favour of a testacy, like, for instance, in *Loftus v. Stoney*[27] where a testator made two wills bearing the same date and wrote on one the words 'last will' and on the other 'duplicate will' and the court held that the 'last will' was the last executed, and the 'duplicate will' was signed first.

4–12   Where it is alleged in a defence that a subsequent will revoked the will propounded by the plaintiff the subsequent will if it is not produced will not be deemed to have that effect unless clear and satisfactory evidence of the contents of it is adduced at the trial. In *In the Goods of Miller*[28] an action was brought to establish the will of the testatrix dated March 10, 1930 as her last will, of which the plaintiff was the surviving executor. The defendants pleaded that the will of 1930 was revoked by a will made between March 10, 1930 and November 11, 1935, and that the will of 1930 was destroyed by the testatrix animo revocandi. It appeared from attendance slips produced by testatrix's solicitor that she attended at his office on two occasions in 1931. An attendance slip dated April 30, 1931, read: 'Attendance on Mrs Miller, going through her will which she altered and asked us to have amended will engrossed.' An attendance slip of May 5 read: 'Attendance on Mrs Miller when she altered her will and we drew a codicil: When she executed both will and codicil.' The testatrix's solicitor in his evidence explained that the note meant the testatrix

---

[25] Above, n.5.
[26] 7 Bro. P.C. 443 at 452.
[27] 17 Ir. Ch. R. 178.
[28] Above, n.6.

executed a new will and codicil on May 5, but he had no recollection of the occurrence apart from the attendance slip, and could not recollect the contents of either document or the persons who witnessed the signature of the testatrix. The next will made by the testatrix was in 1933. On November 7, 1933 she called at her solicitor's office and an attendance slip of that date read: 'Long attendance on Mrs Miller when she stated she wished to make a new will and insisted that she could not call again to sign it and asked us to engross it at once. Taking instructions, engrossing, and attendance to execute.' The solicitor stated that he had no recollection of the contents of that will and that it was more than probable that he was one of the witnesses to it, but he did not remember the name of the second witness. However, he said that when drawing wills it was his practice to dispose of the entire assets and to appoint executors, and if he had departed from his usual practice in the present case he would have remembered it. This will remained in his office until November 13 when it was handed to the testatrix as she said that she wished to show it to a friend. It was never returned to the solicitor. He next heard of the will two years later when on November 11, 1935 the testatrix called to his office in his absence and left a message for him to the effect that she had destroyed her will and did not intend to make a new one. On November 13, 1935 the testatrix saw him in his office and told him that she was not satisfied with certain provisions in her last will and that she had torn it up, and that she thought it was better not to make a new will. On his advice, however, she decided to make a new will but the instructions were not completed at that interview. She never called to his office again and the will was never executed. She died on July 7, 1938. The will of 1930 was kept in the solicitor's office safe but neither the will of 1931, nor that of 1935, was found, or any copy of, or instructions for, either of them. The will of 1930 was propounded on appeal to the Supreme Court. Two propositions were advanced by counsel for the appellant. One, that the evidence was insufficient to establish that either (a) the will of May 5, 1931, or (b) the will of November 7, 1933 had been duly executed, and two, that the evidence was insufficient to establish that either of the aforesaid wills revoked the will of March 10, 1930. Sullivan C.J. disposed of the first proposition without much difficulty. He said it was impossible to hold that the records produced by the testatrix's solicitor even when read in conjunction with his evidence were sufficient to prove the execution of the wills of May 5, 1931 and November 7, 1935. However, the second proposition required more serious consideration. Where one will has been revoked by another of a later date it is well-settled that where the later will is forthcoming, the court, having both wills before it, will be in a position to decide whether the provisions of the two are so inconsistent that they cannot stand together;[29] a similar approach will

---

[29] *Pepper v. Pepper* I.R. 5 Eq. 85; *In Re McFarlane* 13 L.R. Ir. 264; *Reeves v. Reeves*, above, n.2.

be taken in the case of lost wills if there is sufficient evidence of contents.[30] In every case the onus probandi lies on the party setting up the subsequent will as a revocation of the former, and where the later will is not forthcoming the evidence of its contents must be clear and satisfactory.[31] When the contents of the later will have been established then the court has to ascertain from the contents of both wills what the intention of the testator was or the *animus revocandi*. "The intention of the testator in the matter is the sole guide and control."[32] *In Dempsey v. Lawson*[33] it was said by Sir James Hannen that:

> "In this investigation the Court is necessarily to put a construction upon the language of the instrument in question. The intention of the testator conveyed in that language has to be ascertained by reference to the facts with which it was used; but in seeking for the true meaning of the testator, the substance and not the form of the instrument must be regarded. If it can be collected from the words of the testator in the later instrument that it was the intention to dispose of his property in a different manner to that which he disposed of it by the earlier instrument, the earlier instrument will be revoked, and this, although in some particulars the later will does not completely cover the whole subject-matter of the earlier."

Sullivan C.J. taking the foregoing considerations into account held that in the absence of clear and satisfactory evidence establishing the contents of the wills of 1931 and 1935 they could not revoke the will of 1930, and accordingly, that the will of 1930 should be admitted to probate as the last will.

4–13   Once a document is duly executed it may have the effect of revoking a prior instrument regardless of the fact that it contains no revocation clause. In *In the Goods of Brennan*[34] the testatrix gave instructions to her solicitor for the preparation of her will. These instructions were taken down on a sheet of paper by the solicitor which also contained notes of his own. The beneficiaries were her children, the same as in her will, but the distribution of her estate varied. She informed her solicitor that she had a marriage settlement, and he asked her to bring it in to him for consideration. As she was leaving the office she suggested that as a matter of precaution she should sign the instructions. She signed the instructions sheet in the presence of her solicitor and his typist. The instructions sheet was headed "Instructions for new will". The instructions sheet, however, contained no revocation clause and the testatrix never returned to the solicitor's office to execute her will. Her two sons who were named as executors applied for a grant of probate of the "Instructions for new

---

[30] *M'Ara v. M'Coy* 23 L.R. Ir. 138.
[31] *Cutto v. Gilbert* 9 Moo. P.C.C. 131; *Berthan v. Berthan* 18 L.T. 301.
[32] *Lemage v. Goodban*, above, n.19; *In the Goods of Petchell* L.R. 3 P. & D. 153; *Dempsey v. Lawson* L.R. 2 P.D. 98.
[33] Above, n.32 at 105.
[34] Above, n.7.

will" as her last will. Hanna J., having stated that it was the function of the court exercising probate jurisdiction to decide what document or documents the testatrix intended to be her last will and as such admitted to probate, held that the court was entitled to admit parol evidence of the surrounding circumstances to assist it in its inquiry and any statements made by the testatrix prior to the execution of her will.[35] In considering this type of evidence the principle to be followed was stated by Ball L.C. in *O'Leary v. Douglass*[36] to be:

> "In cases of such a character, the testamentary Courts have always admitted parol evidence to show *quo intuitu* the act done. . . . In the Court of Probate, the whole question is one of intention, and the *animus testandi* and *animus revocandi* are completely open to investigation in this Court. Accordingly he received and acted upon the parol evidence of the drawer of a second instrument that it was meant to be in lieu of a former."

Having regard to the circumstances surrounding the giving of the instructions, the statements and actions of the testatrix, and the use of the word "new" in the document signed by her, Hanna J. was satisfied that she intended when she signed the instructions sheet to revoke her prior will and to substitute the executed instructions until a more formal document was drawn up.

4–14 Section 85(2) of the Succession Act also provides for an alternative form of revocation by "some writing" declaring an intention to revoke a prior will and executed in the same way that a will is required to be executed. Thus once the *animus revocandi* is clearly expressed in writing and the writing is duly executed the will to which it refers will be revoked. In *In the Goods of Eyre*[37] the testatrix by her will exercised a power of appointment arising out of a marriage settlement and appointed the proceeds of a policy of life assurance to her daughter who was also her sole executrix. Later she wrote a letter to her daughter which was duly executed by her and two witnesses directing her daughter to destroy the will. An application was made for a grant of letters of administration intestate rather than for probate on the grounds that the letter sent by the testatrix to her daughter declared an intention to revoke her will. Andrews J. held that the letter sent by the testatrix to her daughter was sufficient to revoke the will.

ANIMUS REVOCANDI REQUIRED FOR REVOCATION BY DESTRUCTION

4–15 Another form of revocation recognised by section 85(2) of the Succession Act is revocation by destruction. The act of destruction may be carried

---

[35] *In the Estate of Bryan*, above, n.15.
[36] 3 L.R. Ir. 323 at 330.
[37] Above, n.8.

out by the testator himself, or by some person in his presence and by his direction. The act of destruction whether it be by burning, tearing or otherwise must be carried out animo revocandi. The testator must possess the requisite intention at the time of destruction; the intention must be contemporaneous with the act. It was said by James L.J. in *Cheese v. Lovejoy*[38] that:

> "All the destroying in the world without intention will not revoke a will, nor all the intention in the world without destroying; there must be the two."

Thus where a will is mistakenly destroyed it will not be revoked by section 85(2) because of the absence of the *animus revocandi*, for instance, where a testator destroys his will thinking that it was 'useless' would not be an effective revocation,[39] or where he thought "he was merely disposing of the rubbish."[40] In the latter instances, although the testator may have intended to destroy his will he did not do so animo revocandi. However, where a will is destroyed by mistake the court will first presume that it was destroyed animo revocandi, and probate of it will not issue unless the court is satisfied that it was duly executed and that it was destroyed by mistake.[41] Once the presumption is successfully rebutted and it is established that the destroyed will was duly executed the contents of it may be adduced by affidavit evidence with or without a draft copy exhibited. Where the presumption is rebutted and due execution is established but there is no draft copy of the will available an affidavit made by the draughtsman and witnesses comprising their joint recollections of contents may be admitted to probate.[42] Great weight will also be attached to any declarations or statements made by a testator around the time of the execution of his will and they have always been accepted as evidence in cases where a will has been mistakenly destroyed or lost.[43] Where a will is partially destroyed by mistake the court will admit to probate those parts of the will that still exist and will accept affidavit evidence of the destroyed parts.[44] Even where a will is deliberately destroyed by a third party the court may still presume a destruction *animo revocandi* by the testator especially where the signature of the testator or witnesses' signatures are interfered with and will only allow evidence of contents to be admitted after it is first established that the will was duly executed.[45] The presumption that a will was destroyed animo

---

[38] Above, n.9 at 263.
[39] *Stamford v. White* [1901] P. 46; *Beardsley v. Lacey* 78 L.T. 25.
[40] *Re Jones* [1976] Ch. 200 at 205 *per* Buckley L.J.; *Giles v. Warren* 2 P. & D. 401; *In the goods of Thornton* 14 P.D. 82.
[41] See *Moore v. Whitehouse* 3 Sw. & Tr. 567.
[42] *In the Goods of Legge* 6 N.C. 528.
[43] See *In the Goods of Ball* 25 L.R. Ir. 556.
[44] See *In the Goods of Hogan* 29 I.L.T.R. 64.
[45] *Re Owens* 41 I.L.T.R. 114; See *In the Goods of Body* 4 Sw. & Tr. 9.

revocandi will however always be rebutted where it is established that the testator destroyed his will while of unsound mind,[46] or while drunk.[47]

ANIMUS REVOCANDI AND THE DOCTRINE OF DEPENDENT RELATIVE REVOCATION

4–16 The doctrine of dependent relative revocation was stated by Kenny J. in *In the Goods of Irvine*[48] to mean that:

> If the act of revocation, whether by another will duly executed or by the destruction of the existing will, be without reference to any other act or event, the revocation may be an absolute one; but if the act be connected with some other act or event that its efficacy is meant to be dependent on the other act or event, it will fail as a revocation. If that other act be efficacious, the revocation will operate; otherwise it will not. It is altogether a question of intention, and if, as part of the act of making a fresh will, there will be a revocation of a previous will, that revocation will be absolute provided the fresh will be made."[49]

Thus in circumstances where a testator makes a new will clearly revoking a prior one the revocation will be effective and the new will will be treated as the last will of the testator. The same result will be achieved where a testator destroys a will and then makes a fresh one. However, if the revocation of a prior will is made dependent on making a fresh will the revocation will also be absolute provided a fresh will is made. Where no valid will is made following such a revocation, the revocation will be viewed merely as the first step towards accomplishing the intention of the testator to make a new will. In *Powell v. Powell*[50] the testator destroyed his will with the expressed intention of validating an earlier one and substituting it for the destroyed will. However, such an act could not accomplish the intention as such a process could only be achieved by reviving the earlier instrument. But it was held by Sir J.P. Wilde that such conditional destruction did not operate as a revocation owing to the absence of the *animus revocandi* as the sole condition upon which the destruction was carried out was not fulfilled.[51]

4–17 As was said by Kenny J. in *In the Goods of Irvine*[52] that: "It is alto-

---

[46] See *Brunt v. Brunt* L.R. 3 P. & D. 37.

[47] *In the Goods of Brassington* [1902] P. 1.

[48] Above, n.12 at 489-490.

[49] See *Onions v. Tyrer* 1 P. Wms. 343; *Hyde v. Hyde* 1 Eq. C. 409; *Ex parte The Earl of Ilchester* 7 Ves. 380.

[50] 1 P. & D. 209.

[51] See *Gentry's Case* 3 P. & D. 39; *Dancer v. Crabb* 3 P. & D. 98; *Dixon v. The Solicitor to the Treasury* [1905] P. 42; *In the Goods of Hogan*, above, n.11.

[52] Above, n.12 at 489-490.

gether a question of intention, and if, as part of the act of making a fresh will, there will be a revocation of a previous will, that revocation will be absolute provided the fresh will be made." In *West v. West* [53] it was said by Moore J. that:

> "The intention in turn must be established as a matter of evidence, and it is my duty to see what the evidence is in the present case."

Gannon J. in *In the Goods of Hogan*[54] grounded his view when considering the doctrine on a statement made in Theobald on Wills (7th ed. at p. 750) which was first adopted by Meredith M.R. in *In Re Faris*: [55]

> "The true view may be that a revocation grounded on an assumption of fact which is false takes effect unless, as a matter of construction, the truth of the fact is the condition of the revocation, or in other words, unless the revocation is contingent upon the fact being true."[56]

Gannon J. also adopted the statement by Theobald but substituted the word "is" for the words "may be" appearing at the beginning of the statement. As a result he found that the function of the court in the case before him was not to "effect the intentions of the deceased as they might appear to be but to consider whether or not the formal acts undertaken by the deceased in purported conformity with the requirements of the Succession Act have been performed in the manner prescribed by statute." In furtherance of this view the question of whether or not there was an effective revocation depended on the truth of the facts believed by the deceased to exist at the time of the purported revocation and if the facts did not reflect the belief the will purportedly revoked remained unrevoked.

4–18   In *In the Goods of Irvine*[57] the testator executed a will and a codicil. He subsequently executed another will in printed form containing blanks which were filled in after the execution had taken place. It was admitted by the applicant for a grant of probate that the blank spaces were filled in after execution but he sought to have so much of that will, as revoked all former wills, admitted to probate. The question to be determined by the court was whether in the circumstances the revocation contained in the will executed by the deceased was an absolute revocation, or was a dependent relative revocation. Kenny J. had no doubt that the doctrine of dependent relative revocation was relevant to the case before him. From the evidence he drew the following conclusions of fact: one, that the attempted revocation was merely the first step towards accomplishing the design of the testator to make a new will; two, that it was

---

[53]   Above, n.12 at 37.

[54]   Above, n.11.

[55]   [1911] 1 I.R. 469 at 472.

[56]   See *Thomas v. Howell* 1 I.R. Eq. 198.

[57]   Above, n.12.

dependent and conditional on a will being actually made; and three, that no will was made, and consequently that the intention failed in execution. In *West v. West*[58] after the death of the testator a search was undertaken to discover the testator's will. It was nowhere to be found. However, among his papers included an envelope which was marked "my last will, Made Jan 26, 1918," and also "one made February, 1913, destroyed." The envelope contained a testamentary document (No. 2) which was dated January 26, 1918, and which was drawn up in the same way as a will made by him in February 1913. This document, although signed by the testator, was not witnessed, and thus had no effect as a will. Another draft testamentary document (No. 3) which was not signed by him and from its appearance was incomplete was also found among the testator's papers. The contents of the will of February 1913 were produced in evidence by the testator's solicitors and the executrix named in that will claimed probate in solemn form of the contents as produced in the draft by the testator's solicitors. Moore J. having unreservedly endorsed the statement of the doctrine of dependent relative revocation as expressed by Kenny J. in *In the Goods of Irvine* further stated that the intention in turn must be established as a matter of evidence. Having inferred from the facts that it was prima facie not the testator's intention to die intestate, he found that document No. 2 was intended by the testator in 1918 to be his last will. He also found on the evidence however that the revocation of the earlier will was conditional on the testator's belief that the revocation clause in the later will would be effective, and once it transpired that this belief was unfounded, the doctrine of dependent relative revocation applied, and as a result admitted the will of 1913 to probate. The contents of the destroyed will of 1913 were sufficiently proved from a draft and the draft was admitted to probate as the last will. In *In the Goods of Hogan*[59] the testatrix made her first will in 1977. She made another will in 1979. She later destroyed the will of 1979 in the belief that the will of 1977 would be thereby revived. From on the evidence adduced at the trial, Gannon J. accepted that the testatrix destroyed her will of 1979 in the mistaken belief as to the legal consequences, "namely, the effective disposition by the 1977 will, would ensue." The question therefore which the court had to consider was whether the revocation was an absolute or conditional. Gannon J. stated that the function of the court in relation to the case before him was not to give effect to the intentions of testatrix "as they might have appeared to be but to consider whether or not the formal acts undertaken by the deceased in purported conformity with the requirements of the Succession Act have been performed in the manner prescribed by statute." Adopting this approach there was no doubt that the will of 1977 was revoked but as the purported revocation of the 1979 will was dependent on the truth of facts mistakenly believed

---

[58] Above, n.12.
[59] Above, n.11.

by the testatrix it had no effect, and consequently, the 1979 will remained unrevoked and stood as the last will of the testatrix.

SUMMARY

4–19   Therefore, it can be seen, that whatever mode of revocation is used by the testator, and permitted by section 85 (2) of the Succession Act, it must be carried out animo revocandi. The court when determining whether a testator revoked an instrument animo revocandi may admit extrinsic evidence of the testator's intention to ascertain what document or documents he intended as his last will. Although the court will be guided by Swinburne's maxim that 'no man can die with two testaments', a man's testament may consist of several testamentary documents all comprising his last will. Thus the court's search for the true intention of a testator may involve a scrutiny of several testamentary documents and the admission to probate of those which truly reflect his intention. Although the court in the course of this scrutiny will not fill in blanks or ameliorate deficiencies in testamentary documents it may conduct a comparative analysis of dispositions in documents to ascertain the extent of a revocation between one document and another. The extent of a revocation will be determined by the degree of inconsistency which exists between documents. The analysis may reveal that a later document was intended only to revoke partly an earlier document, or a later document may be viewed as more global in effect and replace an earlier document by implication. In the former the earlier and later documents may all be admitted to probate as the will, while in the latter the later of the two may on its own be admitted to probate. However, the analysis may also result in a stalemate where, for instance, two documents bear the same date and each of them contains a revocation clause, and that they are so inconsistent with each other that they cannot be reconciled and neither can be identified as truly representing the testator's intention. Even where testamentary documents were mistakenly destroyed evidence may be adduced showing their contents for the purposes of this analysis.

4–20   The doctrine of dependent relative revocation may also be applied by the court for the purposes of ascertaining the *animus revocandi* and of identifying the document which is to stand as the last will. When it is established that the revocation was not an absolute one and was made dependent on the happening of some event which did not transpire, where, for instance, the revocation was made conditional on the making of a fresh will which was not made, or where a will was mistakenly destroyed in the belief that a former one would be revived, such revocation would not be absolute owing to the failure of the condition or the mistaken belief thus allowing the will purported to be revoked to remain unrevoked and to be admitted to probate as the last will. Therefore, the search for the last will of the deceased may be conducted by a process of elimination among the deceased's testamentary papers and such a process will be guided by, and sometimes dependent upon, the *animus revocandi.*

CHAPTER 5

Section 27(4) Applications

INTRODUCTION

5–01 In normal circumstances a grant of letters of administration with the will annexed or intestate will be made to the person entitled to apply in accordance with the order of priority set out in Order 79 of the Rules of the Superior Courts. In special circumstances, however, the High Court (or the Circuit Court in a case within its jurisdiction) may make a grant to an applicant under section 27(4) who has not prior title under Order 79 where it is necessary or expedient to do so. The discretionary power of the court under section 27(4) allows it to make a grant to such person as it thinks fit. The facts of a particular case will determine whether the circumstances are truly special for the court to intervene and make a grant under the section. Even where a grant has already been made to an executor or administrator the court may still entertain an application under section 27(4). However, where there is a current personal representative an application under section 27(4) must be accompanied by an application under section 26(2) or section 27(2) revoking the original grant and requiring the removal of the current personal representative and where a personal representative is required to be removed, the applicant must prove serious misconduct or that serious special circumstances require his removal and the court when making a grant may place such limitations on it as it thinks fit.[1] The appointment of an administrator by the court under section 27(4) must be stated in the grant of letters of administration, in the administrator's oath and the administration bond.[2] Moreover, where proceedings are pending to revoke a grant either under section 26(2) or 27(2) a person may be appointed administrator pendente lite by the court.[3]

A BRIEF HISTORY

5–02 It might be of interest to trace briefly the development of the provisions enabling the court to make a grant under section 27(4) of the Succession

---

[1] *Bank of Ireland v. King* [1991] I.L.R.M. 796; *In the Estate of Glynn, Deceased: Ireland and the Attorney General v. Kelly* [1992] 1 I.R. 361; *Re Dunne, Deceased: Dunne v. Heffernan*, unreported, Supreme Court, November 26, 1997.

[2] Rules of the Superior Courts, Ord. 79, r. 22.

[3] Succession Act 1965, s. 27 (7).

Act. For this purpose it might also be useful to look first at the provisions of section 27(4) in order to fully appreciate the evolution of the section. Section 27(4) provides that where by reason of any special circumstances it appears to the High Court (or, in a case within the jurisdiction of the Circuit Court, that Court) to be necessary or expedient to do so, the Court may order that administration be granted to such person as it thinks fit. The original enabling provision was contained in section 78 of the Probate and Letters of Administration Act (Ireland) 1857 but that section postulated certain preconditions which had to exist before any application to the court for a grant and these were:

(a) death intestate;

(b) death testate but without having appointed an executor willing and competent to take probate;

(c) executor resident out of jurisdiction;

(d) necessary or convenient in any such case, by reason of the insolvency of the estate of the deceased or other special circumstances.

The absence of any such preconditions for applications under section 27(4) led McCarthy J. in *In the Estate of Glynn*[4] to conclude that the subsection should be given a liberal interpretation by the court. Section 12 of the Administration of Estates Act 1959 provided that where by reason of any circumstance it appeared to the High Court to be necessary or expedient to do so, the court may, notwithstanding any enactment or rule of law to the contrary, appoint such person as it thought fit to be administrator. It will be seen by contrast that section 12 required only 'any circumstance' to be raised in support of a grant, whereas section 27(4) requires 'any *special* circumstances' to be shown before a grant will be ordered to issue by the court. Thus, while section 78 of the 1857 Act postulated certain preconditions to exist before the court could make an order, section 12 of the 1959 Act went in the opposite direction and allowed any circumstance to be raised, and section 27(4) while not specifying preconditions, requires special circumstances to exist which makes it more restrictive than section 12 of the 1959 Act. The Succession Act, in Part III of the Second Schedule, repealed the whole of the Probate and Letters of Administration Act (Ireland) 1857, and in Part IV of the Second Schedule repealed the whole of the Administration of Estate's Act 1959, thus leaving section 27(4) the only enabling provision in use since January 1, 1967, the date the Succession Act 1965 was enacted. As section 27(9) further provides that the section applies whether the deceased died before or after the commencement of the Succession Act an application under section 27(4) may be made only on the basis of special circumstances existing even before January 1, 1967.

---

[4] Above, n.1 at 366.

The use of section 27(4) by Creditors

5–03 Any creditor of the deceased, perhaps with the sole commercial reason of ensuring payment of a debt owing to him by the deceased, may apply for a grant under Order 79, rule 5(4) and (6)(g) of the Rules of the Superior Courts. Order 79, rule 5(4) provides that a creditor, or indeed, the personal representative of a creditor, may apply for a grant of letters of administration intestate where all other persons entitled to such a grant have first been cleared off.[5] Order 79, rule (6)(g) entitles a creditor with perhaps the same purpose of ensuring payment of his debt to apply for a grant of letters of administration with the will annexed. Or he may simply wait until a grant has been made to the personal representative of the deceased and if his debt remains unpaid he may then institute proceedings against the estate for payment. However, where an attempt to enforce payment of his debt is frustrated owing to the behaviour of the personal representative he may apply to the court for a grant himself under section 27(4).[6] This is what happened in *Bank of Ireland v. King*.[7] In that case the deceased was the owner of a farm of registered land and died intestate. He was survived by his wife and four children. A grant of letters of administration intestate was made to his wife. The plaintiffs instituted proceedings against the deceased's wife for a debt of £34,334.45 owing and due by her and they obtained judgment and costs against her. The plaintiffs registered a judgment mortgage against her one-third interest in the deceased's farm. As the deceased wife failed to vest her interest in the deceased's farm in herself the plaintiffs were unable to realise their judgment mortgage against her. They sought an order of the court requiring an assent to the vesting of her interest in the deceased's farm in herself under section 52(4) of the Succession Act 1965, or in the alternative, an order allowing them to administer the deceased's estate under section 27(4) of the 1965 Act. Costello J. first considered the application under section 52(4) but found that it applied only to a personal representative who failed to assent to the vesting of an interest in the person entitled after the expiration of one year from the date of death of the deceased, and even though a wide interpretation is given by section 52(1) of the Succession Act to the expression 'person entitled' it did not include a judgment mortgagee of lands and was consequently not entitled to have the lands vested in him by a personal representative. But he went on to say that the court had power to revoke any grant of administration where by reason of the special circumstances it is necessary to do so, and it may order that administration be granted to such person as it thinks fit, and may place limitations on the grant.[8] This

---

[5] See *In the Goods of Mahon* 33 I.L.T.R. 24; *In the Goods of Acherton* [1892] P. 104; *In the Goods of Hurwan* [1910] P. 357.

[6] See Succession Act 1965, s. 27 (5).

[7] Above, n.1.

[8] See Succession Act 1965, s. 27(4) and (5).

meant that the court had power to make limited grants for particular purposes. He therefore went on to appoint another person as administrator for the purpose of assenting to the vesting of the interest in the widow of the deceased. He also addressed the question as to whether the assent should be subject to the payment of monies which the personal representative of the deceased might normally be liable to pay[9] and ordered that the new limited administrator should advertise for creditors in one newspaper circulating in the area and if no creditor gave notice of a claim the land should be vested free from the claims of any creditors. He concluded by stating that once the assent was executed then proceedings to realise their judgment mortgage could be instituted by the bank.

The use of section 27(4) by a Beneficiary

5–04 An application may be made to the court under section 27(4) by a beneficiary where the suitability of an executor to take out a grant is called into question,[10] or where his removal is sought.[11] Where an application is made by a beneficiary in a will to have the executor of the will removed and to have him replaced by another person, two matters are required to be established. First, the beneficiary must justify the removal of the executor under section 26(2) of the Succession Act, and secondly, he must show that because of the special circumstances of the case it is expedient and necessary to appoint a new administrator under section 27(4) of the same Act. As an executor is a testator's chosen personal representative the court will be less ready to remove him than it would an administrator appointed under Order 79 rule 5 of the Rules of the Superior Courts.[12] Weighty reasons must be established before the grant of probate will be revoked and cancelled pursuant to section 26(2), and reasons such as a beneficiary feeling frustrated and excluded from what he considers his legitimate concerns in relation to the estate would not be sufficient grounds for the removal of an executor.[13] To justify such a drastic step, the beneficiary seeking the removal must show that the executor was guilty of serious misconduct and/or that there are serious special circumstances requiring his removal.[14] However, if a beneficiary succeeds in showing to the satisfaction of the court that the executor has indeed been guilty of serious misconduct or has established serious special circumstances requiring his removal, the court will remove him under section 26(2) and appoint an adminis-

---

[9] See Succession Act 1965, s. 52 (2).

[10] *In the Estate of S.* [1968] P. 302; *In the Estate of Potticary* [1927] P. 202; *In the Estate of Biggs* [1966] P. 118.

[11] *Re Dunne, Deceased: Dunne v. Heffernan*, above, n.1; *Flood v. Flood*, unreported, High Court, May 14, 1999, McCracken J.

[12] *In re Dunne, Deceased: Dunne v. Heffernan*, above, n.1.

[13] *ibid.*

[14] *In re Dunne, Deceased: Dunne v. Heffernan*, above, n.1; *Flood v. Flood*, above, n.11.

trator under section 27(4).[15] Although it may be observed that, while the expression removal of an executor is used by the courts, the language of section 26(2) provides for the revocation of the grant of probate, and in the case of the removal of an administrator, the revocation of the grant of letters of administration. However, where the application does not involve the removal of a current executor or administrator but rather the appointment of a person as administrator who would not be the person entitled in the order of priority as prescribed by Order 79 rule 5 of the Superior Court Rules, the application will simply be based on section 27(4) only.[16] Where an executor or administrator is removed by the court any payments or dispositions made by him in good faith as a personal representative before his removal may be treated as valid, and indeed, any such personal representative who acted under the revoked grant may retain and reimburse himself in respect of any payments or dispositions made by him which a person to whom representation is afterwards granted might properly have made.[17] Furthermore, a conveyance of any estate or interest in the estate to a bona fide purchaser for valuable consideration by a personal representative will be valid notwithstanding the subsequent revocation of the grant.[18]

5–05 In *Re Dunne, Deceased: Dunne v. Heffernan*[19] was one case in which a beneficiary sought the removal of an executor. In that case the testatrix by her will bequeathed her preference shares in Dunnes Holding Company to her sisters in equal shares and in default to her brothers in equal shares. She died unmarried and without issue and without having revoked or altered her will. There was a history of antipathy between the appellant and the respondent which predated these proceedings. In earlier proceedings between them and other persons the respondent had sold his preference shares in the company for a considerable sum of money. He was concerned that the Inland Revenue Affidavit valuation of the testatrix's preference share of £1 each might result in a liability for capital gains tax in excess of what he had anticipated if the valuation of £1 per share remained. He contended that the shares had a value of £75,000 per share at the date of death of the testatrix. The Inland Revenue Affidavit sworn by the appellant included the preference shares as assets of the testatrix with a valuation of £265. This was done by the appellant on competent legal and taxation advice having regard to the requirements of the company's articles of association. The valuation of the preference shares in the Inland Revenue Affidavit at £265 gave rise to the proceedings. The trial judge ordered that the appellant be removed as executrix of the will on the grounds,

---

[15] *Flood v. Flood*, above, n.11.
[16] *In the Goods of Good*, unreported, High Court. July 14, 1986, Hamilton P.
[17] Succession Act 1965, s. 22 (2).
[18] Succession Act 1965, s. 3 (1) and s. 25 (1).
[19] Above, n.1.

inter alia, that she misconducted herself in making an incorrect averment in the Inland Revenue Affidavit as to the correct valuation of the shares of the testatrix in Dunnes Holding Company. The appellant sought to reverse the decision of the trial judge removing her as executrix of the will.

5–06 Lynch J. in his judgment for the Supreme Court thought that the trial judge approached the case from the wrong perspective by taking the view that the appellant should never have acted as executrix and should have renounced her office in favour of some stranger to the family. He further stated that the family differences which existed prior to the death of the testatrix would not have required the executrix to contemplate renunciation. The fact that the respondent felt frustrated and excluded from what he considered his legitimate concern were not grounds for requiring the removal of the executrix. He stated that:

> "An order removing the appellant as executrix (which would be made by virtue of section 26(2) and not section 27(4) of the Succession Act 1965) and appointing some other person as administrator with the will annexed by virtue of section 27(4) is a very serious step to take. It is not justified because one of the beneficiaries appears to have felt frustrated and excluded from what he considered his legitimate concerns. It would require serious misconduct and/or serious special circumstances on the part of the executrix to justify such a drastic step."

He went on to say that in cases where the person nominated to be executor renounces or where no executor is appointed or on intestacy the right to administration is determined by the Rules of the Superior Courts in Order 79, rule 5, the person entitled to the grant of administration may be passed over more readily and someone else appointed pursuant to section 27(4) than where an executor is appointed and accepts the appointment by proving the will. Where an executor is appointed and proves the will weighty reasons must be established before the grant of probate would be revoked and cancelled pursuant to section 26(2), and the testator's chosen representative thereby removed and someone else not chosen by the testator appointed pursuant to section 27(4) of the Succession Act. Applying the foregoing criteria to the grounds alleged by the respondent he found that the appellant had done nothing wrong in her capacity as executrix and the mistaken perception of the respondent that she had done wrong could not alter the position that she had not. He thought that the alleged conflict of interest was "flimsy in the extreme." The testatrix was entitled to entrust the administration of her estate to her sister notwithstanding the nature and complication of the business enterprise. Accordingly, there were no grounds justifying the removal of the executrix under section 26(2) of the Succession Act. The criteria laid down by Lynch J. were applied by McCracken J. in *Flood v. Flood*[20] but in that case it was held there were

---

[20] Above, n.11.

grounds which justified the removal of the executor because the executor re-fused to repay money which he borrowed from the deceased, his father, by claiming that the money was given to him as a gift.

5–07   Where no personal representative is required to be removed an appli-cation by a beneficiary under section 27(4) must show that the special circum-stances of the case render it necessary or expedient that a grant be made to him. If, for instance, a grant under section 27(4) is required for the purposes of instituting proceedings against a fellow beneficiary who has prior title to a grant the court may refuse to make a grant, under section 27(4) if the grounds relied on by the applicant for instituting such proceedings are insufficient to sustain a claim. Such was the case in *In the Goods of Good*.[21] In that case a daughter of the deceased intestate by a previous marriage applied for a grant of letters of administration intestate under section 27(4) for the limited pur-poses only of instituting proceedings to enforce a contract alleged to have been made between the deceased and his widow relating to her estate and that of the deceased's estate. The deceased's daughter alleged that the deceased and his widow, who both owned property of their own and had children by previous marriages had agreed that the property that each owned on their deaths would pass to his or her children, and would not be left to the surviving spouse or that spouse's children. Hamilton P., having observed that the agreement which the daughter sought to enforce was a verbal one upon consideration of marriage and one not to be performed within the space of one year from the making of it, stated that by virtue of the provisions of section 4 of the Statute of Frauds (Ireland) 1695 no action could be brought unless the agreement or some memorandum or note of the agreement was in writing and signed by the wife of the deceased, or some other person lawfully appointed by her. The daughter of the deceased did not state in her affidavit that it was an agreement in writing, or indeed, that any note or memorandum signed by the deceased was made or was in existence. Accordingly, Hamilton P. held that there were no special circumstances in the case which rendered it either necessary or expedient to order the issuing of a grant pursuant to section 27(4).

5–08   Where it has been established to the satisfaction of the court that spe-cial circumstances exist for the making of a grant under section 27(4) it may be made to a person other than a beneficiary or to a person with the consent of some of the beneficiaries without the need to cite those who do not give their consent.[22]

---

[21] Above, n.16.
[22] *In the Goods of Harte* [1953-1954] Ir. Jur. Rep. 68; *In the Goods of Hogan* [1957] Ir. Jur. Rep. 69; *In the Goods of Potter* [1899] P. 265; *In the Goods of Moffat* [1900] P. 152.

THE USE OF SECTION **27(4)** BY THE STATE

5–09 Where beneficiaries are debarred from succeeding to the estate of a deceased by will because they have been convicted of certain offences against the deceased, such convictions may also preclude them, although it is not expressly provided for in section 120 of the Succession Act, from applying for a grant to the estate on the grounds of public policy, and in such circumstances the State may apply for a grant to the estate under section 27(4) of the Succession Act in the absence of anybody else entitled to apply.[23] However, such persons may once again acquire succession rights to the estate of the deceased if after the act constituting the offence the deceased leaves property to them by will and this may also entitle them to apply for a grant.[24] However, where a beneficiary in a will who is also executor is found guilty of a serious offence against another beneficiary and his interest in the estate is accelerated as a result although he may continue to be entitled as a beneficiary he may not be issued with a grant of probate on the grounds that it would be "utterly wrong that he should be permitted, even in the most formal manner, to administer the estate."[25] Even if a grant has already issued to such an executor before conviction for the offence any application under section 27(4) must be accompanied by an application to remove the executor, or indeed administrator, under section 26(2) or section 27 (2) for the purpose of revoking the grant already made.[26] A question may also arise as to how serious the offence must be to deem it "utterly wrong" to issue a grant to the executor or administrator. Certainly, the murder of a beneficiary by the executor would render it such especially where it accelerates the interest of the executor as beneficiary. This is what happened in *In the Estate of Glynn, Deceased: Ireland and The Attorney General v. Kelly.*[27] In that case the testator, Martin Glynn, by his will made on April 29, 1981 appointed the respondent Michael Kelly his executor. By the terms of his will he devised and bequeathed his farm to his sister Margaret for life with remainder to Michael Kelly absolutely. He later executed a codicil to his will leaving pecuniary legacies to Michael Concannon, and his sole surviving next-of-kin, Michael Donoghue. The testator died on November 15, 1981. His sister, the tenant for life, was murdered on the same day and the respondent was later convicted of her murder. Michael Donoghue, the sole surviving next-of-kin, renounced his right to a grant of letters of administration. The appellants applied to the High Court by notice of motion for an order

---

[23] *In the Estate of Glynn, Deceased: Ireland and the Attorney General v. Kelly*, above, n.1.
[24] Succession Act 1965, s. 120 (1); *In the Estate of Glynn, Deceased: Ireland and the Attorney General v. Kelly*, above, n.1.
[25] *In the Estate of Glynn, Deceased: Ireland and the Attorney General v. Kelly*, above, n.1 at 364.
[26] See *In re Dunne, Deceased: Dunne v. Heffernan*, above, n.1.
[27] Above, n.1.

granting letters of administration with the will and codicil annexed to the Chief State Solicitor under section 27(4). Gannon J. made an order granting liberty to the Chief State Solicitor to apply for a grant of letters of administration limited however to getting in the assets of the deceased for the purpose of preserving them. The appellants appealed against the limitation placed on the grant. McCarthy J. in the course of his judgment for the Supreme Court stated that: "None could doubt the apparent impropriety that will arise if Michael Kelly is permitted to act as executor. He has been convicted of the murder of the testator's sister, who was the life tenant of some twelve acres of land, whose maintenance he had to undertake if the condition set out in the will be enforced, and whose death at his hands accelerated his succession in remainder. It would appear utterly wrong that he should be permitted, even in the most formal manner, to administer the estate. The administration would appear to require the court's assistance in determining whether or not, in the circumstances, the gift in remainder is valid. Failing its validity there will be at least a partial intestacy."[28] The issue was whether or not these facts could be regarded as special circumstances making it necessary or expedient for the court to order that administration be granted to the Chief State Solicitor in substitution for the executor named by the testator. McCarthy J. cited at p. 365 a passage from the judgment of Evans P. in *In Re Crippin* [29] where he said that:

> "In the present case a man who has been convicted of the wilful murder of his wife has, after his conviction, made a will appointing a person his executrix, to administer the murdered wife's estate, and as legatee to be entitled to the murdered wife's property. These are, surely, 'special circumstances'. I therefore pass over and decline to appoint the executrix; and I appoint the applicant as attorney of the deceased woman's sister to be administrator of the deceased's woman's estate on the sister's behalf. If I am right in this exercise of the discretion of the court, there remains nothing which is necessary for me to decide upon this motion."

McCarthy J. went on to say that on grounds of public policy a person who is proved to be guilty of murder or manslaughter of the testator cannot claim to take under the testator's will,[30] and that this was given statutory force by section 120 of the Succession Act, except a share arising under a will made after the act constituting the offence. He did not, however, expressly extend the grounds of public policy to cover the murder of a beneficiary by an executor who was also a beneficiary although he did state in the course of his judgment that it would be "utterly wrong" to issue a grant to such a person. In his view section 27(4) should be given a liberal construction and accordingly he al-

---

[28] *ibid.* at 364.
[29] [1911] P. 108 at 111-112.
[30] *Cleaver v. Mutual Reserve Fund Life Association* [1892] 1 Q.B. 147.

lowed the appeal and made a "the grant of letters of administration not limited to calling in estate but be a grant in ordinary form."

5–10   However, if a testator is in a position to make a new will with the knowledge that his intended executor has been convicted of a serious offence which would normally debar him from succeeding under section 120 of the Succession Act but none the less makes him a beneficiary in his new will it is debateable whether the executor in such circumstances would be precluded from extracting a grant of probate upon the death of the testator. Where the deceased is a murder victim and an application is made under section 27(4) for a grant while the police are still carrying out their investigations the court may not be willing in such circumstances to make a full grant but to maintain the status quo may instead order that a limited grant ad colligenda bona should issue only.[31]

Summary

5–11   Therefore, the High Court, by virtue of the discretionary power given to it under section 27(4), may make a grant of letters of administration with the will annexed or intestate to such person as it thinks fit owing to the special circumstances of a case and that it is necessary or expedient to do so. The Circuit Court is similarly empowered in relation to cases coming within its jurisdiction. The kind of special circumstances required to exist before the court may exercise its discretion include an administrator behaving in such a fashion so as to frustrate a creditor's claim for payment of his debt owing by the estate,[32] or an executor who is convicted of the murder of a fellow beneficiary in order to accelerate his own interest.[33] However, circumstances similar to those found in *In the Goods of Goods* where an order was sought under section 27(4) for the purposes of enforcing a contract will not be viewed as 'special' enough to merit such an order. Moreover, the court when deciding to make an order under section 27(4) may make a limited grant *ad colligenda bona* only[34] or for the sole purpose of allowing the applicant to assent to the vesting of an interest in a beneficiary.[35] Where the conduct of an executor to whom a grant of probate has been made is called in question and the applicant under section 27(4) also seeks his removal, a concomitant application must be made under section 26(2) seeking the revocation of the grant of probate made

---

[31] *Re Nevin*, unreported, High Court, March 13, 1997, Shanley J.
[32] *Bank of Ireland v. King*, above, n.1.
[33] *In the Estate of Glynn, Deceased: Ireland and the Attorney General v. Kelly*, above, n.1.
[34] *Re Nevin*, above, n.31.
[35] *Bank of Ireland v. King*, above, n.1.

to the executor.[36] The type of conduct required for the removal of an executor must be serious, or alternatively, that the serious special circumstances of the case require his removal.[37] The mere fact that a beneficiary feels frustrated and excluded from what he considers his legitimate concerns in relation to the deceased's estate will not be regarded as serious enough grounds requiring the removal of an executor.[38] However, an executor's refusal to pay a debt owing by him to the estate by claiming that the money was given to him as a gift by the deceased will be regarded as serious enough grounds requiring his removal.[39] Similar grounds will have to be established where the removal of an administrator is sought. Where an administrator is required to be removed and the applicant appointed in his place the application under section 27(4) must be accompanied by an application under section 27(2) revoking the grant of letters of administration already made to him. An executor, however, will viewed by the court as the testator's personal appointment and will be less ready to remove him than an administrator appointed under Order 79, rule 5 of the Rules of the Superior Courts.[40]

5–12   Where no grant has been made and the applicant under section 27(4) is not the person next entitled to apply for a grant under Order 79, rule 5 of the Rules of the Superior Courts he will be required to show that special circumstances exist which make it necessary or expedient that a grant be made to him.

---

[36] *In re Dunne, Deceased: Dunne v. Heffernan*, above, n.1; *Flood v. Flood*, above, n.11.
[37] *ibid.*
[38] *In re Dunne, Deceased: Dunne v. Heffernan*, above, n.1.
[39] *Flood v. Flood*, above, n.11..
[40] *In re Dunne, Deceased: Dunne v. Heffernan*, above, n.1 *per* Lynch J.

CHAPTER 6

Extrinsic Evidence of Intention

INTRODUCTION

6–01 Once writing expressing a testator's testamentary wishes has been duly executed in accordance with section 78 of the Succession Act, and it is subsequently admitted to probate, the grant will be conclusive evidence of the testamentary nature of the writing. The efficacy of the testamentary writing will depend however on the clarity of the language used by the testator in expressing his intention. Where the intention is obscured by the language used and the court is asked to ascertain the testator's intention it will first endeavour to interpret the language and construe its meaning, and it will treat the language used by the testator as internal evidence of intention. However, where the testator's intention is obscured by a contradiction appearing in the will the court may admit extrinsic evidence of intention which may be of assistance in the construction of the will in order to explain the contradiction.

6–02 The primary concern of the court in a construction suit will be to ascertain and give effect to the intention of the testator.[1] This would appear to be the one factor which the court will always take into account when it is asked to construe a will.[2] O'Flaherty J. in his judgment for the Supreme Court in *In Re Curtin: Curtin v. O'Mahony and Others*[3] thought that it was the "first duty of a court in construing a will to give effect to the intention of the testator." The court will attempt to ascertain this intention from the language used by the testator. However, this does not mean that the exact words used by a testator will in all cases be followed in their literal meaning. If it is clear from the will as a whole that a literal meaning of a provision would defeat the testator's intention it may become necessary for the court "to do violence" to the language used.[4] The function of the court however is to construe a will and not to venture so far as to make a new will for a testator: "a judge is to tread cautiously so as not offend against the judicial inheritance which is that one is entitled to construe a will but not to make one."[5] The two injunctions laid down by O'Flaherty J. in *In Re Curtin: Curtin v. O'Mahony*

---

[1] *In re O'Toole*, unreported, High Court, June 26, 1980, Barrington J.
[2] *Robinson v. Moore* [1962-1963] Ir. Jur. Rep. 29.
[3] [1991] 2 I.R. 562.
[4] *Re Patterson, Deceased: Dunlop v. Greer* [1899] I.R. 324 *per* Porter M.R.
[5] *In re Curtin: Curtin v. O'Mahony and Others*, above, n.3 at 573 *per* O'Flaherty J.

and Others were applied by Morris P. in *Williams and O'Donnell v. Shuel and Barham*.[6]

6–03   Beyond the language used by a testator the court will be slow to admit evidence of intention *de hors* the will. Extrinsic evidence will be admissible only "to show the intention of the testator and to assist in the construction of, or to explain any contradiction in, a will."[7] Such evidence may be adduced in order to give "unclear or contradictory words in a will a meaning which accords with the testator's intention as thus ascertained."[8] However, if a will is clear, unambiguous and uncontradictionary section 90 has no application.[9]

6–04   Where the court has to decide whether an intestacy ensues because of a provision contained in the will, extrinsic evidence of the testator's intention will not be required as the court will be primarily concerned with the internal evidence provided by the will itself and may also apply the presumption against an intestacy should that be necessary.[10]

THE SCOPE AND EFFECT OF SECTION 90

6–05   Before any construction of the provisions of a will can take place the will itself must have been duly executed and the issuing of a grant of probate or of letters of administration with the will annexed will be deemed conclusive evidence of this fact. On any issue of construction of the provisions of a will arising thereafter, the main function of the court will be to ascertain the intention of the testator. When attempting to ascertain the intention of the testator the court will confine itself to the language used in the will. The useful procedural approach adopted by Carroll J. in *In Re Howell*[11] and first suggested by Lowry L.C.J. in *Heron v. Ulster Bank Ltd.*[12] might profitably be applied when interpreting the language used by a testator. Lowry L.C.J. considered that, having first read the whole will, the following procedure may be adopted:

1.   Read the immediately relevant portion of the will as a piece of English and decide, if possible, what it means.

2.   Look at the material parts of the will and see whether they tend to con-

---

[6]   Unreported, High Court, May 6, 1997.
[7]   Succession Act 1965, s. 90.
[8]   *Rowe v. Law* [1978] I.R. 55 at 73-74.
[9]   *Rowe v. Law*, above, n.8; *In re Collins: O'Connell v. Bank of Ireland*, unreported, Supreme Court, May 19, 1998.
[10]   See *In re Curtin: Curtin v. O'Mahony and Others*, above, n.3.
[11]   [1992] I.R. 290.
[12]   [1974] N.I. 44 at 55.

firm the apparently plain meaning of the immediately relevant portion or whether they suggest the need for modification in order to make harmonious sense of the whole or, alternatively, whether an ambiguity in the immediately relevant portion can be resolved.

3. If ambiguity persists, have regard to the scheme of the will and consider what the testator was trying to do.

4. One may at this stage have resort to the rules of construction, where applicable, and aids, such as the presumption of early vesting, and the presumption against intestacy and in favour of equality.

5. Then see whether any rule of law prevents a particular interpretation from being adopted.

6. Finally, and I suggest, not until the disputed passage has been exhaustively studied, one may get help from the opinions of other courts and judges on similar words, rarely as binding precedents, since it has been said that "No will has a twin brother",[13] but more often as examples (sometimes of the highest authority) of how judicial minds nurtured in the same discipline have interpreted words in similar contexts.

6–06 In *Re Howell*[14] the residuary clause in the will was the subject matter for construction by the court. The text of it was as follows:-

> "I give devise and bequeath my farm in the townlands of Drumpeak and Corinshigo together with the furniture and machinery thereon to my brother Joseph. I give devise and bequeath all my stock and any other assets I may have to my brother Richard."

6–07 Joseph predeceased the testator. A question then arose as to whether the wording of the residuary clause created a full and comprehensive gift. The plaintiff, another brother of the testator, claimed that the words "any other assets" used in Richard's gift could not be construed to include the farm, furniture and machinery which were given to his deceased brother Joseph. Richard claimed that the words "any other assets" included the property in Joseph's gift. Carroll J., following the approach adopted by Lowry L.C.J., held that the immediately relevant portion of the will was "any other assets I may have" and as a piece of English that meant any assets other than the farm, furniture, machinery and stock already mentioned.

6–08 Thus it can be seen that the procedural approach suggested by Lowry L.C.J. and followed by Carroll J. can be of great assistance in interpreting the

---

[13] *In Matter of King* (1910) 200 N.Y. 189 at 192 *per* Werner J.
[14] Above, n.11.

language used by a testator and in attempting to ascertain and give effect to the intention of the testator which is the first duty of the court.[15] However, when endeavouring to ascertain the testator's intention and when interpreting the language used by him, the exact words in their literal meaning need not necessarily be followed by the court if it is plain that to do so would frustrate the testator's intention. If having considered the whole will it becomes clear that to place a literal meaning on a provision in the will would defeat the testator's intention it may become necessary 'to do violence' to the language used.[16] If the testator's intention still remains elusive and cannot be gathered from the language used even where 'violence' is done to the language, the court may then allow the admission of extrinsic evidence "to show the intention of the testator and to assist in the construction of, or to explain any contradiction in, a will."[17] The scope and effect of section 90 of the Succession Act has been subject to two major interpretations by the Supreme Court and on each occasion the court considered the law as it existed prior to the enactment of the Succession Act to measure the extent of the alteration of the law effected by section 90.[18]

6–09   Prior to the Succession Act the general principle applicable at common law as regards the admissibility of extrinsic evidence was very clearly stated by Lord Simon L.C. in *Perrin v. Morgan*[19] to be as follows:

> "The fundamental rule in construing the language of a will is to put on the words used the meaning which, having regard to the terms of the will, the testator intended. The question is not, of course, what the testator meant to do when he made his will, but what the written words he uses means in the particular case – what are the 'expressed intentions' of the testator."

Thus extrinsic evidence of a testator's declarations of intention "as to the meaning to be put on the language of his will was not admissible as direct evidence of his testamentary intention."[20] Kingsmill Moore J. in *In Re Julian*[21] expressed the view that:

> "The Wills Act requires that wills should be in writing, duly witnessed and signed, and to admit direct parol evidence of intention to control the meaning of the will would be to nullify the statute. In two cases only, as far as I know or have been able to ascertain, is such evidence allowed; to rebut or support cer-

---

[15] *In re O'Toole*, above, n.1; *In re Curtin: Curtin v. O'Mahony and Others*, above, n.3 at 573; *Williams and O'Donnell v. Shuel and Barham*, above, n.6; *Robinson v. Moore*, above, n.2.

[16] *Re Patterson, Deceased: Dunlop v. Greer*, above, n.4.

[17] Succession act 1965, s. 90.

[18] *Rowe v. Law*, above, n.8; *In re Collins: O'Connell v. Bank of Ireland*, above, n.9.

[19] [1943] A.C. 399 at 406.

[20] *In re Collins: O'Connell v. Bank of Ireland*, above, n.9 *per* Keane J. (as he then was).

[21] [1950] I.R. 57.

tain bare legal presumptions and to determine which of several persons or things are comprised in a truly equivocal description, that is to say, a description which applies accurately to two different persons or objects."

He also stated that extrinsic evidence of certain circumstances existing at the date of the testator's death may be admitted to show what the testator might have had in mind and which accordingly might assist the court in the construction of the language used in the will. He quoted James L.J. in *Boyes v. Cooke*[22] as saying:

> "You may place yourself, so to speak, in the testator's armchair and consider the circumstances by which he was surrounded when he made his will to assist you in arriving at his intention."

The 'armchair principle' as it came to be called allowed circumstantial evidence to be adduced especially to show a testator's relations with different persons and his knowledge of institutions who claimed to be the object of a gift in his will. In *In Re Julian* the testatrix left a sum of £1,000 "to the Seamen's Institute, Sir John Rogerson's Quay, Dublin." Two institutions claimed the sum, the Dublin Seamen's Institute, Eden Quay, and the Catholic Seamen's Institute, Sir John Rogerson's Quay. One of the objects of each institution was to provide for the religious needs of seamen, in the case of the first by Protestant religious teaching and in the case of the second by Roman Catholic religious teaching. The evidence showed that the testatrix, who was a Protestant, knew the first institute well by visitations and by making subscriptions to it during her lifetime. There was no evidence that she had ever heard of or expressed interest in the second institute. However, Kingsmill Moore J. held that there was no equivocation in the language used by the testatrix and that the relevant rule allowing extrinsic evidence applied only where a description in the will referred accurately to two different objects. Since the only seamen's institute on Sir John Rogerson's Quay was the Catholic Seamen's Institute, and extrinsic evidence of the testator's intention to benefit the other institute was not admissible, the will had to be construed as referring to the Catholic Seamen's Institute. Keane J. (as he then was) in *In Re Collins: O'Connell v. Bank of Ireland*[23] stated that the policy underlying the application of the common law principle was clear because

> "the detailed requirements of the legislature as to the execution, attestation and publication of wills could be circumvented by allowing parol evidence to be admitted as to the intentions of the testator, save in the limited circumstances to which I have referred. However, the strict application of those principles by the court led on occasions to perplexing results, of which *In Re Julian* itself is a remarkable example."

---

[22] 14 Ch. D. 53.
[23] Above, n.9.

However, where extrinsic evidence of the testator's intention was allowed under the common law principle all declarations made by a testator whether before, during and after the execution of the will were admissible. In *Doe d. Allen v. Allen*[24] it was said by Lord Denman C.J. that:

> "The only remaining point is, whether the time when these declarations were made, *viz.* some months after the will was executed, makes any difference. Cases are referred to in the books to show that declarations contemporaneous with the will are alone received: but, on examination, none of them establish such a distinction. Neither has any argument been adduced which convinces us that those subsequent to the will ought to be excluded, wherever any evidence of declarations can be received. There may have more or less weight according to the time and circumstances under which they were made, but their admissibility depends entirely on other considerations."

Although Lord Eldon L.C. in *Langham v. Sanford*[25] thought that most weight was to be given to what was said at the time of execution of the will, he went on to say that it was unfortunate

> "but is certainly settled, that declarations at the time of making the will, subsequent and previous to it, are all admitted: yet we know, that what men state as to their intentions may be conformable to the purpose at the time, but not afterwards; and declarations by a testator, after having made his will, are frequently made for the purpose, not of fairly representing, but of misrepresenting, what he had done."

Thus prior to the Succession Act where extrinsic evidence was allowed in the limited circumstances as prescribed by the common law principle declarations made by a testator before, during and after the execution of the will were admissible to show what he had intended.

6–10 Section 90 of the Succession Act is described as 'new' in the margin and altered the common principle by allowing extrinsic evidence to be adduced as to the intention of the testator where that would assist in the construction of, or to explain any contradiction in, the will. The scope and effect of the section was first considered by the Supreme Court in *Rowe v. Law*.[26] In that case the testatrix, who was separated from her husband and had no children, made her will in 1967. She died in 1972 and probate of her will was granted to the first defendant in 1973. She devised all her estate, which she called her 'Trust Fund', to her trustees upon the following trusts:

1.   To discharge thereout her debts, funeral and testamentary expenses.

2.   To set aside a sum of £1,000 out of the capital of the Trust Fund and

---

[24] 12 Ad. & E. 449.
[25] 19 Ves. 654.
[26] Above, n.8.

directed her trustees to use it to purchase and furnish a suitable cottage for the use and occupation of the second and third defendants during their joint lives and to the survivor of them during his or her lifetime and "as to any balance then remaining" to invest the same in some trustee security and the income therefrom to be paid to the second and third defendant during their joint lives and to the survivor of them during his or her lifetime.

3.   After the death of the survivor of the second and third defendants she directed her trustees to pay the sum of £1,000 or the investments for the time representing the same to a named legatee.

4.   To stand possessed of the Trust Fund then remaining to pay and transfer to the plaintiffs in equal shares as tenants in common absolutely.

6–11   The second and third defendants claimed that the words "as to any balance then remaining" meant the balance of the entire Trust Fund after the payment of debts and the sum of £1,000. The plaintiffs claimed that the words meant any balance of the sum of £1,000 and that they were entitled to the residue after the payment of debts, the £1,000 and a small legacy.

6–12   The first plaintiff stated in his affidavit that he was present when the testatrix gave instructions for the will to the first defendant and that her expressed intention was that the £1,000 was to be applied in the purchase of a suitable cottage for the second and third defendants and that the balance of the estate was to pass to him and the second plaintiff. The statements made by the first plaintiff were contradicted by the first defendant and by two of his employees. A question arose as to whether section 90 of the Succession Act had the effect of allowing the affidavit to be admitted as evidence to assist in the construction of the will.

6–13   The principal point at issue was posed in the form of a question by Henchy J.:

> "where there is clear and unambiguous disposition in a will of portion only of a fund, and there is extrinsic evidence available in a court of construction to show that the testator really intended to make a disposition of the whole fund, does section 90 of the Succession Act, 1965, allow the court of construction to use that extrinsic evidence for the purpose of superseding the clearly expressed intention in the will ?"

He posed the question in that way because he had no doubt that the words "any balance then remaining" did not refer to the whole of the trust created by the will but to the balance then remaining of the portion of it (amounting to £1,000) which was dealt with in the preceding paragraph of the will. He was of the view that if the words in the will prevail the expression "any balance

then remaining" must be held to refer to any balance then remaining of the
£1,000 after it had been applied to purchase and furnish a suitable cottage.
However, there was parol evidence available of certain declarations made by
the testatrix at the time of the making of the will which showed that she intended the expression "any balance then remaining" to refer to the balance of
£1,000 and that her will represented this intention. Counter to this evidence
there was also parol evidence available from her solicitor, who was the draughtsman of the will, to the effect that the testatrix's instructions to him showed that
the balance she had intended was not the balance of the £1,000, but the balance of the trust fund consisting of her whole estate which was valued at
£50,000. Henchy J. considered that if the evidence of the testatrix's solicitor

> "were to be accepted as being correct, and if section 90 of the Succession Act,
> 1965, were to be held to allow it to be used to undermine the true nature of the
> testamentary disposition, it would enable the court to rectify the will by giving
> testamentary effect to a disposition which is not to be found in the will and
> which actually conflicts with the disposition in the will."

6–14   Looking at the pre-Succession Act position as regards the admissibility of extrinsic evidence Henchy J. found that it was an inflexible rule that
where the testator's intention was expressed in the will clearly and unambigu-
ously extrinsic evidence of a contrary intention could not be admitted by the
court for the purpose of overriding the intention expressed in the will. He
went on to refer *Wigram on Extrinsic Evidence in Aid of the Interpretation of
Wills* (5th ed. at p. 8) and approved of the author's statement on the restric-
tions placed on the admissibility of extrinsic evidence. Wigram stated that by
requiring a will to be in writing precludes a court from ascribing to a testator
any intention which his will does not express and in effect makes the writing
the only legitimate evidence of the testator's intention. At the same time, however, the court has a duty to give effect to the intention of the testator which
the will has properly expounded. Thus evidence is admissible which explains
the nature and effect of what the testator has written, but not where it tends to
show merely what the testator intended to have written. Henchy J. also found
that the rule that extrinsic evidence could not be adduced for the purpose of
adding to, varying, or contradicting the terms of a will had been applied firmly
by the courts, even in cases where an interpretation ran counter to the true
intention of the testator.[27] The question then arose as to whether "section 90
overthrew the rule."

6–15   Henchy J. as a result of the analysis carried by him interpreted section
90 as allowing extrinsic evidence to be adduced if it met the double requirement of "(a) showing the intention of the testator *and* (b) assisting in the con-

---

[27] See *In re Huxtable* [1902] 2 Ch. 793; *In re Rees* [1950] Ch. 204.

struction of, or explaining any contradiction in, a will." Any interpretation involving either (a) *or* (b) would produce illogical and unreasonable consequences which the legislature could not have intended. If the section made (a) sufficient for the admission of extrinsic evidence then the court could go outside the will and accept such evidence as to the intention of the testator. This interpretation would run counter to section 78 which lays down the formal requirements for making a will and thus encapsulating the testator's intention. It would be "unreasonable and contradictory" for the legislature to prescribe formal requirements for the purposes of encapsulating the testator's intention in a will and then later on in the same Act to allow in extrinsic evidence of the testator's intention without qualification or restriction. If extrinsic evidence were admissible of the testator's intention without restriction or qualification the door would be open "for fraud, mistake, unfairness and uncertainty."[28] Moreover, since the function of the court in construing a will or in finding an explanation for a contradiction in it necessarily involves a search for the testator's intention, it would be unnecessary for the section to include requirement (b) if requirement (a) on its own were sufficient to allow the admission of extrinsic evidence.[29] The conjunctive "and" in the section connotes "a duality of purpose as a condition for the admission under the section of extrinsic evidence." Therefore, the necessary conditions for the admission of extrinsic evidence are to show the intention of the testator *and* to assist in the construction of, or to explain a contradiction in, the will. The two conditions must be satisfied before the court can allow the admission of extrinsic evidence.

6–16 Applying this interpretation of section 90 to the circumstances of the case extrinsic evidence of the testator's intention on its own was not permitted unless such evidence also assisted in the construction of the will, or explained a contradiction in it. However, as there was no contradiction in the will the court did not require the assistance of extrinsic evidence. Therefore, parol evidence of declarations made at the time of making the will which showed what the testatrix intended by the expression "any balance then remaining" referred to nothing more than the balance of the £1,000 or to the balance of the trust fund of her total estate was not admissible. The admission of such evidence would have involved the rewriting of the will and as such would have been repugnant to section 78 of the Succession Act. The court must take the will as probated and section 90 may not be used for the purpose of supplanting the language used in the will. As the language used by the testatrix was "clear, unambiguous and without contradiction," section 90 had no role to play in its construction. Accordingly, Henchy J. dismissed the appeal.

---

[28] *Rowe v. Law*, above, n.8 at 72.
[29] *ibid.*

6–17   Griffin J. in a concurring judgment was of the view that:

> "on the correct construction of section 90, extrinsic evidence is to be admitted
> only for the stated purpose of assisting in the construction of, or to explain any
> contradiction in a will, and not for the purposes of replacing the dispositive
> intention of the testator as expressed in the will, for that would be outside the
> range of purposes permitted by the section."[30]

He also stated that:

> "If extrinsic evidence of the dispositive intention of a testator is to be admitted
> without qualification, the effect of this would be that a new will could be writ-
> ten for the testator, this will be collected from the statements and declarations of
> the deceased at the time of, before, or after the making of the will, without
> compliance with the provisions of the section."

The minority view of the court was that as expressed in the judgment of
O'Higgins C.J. While he agreed that the language used by the testatrix in her
will was unambiguous and certain, it was clear that section 90 gave primacy to
the intention of the testatrix and that a will should be construed in accordance
with that intention. In the course of his judgment he stated that:

> "The Oireachtas has chosen, and understandably so, to sacrifice the certainty of
> the literal interpretation with its frequently attendant capricious results, in fa
> vour of the somewhat more difficult but more understandable task of ascertain-
> ing the testator's intention. For this reason extrinsic evidence *must* be admitted
> (where it is sought to be so) to 'show the intention of the testator' and 'to show'
> the meaning of the will, and thereby to 'assist in the construction' of the will.
> This may mean in a particular case a substantial change in what has been the
> practise up to this but this is what the legislature has ordained."[31]

He went on to say: "What is permitted by the section as extrinsic evidence of
intention is what was said and done at the time of making the will indicating a
testamentary intention at that time."

6–18   Section 90 was mentioned in a subsequent decision of the Supreme
Court in *In Re Curtin, Deceased: Curtin v. O'Mahony and Others*[32] but the
circumstances of the case did not require extrinsic evidence to be adduced.
However, in *Re Collins; O'Connell v. Bank of Ireland* [33] the circumstances of
the case did require the court to consider the admissibility of extrinsic evidence and section 90. In that case the testatrix by her will left all the contents
of her house to the two plaintiffs. By the residuary clause in her will she left
the remainder of her property to the Sisters of Charity for the charities under

---

[30] *ibid.* at 98.
[31] *ibid.* at 93.
[32] Above, n.3 at 572.
[33] Above, n.9.

their care. There was no specific devise of her house in the will. A close friend
of the deceased said in an affidavit that the deceased wanted the plaintiffs to
have her house because they had a young family and she thought this would
benefit them. The friend also deposed that before the deceased left for hospital where she subsequently died she again said that the house would be "of
good use" to the plaintiffs. Shortly before the deceased's death the first plaintiff said that the deceased told him that she had been to her solicitors and that
she had left her house and contents to him and his wife. She also said that she
was happy with what she had done and that, when she died, the plaintiffs
should get in touch with her solicitors about the house. The solicitor who
prepared the will said in his affidavit that in the course of taking instructions
for her will she indicated that she had been very impressed by the way in
which a named hospice had looked after her husband and that she wanted to
leave the residue of her estate to it. He also said that she had been thinking of
leaving something out of the house to the first plaintiff. He said that having
discussed the matter with her she agreed to leave the contents of the house to
the plaintiffs. He read over the will to her clause by clause and was of the
opinion that she understood the contents and when he had finished reading
she confirmed that that was what she wanted and the will was then executed.
Questions arose as to whether the clause in her will disposing of the contents
of her house only carried into effect the expressed intention of the deceased in
the disposal of her house, whether the deceased could have intended to leave
only the contents of the house to the plaintiffs thereby leaving no specific
bequest of the dwellinghouse which was a major asset of her estate, and whether
the dwellinghouse formed part of the residue of the estate. The appellants
relied mainly on the Supreme Court decision in *In Re Curtin, Deceased: Curtin
v. O'Mahony*[34] having conceded in the High Court that as the will was unambiguous they could not avail of section 90 of the Succession Act because of
the interpretation put on the section by the Supreme Court in Rowe v. Law.[35]
However, the trial judge was satisfied that the case of *In Re Curtin, Deceased:
Curtin v. O'Mahony* was distinguishable from the present case and no grounds
had been established for construing the will other than in accordance with its
terms. From that decision the plaintiffs appealed to the Supreme Court. On
appeal it was submitted on behalf of the appellants that the decision in *Rowe v.
Law* was wrong in law and should be overruled. The respondents submitted
that *Rowe v. Law* was correct in point of law and further submitted that the
trial judge was correct in treating the decision in *In Re Curtin, Deceased:
Curtin v. O'Mahony* as distinguishable from the present case. Keane J. was
however satisfied that the decision of the majority in *Rowe v. Law* was correct
in point of law and should be upheld. In relation to the argument advanced by
the appellants based on the decision in *In Re Curtin, Deceased: Curtin v.*

---

[34] Above, n.3.
[35] Above, n.8.

O'Mahony he had no doubt that the decision in that case was entirely distinguishable from the present case on two grounds. First, the will in *In Re Curtin, Deceased: Curtin v. O'Mahony* if literally construed would have resulted in an intestacy which could not have been the intention of the testator and accepted that there was a presumption against intestacy. He also referred to section 99 of the Succession Act which provides that:

> "If the purport of a devise or bequest admits of more than one interpretation, then, in case of doubt, the interpretation according to which the devise or bequest will be operative shall be preferred."

That provision was clearly intended to ensure that, where the wording of a will allows of more than one construction, it should be interpreted, if possible, so as to avoid an intestacy arising. Although section 99 was not specifically referred to by the court in *In Re Curtin, Deceased: Curtin v. O'Mahony*, it was clear from the observations of O'Flaherty J.[36] that the presumption against intestacy was of paramount importance in that case. No question of intestacy arose in relation to the will in the present case. Secondly, the court reached its conclusion having regard to the language of the will itself and it did not have to consider the extent to which extrinsic evidence of the testator's intention should be allowed under section 90. Keane J. was accordingly satisfied that the decision of the trial judge was correct.

6–18   During the course of a very comprehensive judgment Keane J. considered the law as it existed prior to the introduction of the Succession Act in relation to the admissibility of extrinsic evidence of a testator's intention in the construction of a will. The general principle was that in construing a will the object of the court was to ascertain the expressed intention of the testator. He referred to a passage from the speech of Lord Simon L.C. in *Perrin v. Morgan*[37] as stating the law on the matter as follows:

> "The fundamental rule in construing the language of a will is to put on the words used the meaning which, having regard to the terms of the will, the testator intended. The question is not, of course, what the testator meant to do when he made his will, but what the written words he uses mean in the particular case – what were the 'expressed intentions' of the testator."

The general rule also was that extrinsic evidence of a testator's declarations as to the meaning to be put on the language of his will was not admissible as direct evidence of his testamentary intention. He also referred to the judgment of Kingsmill Moore J. in *In Re Julian*[38] and cited the following passage:

---

[36] Above, n.3 at 573.
[37] Above, n.19.
[38] Above, n.21.

"The Wills Act requires that wills should be in writing, duly witnesses and signed, and to admit direct parol evidence of intention to control the meaning of the will would be to nullify the statute. In two cases only, as far as I know or have been able to ascertain, is such evidence allowed: to rebut or support certain bare legal presumptions and to determine which of several persons or things are comprised in a truly equivocal description, that is to say, a description which applies accurately to two different persons or objects."

Although Kingsmill Moore J. also referred to another category of cases in which extrinsic evidence may be admitted of circumstances existing at the date of death of a testator which might assist the court in the construction of the language used in the will:

"You may place yourself, so to speak, in (the testator's) armchair and consider the circumstances by which he was surrounded when he made his will to assist in arriving at his intention."[39]

Such evidence however was admitted only for the purposes of inferring what a testator intended, and not as direct evidence of intention. This rule, which became known as the 'armchair principle', also allowed evidence to be adduced as to the testator's knowledge of different persons or institutions who claimed a benefit under his will. Thus, as a result of these decisions the statutory requirements as to execution of wills could not be circumvented by admitting extrinsic evidence as to the testator's intention, save in limited circumstances only. The strictures imposed by the decisions at times led to cries of exasperation by judges who felt obliged to follow them:

"I regret to give this decision, for the evidence which I have excluded, if I were allowed to take it into account, would convince me to a moral certainty that the testatrix intended to benefit the Dublin Seamen's Institute. . . . This is by no means the first – and, equally certainly, will not be the last – case in which a judge has been forced by the rules of law to give a decision on the construction of a will which he believed to be contrary to the intention of the testator. . . ."

In that case, as already stated above, the testatrix in her will left a sum of £1,000 "to the Seamen's Institute, Sir John Rogerson's Quay, Dublin." Two institutions claimed the sum, the Dublin Seamen's Institute, Eden Quay, and the Catholic Seamen's Institute, Sir John Rogerson's Quay. One of the objects of each institution was to provide for the religious needs of seamen, in the case of the first by Protestant religious teaching, and in the case of the second by Roman Catholic religious teaching. The evidence established that the testatrix who happened to be a Protestant, knew the first institute well and had subscribed to its funds. There was no evidence of any connection with the Catholic Seamen's Institute. However, as there was no equivocation in the will Kingsmill Moore J. felt obliged by former authorities to hold in favour of

---

[39] *Boyes v. Cooke* 14 Ch. D. 53 *per* James L.J.

the Catholic Seamen's Institute as he was not allowed to admit extrinsic evidence of the testatrix's intention to benefit the Dublin Seamen's Institute.

6–20		Keane J. then considered the extent of the alteration of the law brought about by section 90 of the Succession Act and favoured the construction put on the section by the majority of the court in *Rowe v. Law* which held that extrinsic evidence of the testator's intention was admissible only where it assisted in the construction of a will or that it helped to resolve any contradiction in it. He said that: "Any other construction of section 90, as the judgments of Henchy J. and Griffin J. in *Rowe v. Law* made clear, would have led to a radical and far reaching change in the law which it cannot have been the intention of the Oireachtas to bring about by such, at best, opaque and ambiguous language." He also referred to the minority judgment of O'Higgins C.J. in *Rowe v. Law* who supported a more radical interpretation of section 90 based primarily on its legislative passage through the Oireachtas. O'Higgins C.J. said that:

> "It seems clear that in the section as enacted an indissoluble link has been created between the testator's intention and the construction of the will."

And further that:

> "If section 90 had existed when *In Re Julian* was decided the result would have been otherwise, and I have no doubt that it was passed for the purpose of dealing with that kind of case. Of course, if the section were to be interpreted in the manner in which the learned trial judge interpreted it, no change would be possible in cases such as *In Re Julian* because, as in this case, the words used in the will are unambiguous and clear and no contradiction exists."

Keane J. disagreed with the views expressed by O'Higgins C.J. and his observation in relation to the facts of *In Re Julian*. "A description of the object of the testatrix's bounty as "the Seamen's Institute, Sir John Rogerson's Quay" when there were in fact two seamen's institutes in Dublin, one called "the Dublin Seamen's Institute" and situated at Eden Quay, the other called "the Catholic Seamen's Institute" and situated at Sir John Rogerson's Quay could hardly be regarded as a clear and unambiguous description of the Institute intended to be benefited." Thus the decision in *Rowe v. Law* stands affirmed.

Section 90 and the Presumption Against Intestacy

6–21		In *Re Howell*[40] Carroll J. adopted the procedural approach when interpreting wills suggested by Lowry L.C.J. in *Heron v. Ulster Bank Ltd.*[41] Lowry

---

[40] Above, n.11.
[41] Above, n.12.

L.C.J. suggested, *inter alia*, that one may look at other material parts of the will and see whether they tend to confirm the apparently plain meaning of the immediately relevant portion or whether they suggest the need for modification in order to make harmonious sense of the whole or, alternatively, whether an ambiguity in the immediate relevant portion can be resolved. If, however, ambiguity persists having regard to the scheme of the will, one must then consider what the testator was trying to do. The rules of construction may be applied at this stage as well as aids such as the presumption against intestacy. *Williams and O'Donnell v. Shuel and Barham*[42] is an instance where the court was able to ascertain what the testator was trying to do from the scheme adopted by him in his will. In that case the testator, Harry Lefroy, having made a number of bequests, directed that his residuary estate be sold by his trustees and invested and he further directed that the income therefrom be paid to his wife during her life and after her death as to one moiety thereof to pay the income arising from it to his sister, Hester Margaret Oulton, and after her death "upon trust to divide such moiety into twelve equal shares and to divide such shares among the children of Hester Margaret Oulton in the following proportions, that is to say, to her son Gerald six shares, to her son Ralph three shares, to her three daughters, Dorothy, Noel and Beatrice one share each." The testator then dealt with the second moiety and he directed that the trustees were "to pay the income thereof to my sister, Dorothea O'Grady Lefroy, during her life and after her death upon the same trusts for the said Hester Margaret Oulton and her children as are hereinbefore declared concerning the other moiety." By clause 13 of the will the testator declared that the share of his residuary estate "which is hereinbefore expressed to be given to each of my said nephews and nieces, children of my said sister, Hester Margaret Oulton, shall not vest absolutely in him or her but shall be retained by my trustees and held by them upon the trusts as follows, namely: (a) the income thereof shall be paid to such nephew or niece during his or her life, (b) from and after his or her decease, such share and the income thereof shall be held upon trust for all or any of the children or child of such nephew or niece who being male shall attain the age of 21 years or being female shall attain that age or previously marry and if more than one in equal shares as tenants in common." Clause 13(c) of the will provided: "In the event of the failure or determination of the trusts hereinbefore declared concerning the share of my residuary estate hereby given to any niece or nephew of mine, the share of such niece or nephew including any share accruing to him or her by virtue of this present provision shall go and accrue to the others or other of my said nephews or nieces to whom my residuary estate is hereinbefore given, if more then one in the same share or proportion to which my residuary estate is hereinbefore made devisable and be added to and devolve with their his or her original shares." The three

---

[42] Above, n.6.

surviving nieces and nephew all died unmarried and without issue. A question arose on construction as to whether the share of a deceased nephew or niece was divisible among the surviving nephews or nieces and then to pass to their sons who reach twenty-one years or to their daughters who marry before that time or whether there was a partial intestacy. Morris P. was left in no doubt

> "whatsoever that the scheme envisaged by the testator was that should one of his five nephews or nieces fail by reason of death or otherwise to enjoy the benefits acquired under the will, then the share allocated to that nephew or niece should pass on their death to their sons who reach the age of 21 years or their daughters who marry before that time."

He was also satisfied that it was never the intention of the testator to die intestate insofar as such a share was concerned.

6–22 In accordance with the rules of construction the first duty of a court in construing a will is to ascertain and give effect to the intention of the testator. However, where it is clear that a testator did not intend to die intestate extrinsic evidence of his intention is not necessary.[43] If having considered the will as a whole it is plain that to place a literal meaning on one clause would defeat the testator's intention it may be necessary "to do violence" to the language used.[44] The matter to be ascertained is what was the testator trying to do.[45] Thus where the court has established that the testator did not intend to die intestate, and a literal meaning of a clause in a will would result in such, the court may interpret the language in such a way so as not to defeat the testator's intention, and may suggest the need for modification to make harmonious sense of the whole will. However, in taking this approach the court must bear in mind the dual injunction *viz.*, to ascertain and give effect to the testator's intention but not go so far as to make a new will.[46] Where it is clear that a testator did not intend to die intestate the court may also rely on section 99 of the Succession Act and interpret a devise or bequest which admits of more than one interpretation in a way that renders it operative. In other words, the court may *construe* a will in such a way as gives effect to the intention of the testator and in doing so may also avail of the presumption against an intestacy and the provisions of section 99 of the Succession Act. In *In re Curtin, Deceased; Curtin v. O'Mahony and Others*[47] the testator was at the time of his death a widower without children. His estate consisted of a dwellinghouse, chattels and monies. He left his dwellinghouse to the first defendant abso-

---

[43] *In re Curtin, Deceased: Curtin v. O'Mahony and Others*, above, n.3.
[44] *Re Patterson, Deceased: Dunlop v. Greer*, above, n.4.
[45] *In re Howell*, above, n.11; *Heron v. Ulster Bank Ltd*, above, n.12.
[46] *In re Curtin, Deceased: Curtin v. O'Mahony and Others*, above, n.3; See also *Lynch v. Burke*, unreported, High Court, July 30, 1999, McCracken J.
[47] Above, n.3.

lutely and in the event of her predeceasing the testator then to her husband absolutely. The will then went on to provide that:

> "In the event of I [*sic*] selling the dwellinghouse and lands. . . . I direct that my estate both real and personal which I die possessed of to which at my death I may be entitled be divided in the following percentages subject firstly to payment of my just debts funeral and testamentary expenses."

There followed a number of charitable and other bequests. The percentages purported to add up to 100.5 per cent. The dwellinghouse was not sold. The following questions arose for determination by the court:

(i)   Whether by reason of the fact that the deceased had not sold his dwellinghouse the devise and bequest of the residue of his estate was ineffective?

(ii) If the bequest of the residue of his estate was ineffective whether the residue of the estate of the deceased should be distributed in accordance with the intestacy rules as laid down in the Succession Act 1965?

(iii) If the answer to (ii) was in the negative how should the residue of the estate be distributed?

(iv) If the bequest of the residue of the estate was ineffective what was the effect of the deceased purporting to dispose of 100.5 per cent of his estate?

Lardner J. in the High Court found that the legacies in the will would only take effect if at the time of his death the testator had sold his house, which did not occur.

6–23 Counsel for the Attorney General, who represented the charities involved, had urged the trial judge to consider the provisions of two previous wills of the testator, so as to show the testator's intention by way of extrinsic evidence. The submission was repeated in the Supreme Court. The argument that there is a presumption against intestacy was also repeated in the Supreme Court. In relation to the latter O'Flaherty J. had no doubt that the testator did not intend an intestacy and if that was the result it was due to defective drafting of the will. He also stated that it was the first duty of the court in construing a will to give effect to the intention of the testator. Even without resorting to extrinsic evidence he thought it was clear that the testator could not have intended to die intestate as to most of his estate just because his dwellinghouse had not been sold in his lifetime. He went on to refer to the judgment of Porter M.R. in *In Re Patterson, Deceased; Dunlop v. Greer*[48] and in particular to a passage which dealt with the duty of the court when construing a will. The

---

[48] Above, n.4 at 331.

passage referred to stated that it was the duty of the court "to ascertain, if at all possible, what the testator really meant from the language he has used" and if it is clear not alone that words have been omitted but also what the substance of the omitted clause is, the court may *supply* the place of express words in cases of difficulty or ambiguity bearing in mind that the court is construing a will and not making one.[49] He had no doubt that what the testator intended was that in the event of selling his dwellinghouse in his lifetime that his estate should be divided in the way that he set out in his will, subject to the necessity to make a mathematical adjustment in respect of the addition of the percentages. He then supplied the few missing words to give effect to this intention, *viz.* to insert after ". . . I direct that my estate both real and personal which I die possessed of [and] to which at my death I may be entitled" the words "(including the proceeds of the sale of my dwellinghouse, if sold, but not otherwise)." He continued, however, to say that: "A judge is to tread cautiously so as not to offend against the judicial inheritance which is that one is entitled to construe a will but not to make one. However, two injunctions are on collision course in this case: one is that a court is not entitled to make a will for a testator but on the other hand there is the requirement that effect should be given to the intention of the testator, if at all possible. If the will is given a literal meaning then the intention of the testator is clearly defeated and an absurd result is produced. It seems to me clear that what the testator did intend was to provide for a situation where his dwellinghouse had been sold so that the proceeds thereof could go to and be part of the whole of his estate and, in that event Catherine O'Mahony was to be provided for to the extent of 10 per cent of the whole estate. If, however, the house was not sold (as happened in the circumstances of the case) then she got the "bonus" so to speak of the house together with 10 per cent of the residue."[50] At the beginning of his judgment he referred to *Rowe v. Law*[51] but reserved for further consideration the question whether the majority judgment correctly represented the extent of the amendment of the law effected by the enactment of section 90 of the Succession Act 1965. He did not believe that the admission of extrinsic evidence to prove that the testator made previous wills was necessary in a case where there was no intestacy. He had no doubt whatever that the testator did not intend an intestacy. He consequently refused the request by counsel on behalf of the Attorney General to have extrinsic evidence of the testator's two previous wills admitted as the testator did not intend to die intestate as appeared from a literal reading of the will before the court.

---

[49] *ibid.* at 331-332.
[50] *In re Curtin, Deceased: Curtin v. O'Mahony and Others*, above, n.3 at 573-574.
[51] Above, n.8.

SUMMARY

6–24 Once a testator's writing representing his will has been duly executed in compliance with section 78 of the Succession Act it will be deemed to encapsulate his testamentary wishes. It will also be demonstrative of the fact that he did not intend to die intestate. Any question of his intention which may subsequently arise will therefore involve an interpretation of the language used by him in his will. Although it is the court's duty to ascertain and give effect to a testator's intention it will not go as far as rewriting his will. Nevertheless, in its quest for the testator's intention, the court may broadly construe a will and may even 'do violence' to the language used, or indeed, supply words which were obviously omitted by the testator to give effect to his intention. In carrying out its function the court may also be assisted by the presumption against an intestacy where a valid will exists. In other words, it is the court's duty, if at all possible, to mend the ruptured lines of communication that may exist in the language used by the testator to give effect to his intention. If, having gone to such lengths, the intention still remains elusive due to the use of contradictory language, the court may allow extrinsic evidence to be adduced if such would explain a contradiction and thereby assist in the construction of the will under section 90 of the Succession Act. As a result of two major decisions of the Supreme Court in *Rowe v. Law* and *In re Collins: O'Connell v. Bank of Ireland,* the court will only allow such evidence of intention to be adduced for the purposes of explaining a contradiction and assisting in the construction of a will, but not to explain what a testator intended by the language used by him in his will.

CHAPTER 7

The Issue of Costs in Probate Actions

INTRODUCTION

7–01 Although there is a legal right to costs the liability of a party to pay them is a discretionary matter for the court to decide. This will also be the time during the proceedings when the litigant parties can momentarily rest on their shields while the decision of the court is being pronounced before renewing the fight for costs. Issues of costs in probate actions are governed by the same general provisions which govern all actions in the superior courts. These general provisions prescribe that all "the costs of and incidental to every proceeding" shall be in the discretion of the court.[1] However, notwithstanding this general discretion of the court, *costs will normally follow the event*, unless special cause is shown and where such is shown it must be mentioned in the order for costs, for instance, in a probate action an unsuccessful party may be allowed his costs out of the deceased's estate.[2] But probate actions, unlike other actions, are also governed by special and rather useful provisions in the matter of costs: a party opposing a will may with his defence give notice to the party propounding the will that he merely insists on the will being proved in solemn form of law and intends only to cross-examine the witnesses produced in support of the will, the effect of which will save him from being saddled with the costs of the propounding party unless the court takes the view that there was no reasonable ground for opposing the will.[3] Although the order for costs is usually made at the conclusion of an action there is nothing to prevent the court from dealing with the issue of costs at any stage of the proceedings.[4] In awarding costs, the court may direct: one, that a sum in gross be paid in lieu of taxed costs, or two, that a specified proportion of the taxed costs be paid, or three, that the taxed costs from or up to a specified stage of the proceedings be paid.[5] The court is also empowered to take certain factors into account when awarding costs like, for instance, where the course of the trial is impeded through the neglect of a solicitor for a litigant party making it inconvenient for the court to proceed the solicitor at fault may be personally liable to the other party or parties for such costs as the court may think fit to award,[6] or, as

---

[1] The Rules of the Superior Courts, Ord. 99, r.1(1) and (2).
[2] Ord. 99, r.1 (3).
[3] Ord. 21, r.17.
[4] Ord. 99, r.5 (1).
[5] Ord. 99, r.5 (2).
[6] Ord. 99, r.6.

between solicitor and client, where it appears to the court that costs have been improperly incurred as a result of undue delay or misconduct or without any reasonable cause, such costs may be disallowed and the court may order that the client be reimbursed for any costs already ordered to be paid by him to the other party or parties to the proceedings.[7] Issues of costs in probate actions in the Circuit Court are governed by Order 58 of the Rules of the Circuit Court 1950. The limited defence procedure of cross-examining witnesses only may also be availed of in the Circuit Court under Order 34, rule 13 of the 1950 Rules.

LIABILITY FOR COSTS IN PROBATE ACTIONS

7–02 When determining the liability of parties for costs in probate actions, the court is not confined in exercising its discretion to the immediate and contending parties to the action, the deceased's estate may also be included in the reckoning. Where it is established that the deceased's conduct during his lifetime was the cause of posthumous litigation his estate may be answerable in costs. Where the conduct of a deceased testator is called in question his personal representatives will take up the cause of his estate unless, of course, matters become so intense and calumnies so grievous that the deceased himself may be stirred to forsake the shroud and enter the fray himself a la Banquo; however, even should an apparition come and shake its locks it is unlikely that the composure of the court would be disturbed as it will be concentrated in this instance on the letter and not the spirit. Where it is established to the satisfaction of the court that it was the conduct of the deceased which necessitated the litigation, or that there were reasonable grounds for instituting the proceedings and that such proceedings were conducted bona fide, a litigant party may, even though unsuccessful in either opposing the will or revoking the probate, have his costs paid out of the deceased's estate. The court when deciding to exercise its discretion in awarding an unsuccessful party his costs will be guided by the established rules of practice which will now be discussed.

LITIGATION NECESSITATED BY TESTATOR'S CONDUCT

7–03 The testator's conduct necessitating litigation and involving the revocation of a grant of probate was discussed by O'Daly J. (as then was) in *In the Goods of Mulligan; Mulligan v. McKeown*.[8] In that case the proceedings were

---

[7] Ord. 99, r.7.
[8] [1955] I.R. 112

instituted by a plaintiff who was resident in the United States against the executor of the deceased's will to have the grant of probate revoked on the grounds that the deceased lacked testamentary capacity at the time he made his will. At the trial of the action evidence was given by a medical practitioner who, having examined the deceased a few weeks before his death, was of the opinion that the deceased was certifiably insane. However, notwithstanding such evidence, the jury brought in a verdict in favour of the will. An application was made by the plaintiff, the unsuccessful party, to have his costs paid out of the estate. O'Daly J., in the course of his judgment, referred to *Fairtlough v. Fairtlough*,[9] having stated that it was the first case he was able to discover where a statement of the relevant principles were laid down in ruling the costs of an unsuccessful party revoking a grant of probate. He cited the following statement of principle from the judgment of Dr. Radcliff who was once the presiding judge of the Court of Prerogative in Ireland as follows:

> "The principle of awarding costs out of the fund in testamentary cases is not confined merely to cases where the question arises upon the state in which the deceased has left his testamentary papers. The rule should be taken in a wider view, and wherever it is proper to specially bring the matter before the court for its opinion, the costs may be given out of the estate."[10]

7–04   He also noted that *Fairtlough v. Fairtlough* was cited with approval in the English case of *Davies v. Gregory*[11] by Sir James Hannen. In *Davies v. Gregory* the executors contended that the general rule was that the costs should be allowed out of the estate only in cases where the state in which the deceased left his testamentary papers had given rise to litigation. Sir James Hannen, in the course of his judgment, having noted the reluctance of former courts to grant costs out of the estate beyond the confines of this general rule, questioned the reasoning behind the rule and came to the conclusion that in all cases it was really the conduct of the testator which caused the litigation. He also observed that costs were allowed out of the estate owing to the existence of reasonable doubts as to the testator's testamentary capacity.[12]

7–05   O'Daly J. went on to refer to *Smith v. M'Cashin*[13] which came before Chief Baron Pallis. In that case, the plaintiff, who was heir-at-law as well as one of the next-of-kin of the deceased, sought to have probate revoked on the three grounds of want of testamentary capacity, want of knowledge and approval, and undue influence. It happened that the case was first tried by Gibson J., but the jury failed to agree on a verdict. The second trial which came before

---

[9] 1 Milw. 36.
[10] *ibid.* at 39.
[11] L.R. 3 P. & D. 28; See also *Browning v. Mostyn* 66 L.J.P. 37.
[12] *Frere v. Peacock* 1 Robert. 442.
[13] 32 I.L.T.R. 55.

the Chief Baron resulted in a verdict upholding the will with the exception of some bequests in respect of which it was found that the deceased did not know and approve. On the question of the rights of the respective parties to have their costs of the proceedings, the Chief Baron stated that he had consulted with Gibson J. who was of the opinion that if the verdict in the first trial had been similar to the that in the second he would have given the plaintiff the costs of the action except the costs of undue influence which he would have ordered him to pay.[14]

7–06   In relation to the immediate case before him, O'Daly J. was of the view that if it had been one of opposition to probate of the will propounded by the executor he would have had no hesitation in holding that the testator's conduct and state of health

> "before the will was made and three weeks after its execution, coupled with the subsequent history of his illness, all such matters as causing the litigation which occurred after the testator's death as to the validity of his will."

He also took into account evidence of the testator's condition of insanity. He then posed the question: "Is this case, then, different from a case of unsuccessful opposition to probate?" to which he answered: "I am not satisfied that it is." When the plaintiff had acquiesced in a grant in common form he was resident in the United States and was not informed that the testator was certifiably insane a fortnight before the will was made. He concluded that, in the circumstances of the case and in the light of the principles referred to in the cases, it was proper that the plaintiff should be allowed his costs out of the deceased's estate.

7–07   It should be remembered that *Mulligan* was a jury trial thus making the jury final arbiters of fact in finding in favour of the will, although it is difficult to understand how the jury came to such a conclusion in the light of the medical evidence which, as it turned out, was the basis for O'Daly J. awarding the unsuccessful plaintiff his costs.

7–08   Thus, where it is established that the testator's conduct caused the subsequent litigation or that it was caused by the existence of reasonable doubts regarding the capacity of the testator to make a will, an unsuccessful party will be allowed his costs out of the estate.

LITIGATION ON REASONABLE GROUNDS AND CONDUCTED BONA FIDE

7–09   Even where the testator's conduct did not directly cause the ensuing

---

[14] *ibid.* at 55.

litigation an unsuccessful party may still be allowed his costs out of the estate if it is established that there were reasonable grounds for the litigation and that it was conducted bona fide. This alternative ground was discussed by the Supreme Court in *In the Goods of Morelli; Vella v. Morelli.*[15] In that case, the plaintiff, Concetta Vella, was the only daughter of the testatrix, and the defendant, Guiseppe Morelli, was her only son. By her first will, which was executed in 1950, she left all her property to the plaintiff and defendant in equal shares. In 1955 she made a new will whereby she revoked the will of 1950 and left all her property to the defendant only. The testatrix died in 1962 and a grant of letters of administration with the will of 1955 annexed was made to the defendant. The plaintiff thereafter instituted proceedings claiming, inter alia, that the will of 1955 had not been duly executed. At the trial the witnesses to the execution of the 1955 will gave conflicting evidence in relation to the facts surrounding the execution thereof. The will had been prepared professionally and contained the usual revocation clause. The trial judge however upheld the will of 1955 on the ground that the presumption of due execution had not been rebutted and awarded the defendant his costs but made no order as to the costs of the plaintiff. The plaintiff appealed to the Supreme Court on the issue of costs.

7–10   The plaintiff argued that there was a well-established Irish practice formulated by the courts in the last century on the issue of costs and which was cited in Miller's Probate Practice (1900 ed.) to depend on the answer to two basic questions: (a) Was there reasonable ground for litigation? and (b) Was it conducted bona fide? and that the trial judge had failed to follow this practice when deciding on the issue of the unsuccessful plaintiff's costs. The defendant, on the other hand, submitted that as the Irish practice approximated the English practice in relation to the question of the costs of an unsuccessful party in a probate action that that practice should be adopted as applying the proper general principles.

7–11   Budd J., in the course of his judgment, distinguished between the Irish and English practices for the purposes of deciding which was the more appropriate one to follow in the circumstances of the case.

7–12   For a statement of the English practice he cited a passage from the judgment of Hodson L.J. in *In Re Cutliffe's Estate*[16] as follows:

> "The most convenient case in which to find the principles on which the Probate Court exercises its discretion as to costs is *Spiers v. English.*[17] The headnote

---

[15] [1968] I.R. 11.
[16] [1959] P. 6.
[17] [1907] P. 122.

sets out the principle very clearly in this way: 'The two main principles which should guide the court in determining that costs in a probate suit are not to follow the event are, firstly, where the testator or those interested in the residue have been the cause of the litigation; and, secondly, if the circumstances lead reasonably to an investigation in regard to a propounded document. In this latter case the costs may be left to be borne by those who incurred them; in the former, the costs of unsuccessfully opposing probate may be ordered to be paid out of the estate. Neither of those principles, which, however, are not exhaustive, justifies a plea of undue influence unless there were reasonable grounds for putting it forward'."

7–13 He found that the Irish practice as cited in Miller's Probate Practice (1900 ed.) went back to the time of the Prerogative Court and he referred to the judgment of Dr. Radcliff in *Fairtlough v. Fairtlough*[18] as a starting point. He then referred to a number of later Irish decisions on the matter. Keatinge J. in *Keogh v. Wall*[19] allowed costs out of the estate to a plaintiff in a revocation action who had pleaded undue influence unsuccessfully on the basis that there were reasonable grounds for suspicion. Warren J. in *O'Reilly v. Forde*,[20] in dealing with the matter of costs of an unsuccessful plaintiff, posed the two questions to be considered which were later adopted by Miller's Probate Practice: (a) "Was there reasonable ground for litigation?" and (b) "Was it conducted bona fide?" In *O'Kelly v. Browne*[21] Warren J., when dealing with a motion to vary an order for costs in a probate action, further stated:

"It is the usual practice of this Court, without having regard to the amount or the ownership of the property, if the case has been a proper one for litigation, and the litigation has been properly conducted, to order that the general costs shall be paid out of the assets, *i.e.*, out of the personal estate, for the court has no jurisdiction to order them to be paid out of real estate: *Young v. Dendy*[22]."

Warren J. was also the presiding judge in *Burke v. Moore*[23] a case which involved a question of due execution and where the unsuccessful plaintiff was awarded costs out of the estate. The practice as stated by Warren J. was also followed by the Chief Baron in *Gillic v. Smyth*[24] again a case involving a question of due execution where an unsuccessful defendant this time was allowed his costs out of the estate.

7–14 Having thus distinguished between the two practices Budd J. then briefly undertook a critical review of the English practice. He first found it

---

[18] Above, n.9, at 39.
[19] 9 Ir. Jur. n.s. 418.
[20] 5 I.L.T.R. 54.
[21] I.R. 9 Eq. 353.
[22] L.R. 1 P. & D. 344.
[23] I.R. 9 Eq. 609.
[24] 49 I.L.T.R. 36.

difficult to discover the logical reason for making a distinction between the two types of case dealt with in the English practice. "Why", he asked, "should a party be allowed his costs out of the estate where the testator or those interested in the residue have caused the litigation but not where the circumstances lead reasonably to an investigation in regard to the propounded document?"[25] An investigation of suspicious circumstances surrounding the making of a will was always necessary in the public interest so as to ensure that wills conformed with the statutory provisions dealing with due execution. He failed to understand why the second principle should debar an unsuccessful party from claiming his costs out of the estate who "may be just as free from blame" as a party in the first principle. He thought it reasonable to allow the unsuccessful party his costs out of the estate in either instance.[26] The Irish practice made no such distinction.

7–15 In his view it seemed right and proper that persons having real and genuine grounds for believing, or even having genuine suspicions, that a purported will is not valid, should have the circumstances surrounding the making of that will investigated by the court without being completely deterred from taking that course by reason of fear that no matter how genuine their case may be they will have to bear the burden of what may be heavy costs. In contrast to the English practice, he found the old Irish practice "a very fair and reasonable one" and as such had the result of allaying the reasonable fears of persons faced with making a decision on whether to litigate or not. He then went on to affirm the Irish practice emphasising the qualification that before that practice can operate in any particular case the two questions: (a) Was there reasonable ground for litigation? and (b) Was it conducted bona fide? must first be answered in the affirmative.[27]

7–16 In the present case, having decided to follow the Irish practice, he answered the two questions in the affirmative and allowed the appeal, and accordingly, considered the proper order to make was to allow the plaintiff her costs out of the estate.[28]

7–17 During the course of his judgment Budd J. also made the interesting observation that if the defendant had originally sought probate of the will on motion and had brought to the attention of the court such facts as were in the plaintiff's knowledge before the trial, he was of the view that the defendant would then have been directed to serve notice of motion on the plaintiff and that some investigation by the court would have followed, probably in the

---

[25] Above, n.15, at 31.
[26] Above, n.15, at 31-32.
[27] Above, n.15, at 34-35.
[28] Above, n.15, at 41.

form of a probate action. If such procedure had been adopted in the first place he was of the view that the plaintiff would have been allowed her costs out of the estate, and that a similar result would ensue in the case of a revocation action.[29]

7–18 Thus, the old Irish practice was firmly re-established by the Supreme Court in *Morelli* and the issue of costs of an unsuccessful party in a probate action either challenging a will or revoking a grant will be determined by the answer to the two questions posed: was the litigation reasonable in the circumstances and was it conducted bona fide.

APPEALING AN ORDER FOR COSTS

Until the Supreme Court decision in *Morelli* it was doubtful whether the judicial discretion as regards costs could form the subject matter of appeal unless leave to appeal was given by the court awarding costs, or unless the judge in exercising his discretion had "gone wrong in principle." This was because section 52 of the Supreme Court of Judicature Act (Ireland) 1877 provided that no order made by the High Court of Justice as to costs only, being costs which by law were left to the discretion of the court, should be subject to any appeal unless by leave of the court, then the powers of the appeal court were as wide as those enjoyed in respect of appeals on costs which were not in the discretion of the court: what this basically meant was that where leave to appeal was granted the court of appeal could substitute its own discretion for that of the court in which the order for costs was made.[30] However, Walsh J. in *Morelli*[31] identified certain grounds which always allowed an appellate tribunal to review an order for costs even in the absence of leave to appeal, viz. "if it could be shown that the judge acted arbitrarily, capriciously or recklessly, or that he had based his decision upon grounds which the law did not recognise, or that there was no evidence of the existence of any lawful ground for his decision. In many of these instances the judge was held to have "gone wrong in principle," and thus there grew up the practice that the appellate tribunal would not interfere with the discretion of the judge unless he had gone wrong in principle."

7–20 It was conceded by all the parties in *Morelli* that the necessity for leave to appeal required by section 52 of the 1877 Act did not survive the coming into force of the Constitution of 1937 since that section was not carried over

---

[29] Above, n.15, at 41.
[30] See *Whitmore v. O'Reilly* [1906] 2 I.R. 357, 399.
[31] Above, n.15, at 20-21.

by Article 50 of the Constitution as part of the law of this country.[32] Nevertheless, the defendant contended that the jurisdiction of the Supreme Court to
deal with decisions of the High Court conferred by Article 34.4.3° of the Constitution, and the appeal jurisdiction created by section 24 of the 1877 Act and
vested in the Supreme Court by section 7(2) of the Courts (Supplemental Provisions) Act 1961, should be exercised only on grounds which were referable
to appeals concerning 'non-appealable' discretionary orders. In rejecting this
argument Walsh J. held that such a submission would restrict the jurisdiction
of the Supreme Court which by the terms of the Constitution can only be
restricted within the limits allowed by the Constitution by a law enacted *after*
the coming into force of the Constitution. He concluded his judgment by stating that the Supreme Court is empowered to substitute its own discretion in
any appeal against an order made in the High Court. Thus, since *Morelli*, the
Supreme Court is empowered not only to exercise its own discretion in the
matter of costs following the practice as affirmed by Budd J. but it may also
substitute its own discretion for that of any other court on appeal.

APPEALING AN ORDER FOR COSTS MADE BY A FOREIGN COURT

7–21   As shown above, the issue of costs in a domestic matter is subject to
the court's discretion, and in probate matters the exercise of such a discretion
will follow the well-settled rules of practice, however, the introduction of a
foreign element may complicate matters somewhat. The complication may
arise where proceedings are instituted in an Irish and a foreign court in relation to a similar matter involving the same estate and an order for costs is
made by the foreign court. For instance, where an executor brings an action in
a foreign court to determine the domicile of the deceased at the time of death
and if, after the foreign court has made its decision, he institutes fresh proceedings in an Irish court to determine the same matter, a question may arise
as to the degree of cognisance an Irish court will give to the foreign decision.
The result will be of importance to the executor because if it is held that the
proceedings in the Irish court were superfluous and unnecessary the executor
may be personally saddled with two sets of costs, both Irish and foreign. There
is no doubt that an Irish court is obliged by virtue of the private international
law principle of comity of courts to take cognisance of a foreign judgment.
However, it is not clear whether such comity is also meant to include an order
for costs made by a foreign court. The latter matter was discussed by McCarthy
J. in his judgment for the Supreme Court in *In the Goods of Rowan*.[33] In that

---

[32] *State (Browne) v. Feran* [1967] I.R. 147; See also *Warner v. Minister for Industry and
Commerce* [1929] I.R. 582.
[33] Unreported, Supreme Court, 17 May, 1988.

case the testator died in Ireland. The executor instituted proceedings in Ireland seeking a declaration that the testator died domiciled in Ireland. Proceedings were also instituted in France in relation to the same matter where the testator had some property. The French courts both at first instance and on appeal decided that the testator had acquired a French domicile at the date of his death and made an order for costs and compensation in accordance with French law against the executor. In the Irish proceedings he sought an order that the costs of the French proceedings be paid out of the deceased's estate. Costello J. in High Court,[34] however, refused to make such an order on the grounds that an Irish court would not have granted leave to the executor to institute proceedings in France in the first place, and additionally, that as the French courts had seisen of the case, an Irish court would be precluded by the comity of courts from substituting an Irish order for a French order for costs. On appeal to the Supreme Court on the question of costs, McCarthy J., in the course of his judgment for the court, stated that the Irish legal principle involved was clear:

> "a personal representative is entitled to be indemnified out of the estate in respect of all proper expenses incurred by him in actions relating to the estate, which are brought or defended with the leave of the court, or which, though no leave had been obtained, it was proper to defend."[35]

Unlike Costello J. he went on to differentiate between the French proceedings at first instance and on appeal. He was of the view that as the plaintiff had instituted the appeal proceedings in France based on the advice of his French lawyers, *a fortiori*, he must have been advised to contest the proceedings at first instance. If the plaintiff had sought directions of the French court of first instance and produced the opinion of his French lawyers to the effect that the claim should be contested, McCarthy J. found it difficult to see how that court could have properly refused a direction to defend. However, he stated that very different considerations arose in respect of the appeal and remarked that the weakness of the plaintiff's appeal was reflected by the vigorous language used by the French court of appeal when condemning the executor to pay damages to the beneficiaries. Accordingly, he was prepared to allow the appeal to the extent of varying the order for costs by excluding the costs and expenses incurred by the plaintiff in obtaining advice and defending the French proceedings at first instance.

7–22 On the question of the comity of courts in relation to costs he stated:

> "I do not subscribe to the view that the matter is determined by what is called

---

[34] [1988] I.L.R.M. 65.
[35] McCarthy J. cited *Re Beddoe, Downes v. Cottam* [1893] 1 Ch. 547; *Walters v. Woodridge* 7 Ch. D. 504; *Re Dallaway* [1982] 1 W.L.R. 756.

the 'comity of courts' an imprecise term with criteria that may be difficult to define. The courts will, of course, permit suit upon a foreign judgment."[36]

7–23   Thus, an Irish court will not be precluded by the comity of courts from reviewing a foreign order for costs and may substitute its own discretion by varying the foreign order.

SECURITY FOR COSTS

7–24   When a litigant party requires security for costs from another party to the proceedings he is at liberty to apply by notice to the party for such security.[37] The party on whom such notice is served has forty-eight hours after service to comply with it, and in the event of non-compliance within the specified time the party requiring such costs may apply to the court for an order.[38] However, a defendant who seeks security for costs and who is resident outside of the jurisdiction of the court must show on affidavit evidence that he has a defence on the merits.[39] A plaintiff, on the other hand, who is ordinarily resident out of the jurisdiction but who is temporarily resident within it may be required to furnish such security.[40] Where the court makes an order for security for costs the amount of such security will be determined by the Master of the High Court.[41] As the question of security for costs is one which may arise at the commencement of an action the court when deciding to award them or not will take into account considerations which differ from those applied to the question of costs arising at later stages of the proceedings. Like all issues of costs, however, the issue of security for costs is likewise solely for the discretion of the court, but unlike other issues of costs, there is no rule of practice to guide the court when exercising its discretion. It may, however, take three elements into consideration when exercising its discretion in the matter: one, that an Irish citizen is entitled to sue as of right; two, that the mere absence from the jurisdiction will not disqualify him; and three, that the court has the right to consider all the circumstances.[42]

7–25   In *McNeany v. Maguire*,[43] the plaintiff, who resided in the United States, was one of the deceased's next-of-kin. He entered a caveat and instituted proceedings against the executor challenging the validity of the deceased's will.

---

[36] McCarthy J. cited *Cheshire's Private International Law* (9th edition) at pp. 629 *et seq.*
[37] The Rules of the Superior Courts, Ord. 29, r.1.
[38] *ibid.*
[39] Ord. 29, r.3.
[40] Ord. 29, r.4.
[41] Ord. 29, r.6.
[42] *McNeany v. Maguire* [1923] 2 I.R. 43, 44.
[43] Above, n.42.

The executor applied to the court for an order of security for costs against the plaintiff on the grounds that he resided abroad and had no property in Ireland. Dodd J. in refusing the executor's application held that the plaintiff, though resident in the United States, was an Irish-born subject who, if he had lived in Ireland, could have sued without giving security for costs; moreover, he had entered a caveat. He was also of the view that the plaintiff had shown "a good fighting case" in his affidavit. However, if a plaintiff is "ordinarily resident" out of the jurisdiction for the purposes of Order 29, rule 4 of the Rules of the Superior Courts this may be viewed in a different light from "mere absence" from the jurisdiction which, it will be remembered, is one of the three elements which the court may take into consideration when deciding on whether to make an order security for costs.[44]

THE AMOUNT OF COSTS

7–26   Order 99, rule 10(2) of the Rules of the Superior Courts provides that costs will be taxed on the party and party basis, and on a taxation on that basis all costs will be allowed as were necessary or proper for the attainment of justice or for enforcing or defending the rights of the party whose costs are being taxed. The court in awarding costs may also, where it thinks fit to do so, order or direct costs to be taxed on the solicitor and client basis.[45] However, on a taxation as between solicitor and client all costs will be allowed unless they are of an unreasonable amount or have been unreasonably incurred.[46] Any costs incurred which are of an unusual nature and as such would not be allowed on a taxation on a party and party basis will be presumed to be costs unreasonably incurred unless the solicitor involved informed his client before they were incurred that they might not be allowed.[47] On the other hand, on a taxation as between solicitor and client, all costs incurred with the express or implied approval of the client will be conclusively presumed to have been reasonably incurred.[48] "Client" for the latter purposes will be construed to include a guardian *ad litem* of a person of unsound mind or the guardian *ad litem* or next friend of a person under the age of majority.[49]

---

[44] *ibid.*
[45] Ord. 99, r.10(3).
[46] Ord. 99, r.11(1).
[47] Ord. 99, r.11(2).
[48] Ord. 99, r.11(3).
[49] Ord. 99, r.11(4).

THE ISSUE OF COSTS IN THE CIRCUIT COURT

7–27   In the Circuit Court, the awarding of costs in any proceeding shall be in the discretion of the trial judge, save as otherwise provided by statute or by the Rules of the Circuit Court 1950.[50] Similar to Order 99 rule 1 of the Rules of the Superior Courts, the costs shall follow the event,

> "unless the judge shall for special cause otherwise direct, and in that event such cause shall be stated in the decree or order."[51]

The costs of any *ex parte* or other application including any motion or order may be awarded irrespective of the final judgment in the proceeding, or may be made costs in the proceeding, or may be reserved to be dealt with at the conclusion of the action.[52] Where costs are awarded against two or more parties they are payable jointly and severally unless the judge otherwise orders.[53] The allowance of the expenses of any witness shall be in the discretion of the trial judge and the word 'expenses' shall, in the case of an expert witness, include his reasonable charges in respect of all necessary matters prior to the hearing.[54] The jurisdiction of the county registrar to allow costs is governed by Rules 6 and 7 of Order 58 of the 1950 Rules. Rule 6 provides that:

> "All costs directed to be taxed by the County Registrar (who for that purpose shall have all the powers of a Taxing Master of the High court of Justice) subject as to every item, including outlay and Counsel's fees, to an appeal to the court notice of which shall be given within ten days from the conclusion of the taxation."

Rule 7 provides that:

> "Save as is otherwise provided by these Rules, the costs and fees specified in each scale in the Schedule to these Rules shall be the only lawful fees, costs, charges, and emoluments for the business therein indicated or described, as between party and party, and no other fees, costs, charges or emoluments shall be payable or recoverable therefor."

But where the trial judge or county registrar is of the opinion that there is no appropriate scale of costs, the judge or the county registrar may measure a sum for costs, subject to an appeal to the court from any decision of the county registrar under this rule.[55] However, under rule 14, the trial judge may for special cause order that the costs, as between party and party, in any action be taxed on a scale higher than that otherwise applicable. The county registrar

---

[50] Rules of the Circuit Court, Ord. 58, r.1.
[51] Ord. 58, r.2.
[52] Ord. 58, r.3.
[53] Ord. 58, r.4.
[54] Ord. 58, r.5.
[55] Ord. 58, r.27.

also has power, under Order 15, rule 6, when directed by the trial judge or empowered by the 1950 Rules, to tax bills of costs, including costs as between solicitor and client, and may certify the amount which is due. Furthermore, in any case in which there is no prescribed scale he may, if requested or if he considers it desirable, measure the costs by fixing a reasonable sum in respect of the entire bill or any particular item in it.[56] It will be observed that there are different expressions used in Order 58, rule 27 and Order 15, rule 6 where there is no scale of costs in existence: in Order 58, rule 27 the expression used is "no appropriate scale" and in Order 15, rule 6 the expression is "no pre-scribed scale." However, Murphy J. in *Blackhall v. Blackhall and Rose Blackhall*[57] was forced to conclude that the words "appropriate" and "pre-scribed" were in that context interchangeable. He went on to say that:

> "If an official scale clearly identifies the costs or fees to be paid in respect of particular work, I do not believe it would be open to an officer of the court to conclude that the scale was 'inappropriate' and should be disregarded. If there is to be a departure from the scales, it seems to me that it is a matter either for the judge to invoke the powers conferred on him by Order 58, rule 14 or for the authorities to prescribe new scales of fees."

In *Blackhall v. Blackhall and Rose Blackhall*[58] Gerard Blackhall instituted proceedings against his sisters Eileen and Rose Blackhall in the Circuit Court in relation to the partition of property in Dublin and judgment was given in his favour. On appeal to the High Court Lardner J. ordered that the property in question be sold subject to the approval of the court. Lardner J. further ordered that the plaintiff, Gerard Blackhall, was entitled to his costs of the appeal when taxed and ascertained. The county registrar taxed the plaintiff's costs of the appeal. Rose Blackhall, one of the defendants, issued notice of motion seeking an Order pursuant to Order 61, rule 12 the Rules of the Superior Courts to review the taxation by the county registrar. The review was sought on the grounds that

> "taxation proceeded in spite of a request for an adjournment because of defective procedures by the solicitor and accountant of the plaintiff in that Order 99 of the Rules of the Superior Courts were ignored."

It was also sought on the grounds that the county registrar "failed to observe Order 58, rule 7 of the Rules of the Circuit Court." Many of the objections made by the appellants related to the procedure prescribed by Order 99, rule 30 of the Rules of the Superior Court in relation to the conduct of taxation by the taxing master. It provides by rule 30(6) that:

> "An index or schedule of documents included in each brief, with the number of

---

[56] Ord. 58, r.6.
[57] Unreported, High Court, February 18, 1994.
[58] Above, n.57.

> folios on each, and the page of brief on which the same are respectively copied shall be endorsed in such brief, or annexed thereto and shall be produced on taxation."

Rule 30(8) provides that:

> "Receipts for disbursements charged in the Bill of Costs, together with all Rulings, Orders, Reports and other important documents shall be produced on taxation."

The appellants complained that these and similar regulations were ignored by the county registrar. However, the county registrar in his report made it clear that there were not in fact any disbursements, with the exception of charges for duties which were vouched by the production of the relevant document bearing the appropriate stamp duty so that this complaint had no substance. As regards the index, the county registrar explained that the production of such a document was not required. Murphy J. was of the view that the county registrar was entitled to waive this requirement. He was also satisfied that the

> "non-compliance or dispensation from a procedural requirement of this nature would not affect the jurisdiction of a person exercising a quasi-judicial function."

It seemed to him that the important issue raised in the appeal was the jurisdiction of the county registrar to allow costs, otherwise than by reference to those set out in schedules to the Rules of the Circuit Court. He referred to Order 58, rules 7, 14 and 19 of the Rules of the Circuit Court and stated that it seemed to him that in general party and party costs were to be determined in accordance with costs and fees prescribed in the schedules to the Rules of the Circuit Court as amended from time to time. In his report the county registrar dealt with the contention that he had departed from the prescribed scales in the following terms:

> "Order 58, rule 7 of the Circuit Court Rules 1950 refers to costs in a schedule to the Circuit Court Rules. Since the change in jurisdiction in 1982, it has been the practice by myself, my predecessor and indeed other county Registrars, to allow higher fees than those in the schedule. The Incorporated Law Society gave a guideline on these scheduled items and these to a greater extent had been accepted by me and others as in order. Order 58, rule 7 of the Circuit Court Rules 1950 allows a County Registrar to measure a sum for costs where there is no appropriate scale. I have deemed the 'scheduled costs' as inappropriate in 1993. Order 15, rule 6 of the Circuit Court Rules 1950 permits fixing a reasonable sum in respect of an entire Bill or a particular item."

However, Murphy J. found that if an official scale clearly identified the costs or fees to be paid in respect of particular work it would not be open to an officer of the court to conclude that the scale was 'inappropriate' and should be disregarded. If there is to be a departure from the scales it is a matter "either for the judge to invoke the powers conferred on him by Order 58, rule 14 or for the authorities to prescribe new scales of fees." The plaintiff/respondent contended that the "saving provision" in rule 7 of Order 58 referred back to rule 6 of the same Order. This contention was not accepted by Murphy J. because it seemed to him that the "saving provision" in rule 7 was intended to refer to the succeeding rules and in particular to rule 14. He also found that Order 56, rule 6 did not confer on the county registrar the powers of the taxing master and would not accept that this would entitle the county registrar, or indeed the taxing master, to ignore a scale which was prescribed as the limit of his jurisdiction in a particular circumstance. He concluded by saying that

> "where costs on a party and party basis and the particular fees fall clearly within the prescribed scale then, in the absence of a special direction of the trial judge, the costs allowed may not exceed the prescribed amounts."

As no particular fees or costs were identified in evidence or argument before him as falling within any prescribed schedule, nor were any relevant schedules identified, he was not in a position to allow or disallow particular items. He directed that before the matter was listed for further argument that the appellants lodge with the county registrar the relevant certificate of taxation.

7–28   In any taxation of costs, whenever items appear for disbursement, they must be properly vouched before the county registrar.[59] However, nothing in Order 58 or in the schedule of costs will limit or affect the right of a solicitor to charge costs as between solicitor and client for work done or professional services rendered.[60]

7–29   A party opposing a will may with his defence give notice to the party propounding the will that he merely insists on the will being proved in solemn form of law, and only intends to cross-examine the witnesses produced in support of the will, and will not as a result be liable to pay the costs of the other side unless the trial judge will be of the opinion that there was no reasonable ground for opposing the will.[61]

7–30   Order 13, rule 1 provides that where a party requires security for costs from another party he must apply by notice to such party for such security, and in the event of the latter not complying by notice within seven days after service, the party requiring the security may apply to the court by motion on notice grounded on affidavit. The fact that a plaintiff resides outside the jurisdiction of the court will not be sufficient on its own to entitle the defendant to an order compelling the plaintiff to give security for costs.[62] A defendant must show

---

[59] Ord. 58, r.10.
[60] Ord. 58, r.13.
[61] Ord. 34, r.13.
[62] Ord. 13, r.2.

also by affidavit that he has a defence on the merits before such an order will be made.[63]

Summary

7–31   Thus the issue of costs in a probate action will be solely for the discretion of the court, and when exercising such discretion, especially in relation to an unsuccessful party, it will be guided by rules of practice and procedure when deciding whether or not to allow such costs to be paid out of the deceased's estate, and on appeal an order for costs may be varied or substituted.

---

[63] Ord. 13, r.3.

PART TWO

Related Matters

CHAPTER 8

The Quality of the Spouse's Legal Right

INTRODUCTION

8–01   The entitlement of a surviving spouse to the legal right share is dependent upon two conditions: first, that the surviving spouse is the lawful spouse of the deceased, and secondly, that the deceased died leaving a will.[1] Once these two conditions have been satisfied the quantity of the legal right share in the estate will depend on whether or not there are children: if there are no children the surviving spouse will be entitled to one-half of the estate, if there are children the spouse will have a right to one-third.[2] The legal right share once established will take priority over devises, legacies or bequests and shares on intestacy.[3] The reason why intestacy is mentioned is because a testator may die partially intestate thus making the rules of intestacy applicable to that part of his estate not disposed of by his will. Although the legal right share is expressed to take priority over testamentary gifts and shares arising out of a partial intestacy, it is not expressed to take priority over the debts and liabilities of the deceased.[4] In one case at least the quality of the legal right share was described as having the same effect as a 'debt' due by the estate.[5] Normally, where a debt is due by the estate to a creditor of the deceased the right to claim the debt will survive the creditor and may be claimed by his personal representative for the benefit of his estate. It might be asked, however, does the legal right share have the same effect as other debts due by the estate? While as a debt it will survive the death of the spouse and thus benefit the spouse's estate, but as such it is dependent upon the death of the testator prior to that of the spouse, while the death of a creditor prior to that of the testator will not preclude the creditor's personal representatives from claiming payment for the benefit of the creditor's estate. Thus the survival of the spouse as a 'creditor' is essential for claiming the legal right share and as such it cannot be accurately said to have the same effect as other debts due by the estate. As a result of a more recent decision of the Supreme Court the legal right share was described as having the quality of "an interest arising under a

---

[1]   Succession Act 1965, s. 109(1).
[2]   Succession Act 1965, s. 111(1) and (2).
[3]   Succession Act 1965, s. 112.
[4]   See Succession Act 1965, s. 109(2).
[5]   *In re Urquhart: The Revenue Commissioners v. Allied Irish Banks Ltd* [1974] I.R. 197 at 210.

will or a share arising on intestacy."[6] Thus where the deceased leaves a will, and no provision is made in it for the surviving spouse, the legal right share will be viewed as possessing the quality of a testamentary interest and may be claimed accordingly.

8–02 However, where the deceased leaves a gift in his will to the surviving spouse but is one which is less in value than the legal right share a further right accrues to the surviving spouse to elect between that which is given in the will and the legal right share.[7] This gives rise to the question as to whether the right to elect has a quality similar to that of the legal right itself and as such whether it survives the death of the spouse and may be exercisable by another on behalf of a deceased spouse's estate. Apparently the right to elect is personal to a surviving spouse and as its exercise is discretionary it cannot be exercised by another on behalf of the spouse's estate and that includes the personal representative of the spouse.[8] Therefore, the right to elect exists only for the benefit of the surviving spouse personally within the time prescribed for its exercise.[9] Once exercised in favour of the legal right share, the share may be composed of a blend of a testamentary gift less in value than the share in partial satisfaction and the balance made payable out of the estate.[10] In the event of the death of the spouse after exercising the right of election the value and composition of the legal right share will form part of the deceased spouse's estate.[11]

8–03 Two general points may be made concerning the policy of the Succession Act: one may be described as a quantitative, and the other, as a qualitative, observation. As the general policy of the Succession Act is to improve the condition of the surviving spouse this does not appear to be entirely reflected in the values of the legal right share especially when such values are compared with the values to which a surviving spouse becomes entitled on an intestacy. The legal right share is valued at one-half where there are no children and one-third where are children, on an intestacy a surviving spouse takes the whole estate where there are no children and two-thirds where there are children.[12] A testator who leaves nothing to his spouse is the same as leaving no will as regards that spouse but the effect of leaving a will reduces considerably the amount of the share in the estate to which that spouse becomes entitled. There appears to be no real reason why the values of the legal right shares

---

[6] *Re Cummins: O'Dwyer v. Keegan* [1997] 2 I.L.R.M. 401 at 403.
[7] Succession Act 1965, ss. 114 and 115.
[8] *O'Reilly v. McEntee* [1984] I.L.R.M. 572.
[9] Succession Act 1965, s. 115(4).
[10] See Succession Act 1965, s. 115(3).
[11] *Re Cummins: O'Dwyer v. Keegan*, above, n.6.
[12] See Succession Act 1965, ss. 111 and 67.

and the shares on intestacy should not be the same, and any argument grounded on the general concept of freedom of testation pales in the light of the policy of the Act to benefit a surviving spouse, especially where a will is made deliberately to limit the amount of a spouse's share in the estate. The assimilation of the legal right share with the intestate share would indeed be an improvement in keeping with the policy of the Act and would also eliminate the temptation to use the Act as a means to carry out something which was certainly not intended by it. There is also no real reason why the right to elect between the legal right share and a testamentary gift should not be exercised by a surviving spouse's personal representative if the exercise of such a right would benefit that spouse's estate, as the likely reason for exercising the right to elect in any case is to chose that which is greater in value, subject, perhaps, to a declaration to the contrary in that spouse's will. If such were the case the right could be exercised in favour of that which would be more beneficial to the spouse's estate and bear the quality of an interest arising under a will.

SECTION 112 OF THE SUCCESSION ACT

8–04 Section 112 of the Succession Act provides that:

> "The right of a spouse under section 111 (which shall be known as a legal right) shall have priority over devises, bequests and shares on intestacy."

Section 109(2) provides that references to the estate of the testator are to all estate to which he is beneficially entitled for an estate or interest not ceasing on his death and remaining after all the expenses, debts and liabilities have been discharged. It will be observed that while section 112 provides that the legal right of a surviving spouse has priority over devises, legacies or bequests and shares on intestacy, it does not identify the quality of the right. Similarly, while section 109(2) identifies the extent of the estate which is to be regarded as the subject matter of the legal right, it does not identify the quality of the legal right share nor does it mention it expressly as being payable out of the estate in the same way as the expenses, debts and liabilities of the estate. The logic therefore must be that seeing that section 109(2) precedes section 112 the estate of the testator which forms the subject matter for the discharge of the legal right share is that estate which remains after the expenses, debts and liabilities have been discharged. Section 112, it will be remembered, gives only priority to the legal right over devises, legacies or bequests, it does not identify the right as consisting of a devise, legacy or bequest. Therefore, the only logical interpretation of section 109(2) and section 112 is that a new category of succession right has been created in the form of a statutory right and one which occupies a position of priority to testamentary gifts and one which must first be discharged out of that estate remaining after the payment the expenses, debts and liabilities of the estate. As the whole of Part IX of the

Succession Act is silent on the question of the quality of the legal right, it has been left to the courts to identify it. The Supreme Court on at least two occasions carried out this task.[13] On each occasion the court sought assistance of provisions of the Succession Act other than those found in that Part of the Act which deals with the legal right and, as a result, the court in one case found that quality of the right had the same effect as that of a debt due by the estate,[14] and in the other case, it was found that it had the quality of a testamentary interest.[15] However, one cannot help but feel that that Part of the Succession Act dealing with the legal right provides a sort of a cosmos of its own for identifying the quality of the right, and perhaps the main reason why the Supreme Court looked for provisions outside of it for identifying the quality was the need to fit the right into a recognisable and traditional category of testamentary claims and gifts and to spare confusion in the administration of estates. But those provisions dealing with the legal right are expressed as 'new' in the margins of all the sections in that Part of the Act and serving as a possible indication that some new form of succession right was created and one which had an identity and quality of its own without having to fit it into the traditional categories of testamentary claims and gifts. The right is also distinctive in that it has priority over testamentary gifts after claims against the estate in the form of expenses, debts and liabilities have been discharged. Thus, as a result, the legal right created by the Succession Act would seem to have all the necessary qualities required for an independent succession right which can be asserted by a spouse against the testator's estate as bearing a definite statutory value depending on whether or not there are children, and thereby allowing it to be categorised as a statutory right with a recognisable quality of its own.

THE QUALITY OF THE LEGAL RIGHT AS A DEBT

8–05 Walsh J. in the Supreme Court decision of *In Re Urquhart: The Revenue Comissioners v. Allied Irish Banks Ltd.*[16] stated that the effect of section 46 of the Succession Act was to make the legal right a debt due by the estate. Section 46 provides for the general rules governing the administration of a deceased's estate. Subsection 3 provides that:

> "Where the estate of a deceased person is solvent, it shall, subject to rules of court and the provisions hereinafter contained as to charges on property of the

---

[13] *In re Urquhart: The Revenue Commissioners v. Allies Irish Banks Ltd*, above, n.5; *Re Cummins: O'Dwyer v. Keegan*, above, n.6.

[14] *In re Urquhart: The Revenue Commissioners v. Allied Irish Banks*, above, n.5 at 210 *per* Walsh J.

[15] *In re Cummins: O'Dwyer v. Keegan*, above, n.6 at 403 *per* Barron J.

[16] Above, n.5 at 210.

deceased, and to the provisions, if any, contained in his will, be applicable towards the discharge of the funeral, testamentary and administration expenses, debts and liabilities and any legal right in the order mentioned in Part II of the First Schedule."

Subsection 4 provides that nothing in subsection 3 "affects the rights of any creditor of the deceased or the legal right of a spouse." Subsection 5 makes provision for persons entitled under a will or intestacy to have assets marshalled where a creditor or spouse entitled to a legal right applies an asset in the wrong order. The beneficiary whose property is being taken by the creditor or by the spouse will stand in the place of the creditor or spouse "*pro tanto* as against any property that, in the said order, is liable before his own estate or interest." Subsection 6 provides that

> "a claim to a share as a legal right or on intestacy in the estate of a deceased person is a claim against the assets of the estate to a sum equal to the value of that share."

The effect of section 46 is therefore to make the legal share "a debt due by the estate." In other words, that the legal right share was an administrative matter for the estate. It was also argued in *Reilly v. McEntee*[17] that the right to elect between a testamentary gift and the legal right should be viewed as a chose in action capable of passing on death and that it may exercised by someone other than the spouse. A debt is a chose in action and capable of passing on death and as the legal right had the quality of a debt, ipsa jure, it had the quality of a chose. However, Murphy J. stated that: "If the right to elect was, as the plaintiff argues, a chose in action capable of passing on death then that chose in action would have been liable for estate duty so that presumably it was accepted by the parties in the *Urquhart* case and by implication the court itself that the right of election did not survive the death of the spouse in whom it had vested."[18]

THE QUALITY OF THE LEGAL RIGHT AS A TESTAMENTARY INTEREST

8–06 Barron J. in the Supreme Court decision of *In Re Cummins: O'Dwyer v. McEntee*[19] considered that the net issue for the court to determine was whether section 111 created an interest in the estate or merely gave a right to the spouse to elect to take such interest. In that case at the time of the deceased's death his wife was in a coma and she died twelve hours after his death. Both the deceased and his wife made wills. There were no children of the marriage. The deceased left nothing to his wife in his will. Barron J. re-

---

[17] Above, n.8.
[18] *ibid.* at 576.
[19] Above, n.6 at 403.

ferred to the wording of section 111 of the Succession Act and in particular
the expression "shall have a right to" and considered that it was not just a
question of construing the word "right" in the context in which it was used
because section 112 of the same Act provided that "the right of a spouse under
section 111 is to be known as a legal right." He found the expression defined
in section 3 of the Act as meaning "the right of a spouse under section 111 to
a share in the estate of the deceased person." He found the word "share" in
relation to the estate of a deceased was also defined in section 3 to include
"any share or interest, whether arising under a will, on intestacy or as a legal
right, and includes also the right to the whole estate." He went to say that:
"From these definitions, two matters are clear. First, the surviving spouse has
a right to a share in the estate, and secondly, this right has the same quality as
an interest arising under a will or a share arising on intestacy. The two latter
interests vest on death. In my view the former does also."[20] He also found that
a similar view was expressed by Walsh J. in *In Re Urquhart: The Revenue
Commissioners v. Allied Irish Banks Ltd.*[21] when he said, referring to the sections in Part IX of the Act, that:

> "In my opinion, the whole of this structure presupposes and is based on an
> assumption implicit in the statute, in addition to what is expressly stated in
> section 111, that a legal right arises on the moment of the death of the testator.
> Where there is no legacy or devise or where there is a legacy or a devise ex-
> pressed to be in addition to the legal share, the legal share vests upon the death."

Barron J., having approved of the construction of Part IX of Act by Walsh J.,
went to express the view that it was "not appropriate to submit that to construe
section 111 as creating a vested interest is to frustrate the intentions of either
or both of the deceased and the surviving spouse." He concluded by saying
that:

> "It must be presumed that in the absence of a renunciation under section 113
> that both spouses realised that the survivor of them would be entitled to the
> legal right and, even accepting that this was an interest conditional on accept-
> ance, so could distribute the relevant assets as he or she wished. It is important
> that the law should be certain so that those who rely upon it when they make
> their wills should be in no doubt as to how their assets will be distributed not
> only in expected circumstances but in unexpected circumstances also."

He therefore decided that the deceased's spouse became entitled to one-half
of the estate on his death. Barron J., while affirming the construction placed
by Walsh J. on Part IX of the Act, did not adopt the view that the legal right
share had the effect of a debt due by the estate, but instead thought that the
legal right had "the same quality as an interest arising under a will, or a share

---

[20] *ibid.*
[21] Above, n.5 at 211.

arising on intestacy." In other words, that the legal right was a distributive, and not an administrative, matter.

THE PERSONAL QUALITY OF THE RIGHT OF ELECTION

8–07 The right of election under section 115 of the Succession Act presents the surviving spouse with the option of "taking" a gift in the will or the legal right share. Once exercised in favour of the legal right share the same question as regards the quality of the right may arise as hitherto discussed. However, in relation to the right of election it may first be more a question of quantity than quality. Naturally, if the value of the legal right share is greater than the value of a testamentary gift, sentiment apart and human nature being what it is, the value of the right may be the determining feature when deciding to elect between the two. The time for ascertaining the value of the legal right is when all the expenses, debts and liabilities of the deceased have been discharged,[22] and the value of the right may then be computed by reference to section 111 of the Act. The question of quantity of the right therefore precedes any question of quality, and the question of quality will depend on the exercise of the right of election in favour of the right. The condition precedent for the acquisition of the legal right share is the exercise of the right of election in its favour by the spouse.[23] It is personal to the surviving spouse of the testator and it must be exercised within the time prescribed for doing so.[24] The right of election itself does not bestow any property rights nor does it have the quality of a chose in action.[25] A failure to exercise the right with the time prescribed entitles the spouse, or the spouse's estate, to the testamentary gift only. However, when exercised the spouse will become entitled to the value of the right as determined by section 111, and the spouse's estate in the event of death immediately afterwards. The questions as to when and by whom the right of election may be exercised were considered by Walsh J. in the Supreme Court in *In Re Urquhart: The Revenue Commissioners v. Allied Irish Banks Ltd.*[26] and by Murphy J. in the High Court in *Reilly v. McEntee*[27] respectively.

8–08 In *In Re Urquhart: The Revenue Commissioners v. Allied Irish Banks Ltd.*[28] a question arose as to whether one-half of the testator's estate went to the surviving spouse as of right by virtue of section 111 and whether the joint

---

[22] See Succession Act 1965, s. 109(2).
[23] *In re Urquhart: The Revenue Commissioners v. Allied Irish Banks Ltd*, above, n.5 at 211-212.
[24] *Reilly v. McEntee*, above, n.8 at 575-576; Succession Act 1965, s. 115(4).
[25] *Reilly v. McEntee*, above, n.8 at 576.
[26] Above, n.5.
[27] Above, n.8.
[28] Above, n.5.

effect of sections 111 and 115 conferred a right to *claim* only one-half of the estate as distinct from a right to *take* one-half of the estate. In that case the testatrix left a legacy to her husband on condition that he survive her by one month. In fact he survived her by one day and died without having exercised his right to elect between the legacy in the will and the share as a legal right. It was claimed by the plaintiffs that the husband had power to dispose of his legal share at the time of his death and that the effect of section 111 was to confer on him a vested right to one-half of the estate which took effect on the death of his wife and continued to be effective unless divested by an election made under section 115 within the period set out in that section and, as he died without making any such election, he was competent to dispose of the one-half share of the estate at the date of his death. However, the defendants disputed this claim on the ground that the husband had never elected to take the legal share in his wife's estate under section 115 and that therefore he was not entitled to any share of the estate or to any benefit under the will as the gift to the husband under the will lapsed as he did not survive his wife by one month. In his judgment, Walsh J., stated that the provisions of section 115 must be read in the light of section 114, and where a devise or legacy is left to a spouse it will be deemed to have been intended by the testator to have been made in satisfaction of the share as a legal right of the spouse. "In the latter event, of course, the right of election under s. 115 arises." He was of the opinion that

> "the whole structure presupposes and is based on an assumption implicit in the statute, in addition to what is expressly stated in s. 111, that a legal right arises on the moment of death of the testator. Where there is no legacy or devise or where there is a legacy or devise expressed to be in addition to the legal share, the legal share vests upon the death. But when a testator in his will makes a devise or bequest to a spouse and it is not expressed to be in addition to the share as a legal right, then the spouse has a statutory right to take the share as a legal right – but that share does not vest until he takes it. If the spouse does not take the share as a legal right, then the legacy or devise under the will which vested in the spouse at the death of the testator will remain vested in the spouse without his taking any step in relation to it. The spouse can never have both. This result flows from the joint effect of s. 114, sub-s. 2, and section 115."[29]

The right to take the legal share requires a "taking" to vest the share in the spouse. The "taking" may take the form of "an actual taking, as by express election to take it instead of the legacy, or it may be a constructive taking by dealing with the legal share in a manner which is inconsistent with any explanation other than that the spouse, in so dealing with it, has elected to take the legacy."[30] Therefore, the spouse is not competent to dispose of the legal share until he or she has made a formal election or has dealt with it in such a way. As

---

[29] *ibid.* at 211.
[30] *ibid.* at 211-212.

Walsh J. succinctly put it: "if the spouse does not take it he does not get it."[31] If the death of the spouse takes place before the right to elect is exercised the legal share does not form part of the spouse's estate because the spouse has done nothing before death to take the share as a legal right. Walsh J. found support for his view by referring to the terms of section 115(5) which provides that in the case of the surviving spouse being of unsound mind the right of election must be exercised either by the committee of that spouse, or where there is no committee, by the High Court or the Circuit Court as the case may be. "Failure of any of these bodies to act will result in a position where the legal right, which the surviving spouse had been entitled to take, had not in fact been taken."[32] In his view the true construction of section 115, in the light of the other sections of Part IX is that the spouse is entitled to take the share as a legal right referred to in section 111, but it must be taken. He concluded by describing the legal share as a statutory offer which is not binding on a spouse until it is accepted.[33] Therefore, although the husband, at the date of his death, was entitled to take the legal share, but as he did not do so, before his death, it was not property which he was competent to dispose of.

8–09 In *Reilly v. McEntee*[34] Murphy J., having approved of the principle enunciated by Walsh J. in *In Re Urquhart: The Revenue Commissioners v. Allied Irish Banks Ltd.*,[35] stated that:

> "If the election is not made for whatever reason prior to death then the property comprising the legal right cannot in my view form part of the estate of the spouse entitled to exercise such right."[36]

However, he went on to consider whether the right of election itself, as distinct from property rights that it might confer, passed on the death of the spouse to her personal representative. In that case the surviving spouse sought and obtained a grant of letters of administration intestate to the deceased's estate and went into possession of his property. A will was later discovered during the lifetime of the spouse under which the deceased left all his property to his spouse for life and on her death to his nephew absolutely. It was finally admitted to probate after the death of the spouse although preliminary steps seeking a grant were taken before her death. It was claimed that the right to elect between the gift in the will and the legal share survived for the benefit of her estate and as such was exercisable by her personal representative. However, Murphy J. stated that the

---

[31] *ibid.* at 211-212.
[32] *ibid.* at 212.
[33] *ibid.* at 215.
[34] Above, n.8.
[35] Above, n.5 at 212.
[36] Above, n.8 at 575.

"right of election is expressed throughout s. 115 as being a right which may be exercised by the spouse and, subject only to the particular case of the surviving spouse being a person of unsound mind where the right is expressed to be exercisable by the committee of the spouse's estate or the court, the election is expressed to be exercisable by the spouse and not by any person other than the spouse."[37]

Even though the right of election may be a very valuable right and may enable a spouse to exchange a nominal testamentary gift for a more substantial share in the estate, it is not the value of the right which is in issue but rather the identity of the person by whom it is exercisable. The section does not transmit the right to elect to any other person. According to Murphy J.:

"the purpose and intent of the legislation is to give to the surviving spouse a personal discretion as to whether he or she would take under the will or under the Act."[38]

He then considered whether the right to elect was a chose in action and having referred to the *Urquhart* case stated that:

"If the right to elect was, as the plaintiff argues, a chose in action capable of passing on death then the chose in action itself would have been liable to estate duty so that presumably it was accepted by the parties to the *Urquhart* case and by implication by the court itself that the right of election did not survive the death of the spouse in whom it had vested."

Accordingly, he held, that the plaintiff was not entitled to the relief claimed.

A Suggested Alternative Construction of Section 114(2)

8–10　It is clear that the general aim of Part IX of the Succession Act is to benefit the surviving spouse of the testator by giving a legal right to a share in the estate. Where a testator leaves nothing to his spouse by will the spouse may claim a legal right share in the estate in accordance with the value of that share as specified by section 111. While there is nothing preventing a testator from freely disposing of his property but if he ignores the legal right of his spouse in doing so his estate will be answerable in the amount prescribed by section 111. The legal right even takes priority over the way in which a testator disposes of the property in his will.[39] The right however may be voluntarily renounced by a spouse in an ante-nuptial contract in writing or in writing after marriage and during the lifetime of the testator.[40] On the other hand, a testator may increase the value of the spouse's share in the estate by providing

---

[37] *ibid.* at 575.
[38] *ibid.* at 576.
[39] Succession Act 1965, s. 112.
[40] Succession Act 1965, s. 113.

that a gift to his spouse shall be in addition to the legal right share.[41] It can be seen that the provisions of Part IX of the Act so far are obviously in support of the aim of benefiting the surviving spouse. A definite right is given, it has priority over gifts in the will, it may be renounced by act of the spouse, and it may be increased but not decreased by the testator. However, when it comes to section 114(2) it is provided that a gift to a spouse by will shall be deemed to have been intended by the testator to be in satisfaction of the legal right. While this obviously presumes that the gift to the spouse is a valid one, does it presume anything more? Walsh J. in *In Re Urquhart: The Revenue Commissioners v. Allied Irish Banks Ltd.*[42] stated that section 114(2) must be read in conjunction with section 115 which gives the surviving spouse a right of election between the gift and the legal right. As a result, he was of the view that there must be a "taking" of the legal right share otherwise the spouse would be entitled only to the testamentary gift. This view was later affirmed by Barron J. in *Re Cummins: O'Dwyer v. Keegan.*[43] Thus, the right of election will not survive the death of the spouse and will lapse if not exercised within the time prescribed by section 115(4). Does this mean that as a result of the wording of section 114(2) once something is left to the spouse it will be deemed to have been intended by the testator to be in satisfaction of the legal right share? To take an extreme case, for instance, can it be said that a testator whose estate is worth say 5 million pounds and who leaves his spouse 5 pence in his will intended the 5 pence to be in satisfaction of the legal right share? Was section 114(2) designed by the legislature to deal with a situation similar to or perhaps less extreme than the foregoing instance? It was said that section 114(2) should be read in conjunction with section 115, but section 114(2) is part of section 114 to govern situations coming within the provisions of section 114, and if that is the case must section 114(2) be so read. It is suggested that section 114(2) is part and parcel of the increasing crescendo of provisions which go in support of a spouse's legal right and has its own part to play in the protection of it. Therefore, it is felt, that section 114(2) may be interpreted in a way which preserves the legal right share and not in a way which diminishes it, as a testator cannot be deemed to have satisfied the legal right share by leaving something in a will which is less than the value of legal right share. It is further thought that as a result the type of testamentary gift envisaged by section 114(2) is one which is greater, and not less, than the value of the legal right share. Section 115 then goes on to give a right of election to a spouse to choose between the gift in a will and the legal right share and in default of exercising the right will be entitled only to the testamentary gift. It is suggested that the purpose of section 115 is to present the spouse with the choice of electing between a gift of greater value and the legal right share for any number of

---

[41] Succession Act 1965, s. 114(1).
[42] Above, n.5.
[43] Above, n.6.

reasons, for instance, that residuary beneficiaries should receive the benefit of the surplus or those entitled in the case of a partial intestacy. In the event of a spouse being left a number of testamentary gifts that spouse may "further elect to take any devise or bequest less in value than the share in partial satisfaction thereof."[44]

SUMMARY

8–11   While Part IX of the Succession Act created a new succession right in the form of a legal right it is silent on the question of the quality of the right. Although section 109(2) of the Act provides that references to the estate of a testator means that estate which remains after expenses, debts and liabilities have been discharged, it does not specify that the legal right should be discharged as a debt due by the estate or that it should be discharged out of the estate remaining after the expenses, debts and liabilities have been discharged. Furthermore, although section 112 gives the legal right priority over testamentary gifts, it is not a testamentary gift, for if that were the case the section no doubt would have stated that the legal right should have priority over *other* testamentary gifts, therefore, in the quest for the quality of the right section 112 is only helpful to the extent that it does not specifically give the legal right the quality of a testamentary gift. However, by the wording it is clear that section 112 created a new succession right in the form of a legal right. Due to the positing of the legal right somewhere between the expenses, debts and liabilities and testamentary gifts, the courts in an attempt to identify the quality of the right have either placed it in the category of debts due by the estate and making it an administrative matter,[45] or described it as having the quality of a testamentary gift and thus making it a distributive issue,[46] and on each occasion found justification for the view by looking at statutory provisions outside of the Part of the Act creating the legal right. The question of quality of the right arises on the death of the testator and in circumstances where the spouse is either left nothing in the will or where the will states expressly that a gift to a spouse is to be in addition to the legal right share. However, in circumstances where the spouse is left a gift in the will but which is not expressed to be in addition to the legal right, the gift in the will will be deemed to have been intended by the testator to be in satisfaction of the share as a legal right by section 114(2), and in such circumstances the spouse by section 115 is given a right of election to choose between the gift and the legal right, but the courts have held that the right must be exercised personally by the spouse in

---

[44] Succession Act 1965, s. 115(4).

[45] See *In re Urquhart: The Revenue Commissioners v. Allied Irish Banks Ltd*, above, n.5 at 210.

[46] See *Re Cummins: O'Dwyer v. Keegan*, above, n.6 at 403.

order to vest the legal right share otherwise the spouse will be entitled to the testamentary gift only.[47] Once the right of election is exercised in favour of the legal right this will give rise to the same question of the quality of the right.

8–12 However, as suggested by the author, the legal right is a 'new' succession right and accordingly the search to define its quality cannot wholly be accommodated by reference to traditional categories in the form of debts or testamentary gifts. The legal right is a statutory right of succession to a defined portion of the testator's estate. As such it is *sui generis* and carries its own quality. It is expressed by section 112 to have priority over testamentary gifts and as such gifts are discharged out of the testator's estate and as the testator's estate has been defined for the purposes of Part IX of the Act as meaning all that remaining after expenses, debts and liabilities have been discharged, it seems that the legal right share is payable out of the estate remaining after the expenses, debts and liabilities have been discharged though in priority to testamentary gifts. The legal right created by the Succession Act is a succession right, and not an administrative charge, and by section 112 the share which it represents must first be paid out of the 'distributive' estate of the testator.

8–13 It was also suggested by the author that an interpretation of section 114(2) and section 115 might yield a plausible result by reference to the sections contained in that Part of the Act which deals with the legal right without looking at other provisions of the Act. As all of the preceding sections in the Part go in support of the legal right sections 114(2) and 115 should not be interpreted as going against this strong stream of support in favour of preserving the legal right share. It will be remembered that section 114(2) provides that any gift to the spouse by will will be deemed to have been intended by the testator to be in satisfaction of the legal right. Section 115 gives the spouse a right of election between any such gift and the legal right. It will also be remembered that the general aim enshrined in Part IX is to benefit the spouse even at the expense of other beneficiaries and implicit in this is that the spouse may also be generous in the exercise of the right of election insofar as they are concerned. Thus the provisions should first be interpreted to preserve the legal right and not to diminish it. With this view in mind, section 114(2) might be interpreted as preserving the legal right and that a testator could not be deemed to have intended a gift to be in satisfaction of the legal right which is something less in value than the share which it represents. Rather, the purpose of section 114(2) is to deal with a situation where a spouse is left a gift which is greater in value than the legal right share and that the purpose of the right of election in section 115 is to give the spouse the option of taking the value of

---

[47] See *In re Urquhart: The Revenue Commissioners v. Allied Irish Banks Ltd*, above, n.5; *Reilly v. McEntee*, above, n.8.

the legal right share only and thereby benefiting other beneficiaries if the spouse so wishes. This would also reflect the priority which the legal right has over testamentary gifts and that any such gift which tends to diminish the right and not preserve it would not be in keeping with the priority given to it by section 112.

8–14 It is also the author's view that there is no reason why the quantitative values of the legal right share should not be on par with those arising on an intestacy. The question might be asked why should a spouse receive more by way of intestacy and be entitled to something less where that spouse is left nothing by will. In other words, should the existence of such a will be a sufficient reason for the difference in values between the two rights especially where a spouse is concerned and also that an equalising of values does not mean a blurring or an abolition of the concepts of freedom of testation and intestacy. Both rights are statutory rights and the shares which they represent are payable out of the *estate* of the deceased.

CHAPTER 9

Section 117 Applications

INTRODUCTION

9–01 Where a testator has failed to make proper provision for his children by will or otherwise in accordance with his means they may apply to the court to have such provision made for them out of the estate.[1] A testator has a moral duty to make proper provision for his children and the court will assume the role of a prudent and just parent when deciding whether he has failed to fulfil this duty.[2] Where it is established that a testator has failed in his moral duty to make proper provision for his children in accordance with his means, the court in deciding the extent of the provision for any child of a testator, may take into account the situation in life of each child and any other circumstances which may be of assistance in arriving at a decision that will be as fair as possible to the child to whom the application relates, and to the other children.[3] However, an order made by the court under section 117 will not affect the legal right of a surviving spouse or if the spouse is the father or mother of the child, any devise or legacy to the spouse or any share to which the spouse is entitled on an intestacy, and such provision for a child can only be made out of the estate remaining after first deducting the value of the legal share of a surviving spouse, or any testamentary gift to the parent of a child or a share on an intestacy.[4] The relationship of testator and spouse thus takes precedence over the relationship of testator and child and this is reflected in the absolute nature of the right which a spouse has to a share in the estate.[5] The child of a testator must establish to the satisfaction of the court that the moral duty to make proper provision for him has not been fulfilled. An application under section 117 must be made within six months from the first taking out of a grant to the estate.[6]

9–02 Although the expression "moral duty" used in section 117 smacks of the language of natural law, it was described as a "legal duty" by Keane J. (as

---

[1] Succession Act 1965, s.117(1).
[2] *ibid.*
[3] Succession Act, s.117(2).
[4] Succession Act 1965, s.117(3).
[5] Succession Act 1965, s.111.
[6] Succession Act 1965, as amended by the Family Law (Divorce) Act 1996, s. 46.

he then was) in *E.B. v. S.S.*[7] and given the force of positive law by the Succession Act. Usually, a 'duty' creates a corresponding 'right', however, the duty created by section 117 does not give rise to a right in the strict sense of the word, but rather to an entitlement to make a claim. The nature of the moral duty under section 117 has been subject to at least two different interpretations by the courts. It is certainly based on the relationship between testator and child and arises out of such a relationship though according to Kenny J. in *In the Goods of G. M.: F.M. v. T.A.M.*[8] it

> "does not of itself and without regard to other circumstances create a moral duty to leave anything to a child,"

and he went on to specify such facts as should be taken into account by the court. This view was adopted by Finlay C.J. for the Supreme Court in *In the Estate of I.A.C.: C. v. W.C.*[9] On the other hand, Keane J. for the Supreme Court in *E.B. v. S.S.*[10] was of the view that the Oireachtas had transposed the moral duty into a legal duty owing by parents to their children and enforceable in the terms laid down in section 117, which would seem to suggest that the relationship of parent and child creates this legal duty and that that relationship activates the provisions of section 117 for the purposes of deciding, whether a testator had failed to fulfil this duty by will or otherwise to make proper provision for his children in accordance with his means. McCracken J. in *McDonald v. Norris*[11] apparently following the reasoning of Keane J. said that there is an assumption in the Succession Act that a moral duty exists in general for a testator to make provision for his children and that the provisions of section 117(2) must be considered when deciding whether there has been a failure of such duty. Section 117(2) provides that:

> "The court shall consider the application from the point of view of a prudent and just parent, taking into account the position of each of the children of the testator and any other circumstances which the court may consider of assistance in arriving at a decision that will be as fair as possible to the child to whom the application relates and to the other children."

Thus, according to the views of Kenny J. and Finlay C.J. the moral duty is not created merely by the relationship of testator and child but is also dependent on other circumstances for its existence, while according to Keane J. and McCracken J. the relationship of testator and child created a 'legal duty' and that the provisions of section 117(2) must be considered in deciding whether there has been a failure of such duty. However, whatever the nature of the

---

[7]   [1998] 2 I.L.R.M. 141.

[8]   106 I.L.T.R. 82 at 87.

[9]   [1989] I.L.R.M. 815 at 819.

[10]   Above, n.7.

[11]   [1999] 1 I.L.R.M. 270; See unreported, Supreme Court, November 25, 1999, *per* Barron J.

moral duty one thing is clear and that is there is a high onus of proof on the applicant child to establish a positive failure in moral duty by the testator. Where it is established that a testator has failed to fulfil his moral duty to make proper provision it then becomes a question of assessing the value of the child's share in the estate. The value of a child's share will also depend on the condition in life of a particular child, and where there are other children it does not follow that they will all become entitled to an equal share because the maxim 'equality is equity' is not applicable to section 117 applications.[12] Furthermore, running counter to the moral duty of a testator is the behaviour of a child towards him, and while certain criminal behaviour under section 120(4) of the Succession Act will preclude a child from making any application under section 117, behaviour other than criminal may affect the moral duty and may be taken into account by the court in assessing the fulfilment of such duty.[13] However, notwithstanding the differences in interpretation of the nature moral duty, the facts of a case will be of paramount importance and each case will be judged on its own individual merits.

9–03 There is also an underlying principle of law at play here, *viz.* freedom of testation. Under this principle a testator is entitled to dispose freely of his property in the way he chooses. However, where a testator makes a will which does not take due cognisance of his moral duty towards his children such duty may be enforced against his *estate*. His will will stand as drafted and executed but his estate can only be distributed subject to the order of court. It is not the function of the court to re-draft the will of a parent-testator, its function is to enforce the legal duty against the estate in the way its thinks fit.[14] When section 117 is relied on the court will not be confined in its investigations to the will only, it may also take account any inter vivos gift given to a child in deciding whether proper provisions has been made for a child, as section 117 provides that proper provision may be made by will "or otherwise."

9–04 Therefore, applications under section 117 are confined to the children of a testator and the onus of proof is on them to establish that the testator has failed in his moral duty to make proper provision for them in accordance with his means by will or otherwise, and the court must consider such applications in the light of the provisions of section 117(2) and any order of court made on foot of such applications must not affect the rights of a spouse under section 117(3).

---

[12] *E.B. v. S.S.*, above, n.7.
[13] Above, n.11.
[14] *In the Goods of J.H.: M.F.H. v. W.B.H.* [1984] I.R. 599.

THE APPLICANTS UNDER SECTION 117

9–05 Only the child or children of a testator may apply to the court under section 117. Originally such applications could only be made by children coming within the definition of children in the Succession Act. However, since the enactment of the Status of Children Act 1987 an illegitimate child of a testator may also apply to the court under section 117. As there are no age limits specified in the Succession Act middle aged or even elderly offspring may apply for proper provision to made for them out of the estate. Although the moral duty of a testator is owing to his children only, other relationships may also create moral obligations which may impinge on or affect the moral duty of a testator to make proper provision for his children, for instance, where the testator has been the sole support of elderly parents any provision for them in a will may be taken into consideration by the court in assessing the moral duty owing to children,[15] and perhaps, the grandchildren of a testator, however, the needs of the latter will not be a factor which would justify the court in setting aside the findings against their parent who has failed to establish the moral duty.[16] Furthermore, although the court must make a decision which is as fair as possible to the applicant child, the same consideration will be given to other children of the testator who have not applied to the court.[17] In the context of section 117 (2) the expression "other children" has been held to mean any other child who is also an applicant or who is a beneficiary under the will and whose testamentary benefit may be affected by a court order.[18] Although the court is not required to take into account a provision or lack of provision made for children who are not covered by either category, any provision for such children as already exists cannot be affected by a court order under section 117. Thus a court order under section 117 will not affect any benefit given to children during the lifetime of the testator and who are not within either category of "other children" for the purposes of section 117 regardless of the fact that they may have received more than would have been considered as proper provision under a section 117 application. The latter type of benefit may even include an equity based on a form of proprietary estoppel established against the testator during his lifetime and which was subsequently satisfied by a court decision.[19] However, certain criminal behaviour by a child against the deceased or against the spouse or any child of the deceased and which has led to his conviction for an offence punishable by imprisonment for a maximum period of at least two years or by a more severe penalty will pre-

---

[15] See *L. v. L.* [1978] I.R. 288.
[16] *E.B. v. S.S.*, above, n.7.
[17] Succession Act 1965, s. 117(2); *In the Goods of J.H.: M.F.H. v. W.B.H.*, above, n.14.
[18] *In the Goods of J.H.: M.F.H. v. W.B.H.*, above, n.14.
[19] See Chap. 10.

clude him from making an application under section 117.[20] This provision seems to set a climate of behaviour for the child of a testator when the moral duty is being considered and although such behaviour may not be criminal as envisaged by section 120(4) of the Succession Act, it may be serious enough for a court to take such behaviour into consideration when deciding on whether or not the moral duty has been fulfilled *vis-à-vis* that child.[21]

9–06   It must also be borne in mind that there is a statutory period for making an application under section 117 and the legal disability of age which usually extends the statutory period is not applicable to applications made under section 117.[22] The prescribed time for bringing an application under section 117 is six months from the first taking out of a grant.[23] This means that time will run against a child of the testator when a grant of probate or letters of administration with the will annexed has issued and even though a subsequent grant *de bonis non* may issue, time will continue to run from the date of the original grant and will not commence afresh from the date of the subsequent grant. Normally, unless the passing of a time period for an action is pleaded as a defence, a claim will be decided on its merits. However, where the time period for a section 117 application has expired all claims made under it will become statute-barred. Part IX of the Succession Act which deals with the limitation of actions is also of no assistance to a claim based on section 117 which is out of time. Section 126 which amends section 45 of the Statute of Limitations 1957 provides that no action may be brought after six years in respect of any claim to the estate of a deceased person or to any share or interest in such estate, whether under a will, on intestacy or under section 111 of the Succession Act, and section 127 which amends section 49 of the Statute of 1957 provides that where the person to whom a right of action accrued was under a disability has three years from the cessation of the disability to bring such actions as set out in section 126. Section 117 applications do not come within the compass of these provisions and the period of six months remains regardless of the fact that the applicant child is under the legal disability of age which would otherwise entitle him to rely on such provisions if the action were one coming within the scope of sections 126 and 127. An application made under section 117 is viewed not as a claim under a will but rather as a claim made "independently of the will and against its provisions."[24]

---

[20]   Succession Act 1965, s.120(4).

[21]   McDonald v. Norris, above, n.11.

[22]   *M.P.D. v. M.D.* [1981] I.L.R.M. 179.

[23]   Succession Act 1965, as amended by the Family Law (Divorce) Act 1996, s.46.

[24]   *M.P.D. v. M.D.*, above, n.22 at 184, *per* Carroll J.

THE MORAL DUTY OF A TESTATOR

9–07   Although the relationship of testator and child is necessary to the creation of the moral duty the existence of such a relationship alone without regard to other circumstances will not be sufficient to establish the duty.[25]
Moreover, although the moral duty may be found to exist an order of the court
must not affect the legal right of a surviving spouse or any devise or legacy
left to a spouse or any share to which that spouse is entitled to on intestacy.[26]
As a result of section 117(3), it was the view of Kenny J. in *In the Goods of
G.M.: F.M. v. T.A.M.* that because a testator may leave the whole of his estate
to his spouse the moral duty created by section 117 is not an absolute one,
"nor is it an obligation to each child to leave him something." However, section 117(3) also provides that any devise or legacy left to a spouse or any share
to which that spouse is entitled to on intestacy cannot be affected by an order
where the spouse is the father or mother of the applicant child, thus if the
surviving spouse is not the father or mother of the applicant child an order
made by the court under section 117(1) may affect such devise or legacy or
share on an intestacy. This latter may become an issue on the remarriage of a
testator on the death of a former spouse, or indeed, where the applicant child
is the illegitimate child of a testator.[27] However, the legal right of a spouse
will not be affected by the relationship between surviving spouse and child of
the testator; the legal right which is an absolute right arises out of the relationship of testator and spouse only.[28] The situation created by section 117(3)
may cause problems for the surviving spouse who is not the father or mother
of the applicant child and who is contemplating the exercise of the right of
election between a gift in the will and share to which that spouse is entitled as
a legal right.[29] The main problem arises out of the time period for making an
application under section 117 and the time within which a surviving spouse is
allowed to exercise the right of election under section 115. A child of the
testator has six months from the first taking out of a grant to make an application; a surviving spouse has six months from the time the personal representatives of the testator notified him of the right of election or one year from the
first taking out of the grant.[30] By section 117(3) an order of the court must not
affect the legal right of a spouse but what if the time period for a spouse to
exercise the right of election has not elapsed before the court makes an order.
A spouse who has the luxury of time may decide to await the outcome of the

---

[25] *In the Goods of G.M.: F.M. v. T.A.M.*, above, n.8.
[26] Succession Act 1965, s.117(3).
[27] See Status of Children Act 1987.
[28] See Succession Act 1965, s.111.
[29] See Succession Act 1965, s.115(4).
[30] Succession Act 1965, s. 117(6) as amended by the Family Law (Divorce) Act 1996,
s.46.

application to see how it might affect the devise or legacy left to him, and accordingly, delay the exercise of the right of election should the court order adversely affect the testamentary gift in terms of value. It would be an easy matter for the court to take into account the amount left to the surviving spouse or the value of the legal right if the spouse elects to take it where the spouse is the father or mother of the applicant child as no order of court may affect the amount left to the spouse or the value of the legal right. However, there is no such clear-cut basis for evaluation in the case of a spouse who is not a parent of the applicant child unless of course the court order only affects the testamentary gift to such a spouse to the extent and value of the legal right so as to avert any further action should such a spouse subsequent to the court order exercise his right of election in favour of the legal right share. Thus, it would seem that, while the moral duty may not arise by the virtue of the relationship of testator and child only, nevertheless, if it is found to exist when other circumstances are taken into consideration, the relationship of testator and spouse may be affected by a court order following an application by a child who is not a child of the surviving spouse. This obviously is an unsatisfactory state of affairs for such a spouse and perhaps one in need of reform, and, as a corollary, it may also be viewed as a further inroad on a testator's freedom of testation when making provision for his spouse.

9–08 Notwithstanding the foregoing which might be viewed as exceptional, the existence of the moral duty to make proper provision for his children will be gauged by the facts existing at the date of death of the testator and "must depend upon:-(a) the amount left to the surviving spouse or the value of the legal right if the survivor elects to take this, (b) the number of the testator's children, their ages and their positions in life at the date of the testator's death, (c) the means of the testator, (d) the age of the child whose case is being considered and his or her financial position and prospects in life, (e) whether the testator has already in his lifetime made proper provision for the child. The court must decide whether the duty exists and the view of the testator that he did not owe any is not decisive."[31] In *In the Goods of G.M.: F.M. v. T.A.M.* the testator left all his property in Ireland upon trust for his wife for life and after her death for two nephews. Although there were no children of the marriage the testator's wife decided to adopt a boy without informing the testator until the boy who was English came to live with the testator and his wife in Ireland. There was no formal system of adoption in Ireland at the time. However, with the enactment of the Adoption Act 1952 a formal system of adoption was introduced into Ireland, and two years after the 1952 Act the plaintiff was legally adopted by the testator and his wife. At the time when the plaintiff applied to the court under section 117 he was 32 years, married and had two

---

[31] *In the Goods of G.M.: F.M. v. T.A.M.*, above, n.8 at 87 *per* Kenny J.

children of his own. In holding that the testator had failed in his moral duty to make proper provision for his adopted son, Kenny J. ordered that proper provision be made out of the estate and that the question must be decided from the point of view of a prudent and just parent. On this basis he ordered that the plaintiff be given one-half of the testator's estate excluding any immoveable property owned by the testator in England.

9–09　When deciding whether a testator has fulfilled his moral duty towards his children the fact that he did not give them all an equal share will not necessarily mean that he had failed in his moral duty in relation to those who received less. As was said by Keane J. in delivering the majority decision for the Supreme Court in *E.B. v. S.S.*[32] that "it is not necessarily an answer to an application under s. 117 that the testator has simply treated all his children equally. The maxim 'equality is equity' can have no application where the testator has, dividing his estate in that manner, disregarded the special needs (arising, for example, from the physical or mental disability) of one of the children to such an extent that he could have failed in his moral duty to that child." However, he also thought that it was an "understandable anxiety of parents" to effect an equal distribution of their property among their children so far as possible in order to avoid sibling disaffection after their deaths. If such is the declared intention of a testator it may be taken into consideration by the court, "although not a decisive factor." In *E.B. v. S.S.*[33] the testatrix, before her death, divided the shares she held in a company among her children. The plaintiff sold his shares which realised at £275,000. In a subsequent will the testatrix left the bulk of her estate to charity. Before she made the subsequent will the testatrix was aware that the plaintiff had dissipated all of his money and that he was experiencing financial and marital problems but he was nevertheless excluded from her will. However, Keane J. was of the view that, although the court "cannot disregard the fact that parents must be presumed to know their children better than anyone else and in many cases that obvious fact would be of little weight where it is established that a child had been treated in a manner which points clearly to a failure of the moral duty, in the present case knowledge of the plaintiff's circumstances was of 'considerable significance' where even the most favourable view of the plaintiff's case, and that it cannot be suggested that he was treated with anything other than generosity and support by both his parents up to the time the shares were transferred to him. Against the plaintiff's background the testatrix's decision not to make further provision for him may well have been prompted not merely by the concern that her money should go where she could be sure it could do most good, but also by the belief that, since the provision of significant finan-

---

[32] Above, n.7 at 150.
[33] Above, n.7.

cial assistance had not in the past produced the best results, it might not have been in his own interest to provide him with further funds, even through the mechanism of a trust."[34] In the circumstances Keane J. concluded that the plaintiff had failed to establish that the testatrix had not fulfilled her moral duty to him. In the course of his judgment he stated that the Oireachtas "has transposed the moral obligation which she, in common with all parents, owed to their children into a legal duty enforceable in the terms laid down in section 117." He also remarked, however, that the "extremely ample provisions" afforded to the children of a testator under section 117 were not to be extended to grandchildren and that therefore the needs of the plaintiff's children were not a factor to be taken into consideration by the court.

9–10 In assessing whether a testator has failed in his moral duty the court may also take into consideration the behaviour, or rather misbehaviour, of the child towards him during his lifetime.[35] The kind of misbehaviour envisaged here is not of the criminal variety which is governed by section 120 of the 1965 Act and which precludes the making of an application under section 117. It is a kind of behaviour engendered by 'bad feeling' between testator and child and may be taken into account by the court when deciding whether a testator has failed to fulfil his moral duty in regard to a particular child, and although a testator is not obliged to treat all his children on an equal basis the reason for his not doing so may be of importance when deciding whether he has failed to fulfil his moral duty relation to a particular child.[36] The question which McCracken J. in *McDonald v. Norris* had to decide was whether "a prudent and just parent, in the circumstances of the present case and given the behaviour of the plaintiff, reached a decision which was in accordance with his moral duty to the plaintiff."[37] In that case the plaintiff was a son of the testator who died in 1993. The defendant was executrix of the will. The deceased by his will left all his property in trust for the executrix's daughter. The plaintiff was left a legacy of £5,000. The plaintiff worked on the family farm from an early age. The defendant and her family were related to the testator and before his death he had become friendly with her and her family. In 1980, the relations between the testator and the plaintiff had deteriorated so much that the testator went to reside with the defendant's family. In 1982, the plaintiff occupied the family farm and worked it for his own benefit; he also opened a quarry on the lands. At one stage matters became so violent that the gardai were involved. This was followed by injunction proceedings being taken against the plaintiff for possession of the family farm. The plaintiff entered a defence and counterclaim for the work he had carried out on the farm. The deceased

---

[34] *ibid.* at 150-151.
[35] *McDonald v. Norris*, above, n.11.
[36] *ibid.* at 280-281.
[37] *ibid.* at 279-280.

was granted an injunction and the plaintiff was awarded £11,000 for work done. However, the plaintiff succeeded in obtaining a stay on the injunction for a year after which he had to vacate the farm. The plaintiff remained on the farm and paid the deceased the sum of £2,000 to permit him to do so until the middle of 1985. He continued to remain on the farm after the year had passed as a result of which the testator had to seek an attachment and committal order to enforce the injunction. The order was executed and the plaintiff received a prison sentence of eleven months. While the plaintiff was in prison his wife and son continued to work the farm and quarry. In 1986, the testator transferred part of the farm to the plaintiff's brother. After that a campaign of vilification was conducted in the locality against the deceased and the defendant's family which included threats and damage to property. In 1988, because of his threatening behaviour, the plaintiff was bound over to keep the peace for two years by the District Court. After the testator's death in 1993 the plaintiff applied to the court under section 117 claiming that the deceased had failed to fulfil his moral duty by not making proper provision for him in accordance with his means. McCracken J. was of the view that the testator was entitled to consider that he had already conferred a considerable benefit on the plaintiff during his lifetime in spite of the plaintiff's "appalling behaviour." He was also of the view that a moral duty existed but was affected by the plaintiff's behaviour and that the scheme of the Succession Act implied that among the circumstances which a court may take into account in assessing the fulfilment of the moral duty was the behaviour of the plaintiff towards the testator which, while not absolutely precluding him under section 120, nevertheless is a circumstance which should be taken into account together with the benefit which the plaintiff had in fact received during his lifetime. He further thought that the judgment of Keane J. in *E.B. v. S.S.* did not support the view that there may be cases where a child though in serious need may be owed no moral duty by a testator. Turning to the facts of the present case he looked at what benefit the plaintiff received during the testator's lifetime. He got a roof over his head, he got food from the local shop and he got a small acreage of land on which he grew cereals. He had use of a farm of 400 acres for which he paid nothing. He developed his own herd of cattle on the farm, he worked a quarry on the lands and he tilled some of the lands. The plaintiff did not receive the benefit by a voluntary act of the testator but rather took it against his will. Later even though he paid a rent of £10 an acre and a sum of £1,000 for the unlimited use of the quarry for a year both sums of money were gross undervalues. McCracken J. thought that the plaintiff received "a very real and substantial benefit" during the lifetime of the testator. The testator also left the plaintiff a legacy of £5,000 and in the light of the wording of the will he did so in full knowledge of the provisions of section 117. Accordingly, McCracken J. was satisfied that in all the circumstances the testator's moral duty was fulfilled by giving a legacy of £5,000 to the plaintiff and was of the view that the plaintiff had not discharged the onus of proof which is on him to show the failure of such moral duty.

9–11   The decision of McCracken J. was appealed to the Supreme Court.[38] Even though the Supreme Court recognised that the behaviour of a child towards the testator was a factor to be taken into account when deciding whether the testator had fulfilled his moral duty, it was also of the view that it was for the court to determine to what extent account should be taken of such behaviour. The testator owed a moral duty to his son commencing from the date of birth and assessable at the date of death of the testator. But was his behaviour over a period of time so grave that it extinguished or diminished the duty? Barron J. in a unanimous judgment for the Supreme Court stated that when judging "a child's behaviour towards a parent, it is important to determine whether that conduct would have been the same had a stranger been involved. It should not be overlooked that parents and children have the same genes and that an uncompromising stubbornness in the one is likely to be mirrored in the other. This situation would not have developed had the applicant been farming in a stranger's lands." In the light of the facts Barron J. held that the testator had failed in his moral duty and the behaviour of the son, though appalling, was not so grave as to extinguish or diminish such a duty. Also the benefits which the applicant derived from the land and quarry were not in the nature of advancements and had been overstated somewhat in the High Court. Reversing the judgment of McCracken J., he held that the applicant was entitled to have the moral duty fulfilled by having the entire land transferred to him. As regards the will benefiting the defendant's daughter, the testator did not owe her a moral duty at his son's expense. The judgment of Barron J. is typical of the humane approach adopted by him to succession matters involving the immediacy of a family and his understanding of the problems which may arise out of so close a relationship, and how the ebb and flow of emotions can alternate between good and bad feelings during a lifetime and their stopping up at death cannot make that point in time solely the time for judging whether behaviour by a child towards his parent was so serious as to diminish or extinguish the moral duty. The moral duty is a continuous duty commencing from the date of birth and lasting until the date of death.

9–12   Regarding the onus of proof resting on the applicant, Finlay C.J. in *In the Estate of I.A.C.: C.F. and F. v. W.C. and T.C.*[39] was of the view that the phrase 'failed in his moral duty to make proper provision for the child in accordance with his means' placed a relatively high onus of proof on an applicant seeking relief under section 117. Having adopted and approved of the general principles applied by Kenny J. to an application under section 117 in *In the Goods of G.M.: F.M. v. T.A.M.*[40]

---

[38] Above, n.11.
[39] Above, n.9 at 819.
[40] Above, n.8 at 87.

"as being a correct statement of the law" he went on to add a qualification to it. He thought that it was not sufficient "to establish that the provision made for a child was not as great as it might have been, or that compared with generous bequests to other children or beneficiaries in the will, it appears ungenerous. The court should not, I consider, make an order under the section merely because it would on the facts proved have formed different testamentary dispositions."[41]

He emphasised that a "positive failure in moral duty must be established." The facts of the case were that the deceased was a widow and was survived by four children: T., a son aged 44; W., a son aged 42; C. and Ch., twin daughters, aged 41. The situation of each of the four children at the date of the testatrix's death was as follows: T. was a permanent invalid, as a result of sustaining brain damage; W. was married with three sons and was the owner of the family business which had been transferred to him by his mother during her lifetime; C. was separated from her husband and had four children, and had a job and a house of her own.; Ch.'s marriage was in difficulty during the lifetime of the testatrix and broke up after the testatrix's death. By her will the testatrix left £30,800 to T., £62,900 to W., £12,900 to C. and £13,100 to Ch. The trial judge was of the opinion that the testatrix had failed in her moral duty to make proper provision for C. and Ch., and made provision for them out of the estate by varying the devise of a premises to W. so as to make C. and Ch. joint tenants with him of those premises in shares of one-ninth to C. and two-ninths to Ch. W., the first-named defendant, appealed this decision to the Supreme Court. Finlay C.J., in the course of his judgment remarked that where evidence has been given of a testator's support for his children during his lifetime, and where the relationship between a testator and his children was one of caring and kindness, the court should be reluctant to vary his dispositions by will. However, this approach would differ and different considerations would apply where a "marked" hostility existed between a testator and one of his children. Applying these principles to the facts of the case before him he came to the following conclusions. He was of the view that while the provision for Ch. was a proper one at the time of the making of the will in 1981 it ceased to be so at the date of death of the testatrix in 1985. The testatrix was aware of the difficulties in Ch.'s marriage and should have made provision for the probability of the break-up of that marriage bearing in mind that of the four children Ch. had received the least financial benefit from her and that proper provision for her involved either a further gift by will or the making of a gift inter vivos. The testatrix by her provision for C. during her lifetime indicated in a definite way her appreciation of the particular problems facing a daughter whose marriage had in fact broken up. Finlay C.J. was of the view that as a logical consequence she would have made improved provision for Ch. seeing that she was aware of the likelihood of Ch.'s marriage breaking up also. He

---

[41] *In the Estate of I.A.C.: C.F. and F. v. W.C. and T.C.*, above, n.9 at 819.

felt, however, that C. and Ch. could not be treated on an equal basis in assessing the moral duty because the testatrix had made provision for C. not only in her will but also by gifts made to her by the testatrix during her lifetime valued at £20,000. Moreover, at the time of the testatrix's death C. was employed and owned a house subject to a small mortgage and also her husband provided her with reasonable maintenance for her children. Accordingly, he allowed the appeal by setting aside the finding of a failure properly to provide for the plaintiff, C., by affirming the finding of a failure to provide for the plaintiff, Ch., and by affirming the appropriate variation in the administration of the estate of the testatrix and to declare Ch. entitled to two-ninths share in the premises which were devised to W.

"THE QUANTUM OF WHAT IS PROPER PROVISION"

9–13   There are two issues required to be determined by the court in all proceedings under section 117. The first issue which the court must determine is whether a testator has failed in his moral duty owed to his children, and the second issue concerns the provision which the court should make for them out of the testator's estate.[42] As the court is required to make an order which is just and in furtherance of this it must consider any application under section 117 from the point of view of a prudent and just parent, "taking into account the position of each of the children of the testator and any other circumstances which the court may consider of assistance in arriving at a decision that will be as fair as possible to the child to whom the application relates and to the other children."[43] Because of this requirement a parent must weigh up carefully all his moral obligations,[44] and these obligations are not necessarily confined to the children of a testator: a testator may have aged and infirm parents who are dependent on him and to whom he owes a moral duty to support. Among the children themselves the moral duty owing to each may vary with their circumstances in life: an exceptionally bright child may make it morally wrong not to have his intellectual talents fostered or a child who is mentally retarded may require greater provision to be made for him in order for a testator to fulfil the moral duty owing to that child. However, it must be emphasised, that the moral duty which a testator may owe to parents who are dependent on him is a circumstance only which the court may take into consideration in assessing the quantum of what is proper provision for the children of a testator under section 117(2), it is not in the nature of a legal duty which a testator owes to his children under section 117(1); furthermore, any such moral duty owing by a testator to his grandchildren was expressly discounted by Keane J.

---

[42] See *L. v. L.*, above, n.15.
[43] Succession Act 1965, s.117(2).
[44] *L. v. L.*, above, n.15.

in *E.B. v. S.S.* Thus, it would seem that moral obligations other than the moral duty owing to the children of a testator may also be taken into account which the court may consider to be of assistance in arriving at a decision that will be as fair as possible to the applicant child and to the other children. Nevertheless, it was held by Costello J. in *L. v. L.* that a testator when acting as a prudent and just parent towards his children "would have to bear in mind his obligations to his own parents who are dependent on him and that the provision he makes for his children may have to be reduced because of these other obligations." Therefore, where a child of a testator claims under section 117(1) that proper provision has not been made for him, the court, when determining whether such is the case, "must bear in mind all the moral duties which a testator may have had and all the claims on his resources thereby arising."[45] The view of Costello J., that all moral obligations and all claims on his resources thereby arising must be taken into account, was approved of by McWilliam J. in *JH v. Allied Irish Banks* an unreported judgment delivered on November 17, 1978, and it was also cited by Barron J. in *In the Goods of J.H.: MFH v. WBH*[46] as demonstrating the approach which the court adopts "in the exercise of its jurisdiction under the section."

9–14   In exercising its jurisdiction the court is required by section 117(3) to look at matters from the point of view of a prudent and just parent, and to take into account the position of each of the children and any other circumstances which it may consider of assistance. Once this done, the court must then reach a decision which is as fair as possible to the applicant child, and where there are other children, to those other children also. The expression "other children" was held by Barron J. in *In the Goods of J.H.: M.F.H. v. W.B.H.* to mean "any other child who is also an applicant or who is a beneficiary under the will and whose benefit thereunder may be affected by the exercise of the court's powers," and that the court should not be required to take into account provision or lack of provision made for children not in either of these categories.[47] Thus the position of a child who is not an applicant to the court or who is excluded from the testator's will will not be taken into account by the court when determining whether proper provision has been made for the "other children" the presumption being that such a child must have benefited 'otherwise' than by will for otherwise such a child would also apply to the court under section 117, but should a child receive such a benefit it cannot be affected by an order of the court under the section. This latter may be of importance to a child of a testator, for instance, who has established an equity to such of the testator's estate which is worth more than any share he would likely receive if

---

[45] *L. v. L.*, above, n.15.
[46] Above, n.14 at 606.
[47] *ibid.* at 606-607.

he pursued an application under section 117.[48] However, in relation to children who have applied to the court a balance must be struck between them on the basis of what is just by having regard to the provisions of the will and all other matters which the court is required to take into account.

9–15 Barron J. thought that the provisions of section 117 clearly required the court to be fair in all the circumstances. Since the court must determine whether or not proper provision has been made in accordance with the testator's means, "it follows that "proper" means what is fair in the light of matters which it has to consider and that the standard to be applied depends on the means of the testator."[49] The court has to decide whether or not any or any further provision ought to be made out of the estate for a child, and if so what further provision would discharge the moral duty. In assessing this the court must take into account the provisions of section 117(2). These provisions require that the position of the applicant child cannot be taken in isolation. "The quantum of what is proper provision in any particular case is not an absolute but is dependent on all matters which the court may take into account."[50] It is the duty of the court to take all matters within the compass of section 117(2) into consideration and to make its decision in this overall context. Barron J. was of the view that, while an applicant child might require particular provision to be made for him out of the testator's estate, the court must also take into account the moral claims of others which may require such provision to be reduced or to be omitted entirely. Although it would appear that the time for assessing the moral duty is the date of death of the testator, the court in its quest to be fair in the circumstances is not confined to that date alone and may look to events which are subsequent to that date. Having taken all such considerations into account the court is empowered to order such provision for the applicant child out of the estate as the court thinks just, and when making such an order the court will have regard not only to the interests of the applicant child but also to the interests of the other children "and such other person to whom the testator owed a moral duty."[51] However, the court is not empowered by section 117 to re-write the will of a testator, its power is one of intervention in the estate where it is established that a testator has failed in his moral duty to make proper provision for a child in accordance with his means by will or otherwise out of his estate, although should the court uphold the claim of a child there will have to be a variation in the distribution of the estate to take into account the provision ordered for that child by the court. In the final analysis, each particular case must stand on its own facts.

---

[48] See Chap. 10.
[49] Above, n.14 at 607.
[50] *ibid.*
[51] *ibid.* at 607-608.

9–16   In *In the Goods of J.H.: M.F.H. v. W.B.H.*[52] the testator left a bungalow to his wife for life and after death to a grandson and left the remainder of
his estate which included a farm to one of his nine children. Four of his children lived on the farm with the residuary beneficiary. Two of the four children
had some form of steady employment and one of the remaining two suffered a
disability and was cared for and looked after by one of the children who was
employed. These four children applied to the court under section 117 claiming
that the testator had failed in his moral duty to make proper provision for them
by will in accordance with his means and that such provision be made for
them out of the testator's estate. Barron J. in deciding the 'quantum' of the
provision to be made for them out of the estate having taken into account the
provisions of section held that each of the plaintiffs should be entitled to a
licence to reside in the family home until marriage, otherwise for life, and in
the event of marriage each should they so wish be provided with a site to build
a home. In the case of the child with a disability she should further have an
exclusive licence in common with such other member of the family who may
be living in the family home and looking after her to use and occupy a part of
the estate specified on a map, subject to the right of the residuary beneficiary
to use the farm buildings for the purposes of his business as a farmer or as a
contractor. The residuary beneficiary was also to provide her with maintenance as long as she remained unemployed and was not in receipt of social
welfare payments. The lands were to be stocked with a limited number of
cattle for her benefit and the member of the family looking after her. Furthermore, as the lands were the subject matter of a planning application and should
they come within the category of development land, the four children in common with the residuary beneficiary should be entitled to an equal one-fifth
share in the proceeds of a sale of such land. Until such time the residuary
beneficiary was entitled to use them for agricultural purposes subject to the
payment of a reasonable conacre rent for them to the four other children. Barron
J. thought that such an arrangement would be one which a prudent and just
parent would have wanted in order to benefit such of his children who were
weakest financially, a category into which each of the plaintiffs fell.

9–17   In *J. de B. v. H.E. de B.* [53] Blayney J. considered the "quantum of what
is proper provision" where a child of the testator had received financial assistance during the lifetime of the testator and was left a legacy in the will and
whether, in such circumstances, the testator had already in his lifetime made
proper provision for him. In that case the testator left his main assets which
consisted of a farm, stock and machinery to his wife for life and after her death
the remainder interest was left to his eldest son H. H.'s remainder interest was
charged with the payment of the deceased's debts, funeral and testamentary

---

[52]   Above, n.14.
[53]   [1991] 2 I.R. 105.

expenses and with the payment of legacies. The plaintiff was the youngest son. After having spent six years at university he became a musical producer. He was married with three children. His annual income amounted to £16,500. The testator in his lifetime provided him with financial assistance when the mortgage on his house fell into arrears. He also gave him a gift of a painting which had a value of between £800 and £1,000. He was also left a legacy of £5,000. The net value of the deceased's estate amounted to approximately £200,000. The plaintiff applied to the court under section 117 to have proper provision made for him out of the deceased's estate. The first question which Blayney J. had to decide was whether by applying the criteria laid down by Kenny J. in *In the Goods of G.M.: F.M. v. T.A.M.* and the additional principle enunciated by Finlay C.J. in *In the Estate of I.A.C .: C.F. and F. v. W.C. and T.C.* a positive failure had been established by the plaintiff. He pointed out that one of the criteria laid down by Kenny J. and approved by Finlay C.J. in the Supreme Court which may be taken into account for the purposes of determining the existence of the moral duty to make proper provision was whether the testator had already in his lifetime made proper provision for his child. He cited the following passage from the judgment of Kenny J.: "The obligation to make proper provision may be fulfilled by will or otherwise and so gifts or settlements during the lifetime of the testator in favour of a child or the provision of an expensive education for one child when the others have not received this may discharge the moral duty."[54] Blayney J. accordingly thought that it was relevant to bear in mind then the plaintiff's third level education at the end of which he was awarded an M.A. degree and that the deceased had helped him to pay off a debt of £4,000 and gave him a gift of a painting worth between £800 and £1,000 during his lifetime and prior to making his will. At the date of his death the testator's only assets consisted of his farm, machinery and stock. He had debts amounting to £22,663. The farm was the sole means out of which he could make provision for his wife and children by will. By his will he left the farm, machinery and stock to his wife for life with remainder to his eldest son H. absolutely. H. and his family at the request of the testator and his wife lived on the farm since 1970. He had no other house and used the land for training horses. According to the evidence of another son the testator had always intended to leave the farm to H. In these circumstances Blayney J. asked would it have been fair for the testator to have encouraged this expectation and then to have failed to fulfil it. It was also established in evidence that the plaintiff in 1984 had written a letter to the testator suggesting that he should leave a 40 acre field to him for the purposes of building a house for himself and his family and deriving some income from it and that he would supplement this income in various other ways. The testator failed to reply to this letter. Blayney J. was of the opinion that the testator's failure to leave the

---

[54] Above, n.8. at 87.

plaintiff these lands could not be said to be a failure in his moral duty to the plaintiff. In fact the testator could justifiably have taken the view that in the particular circumstances he had a moral duty to leave the entire farm to H and that that duty took precedence over any duty he might have had towards the plaintiff.[55] Blayney J. then went on to consider whether the testator ought to have made further provision for the plaintiff by giving him more than the £5.000 legacy. However, as the only way this could have been done was by charging the farm with the increased amount it would not have been fair to H. There were also two other children of the testator who had stronger claims than that of the plaintiff's but who had settled them and were charged on the remainder interest of H. Could further provision for the plaintiff be similarly charged ? In the opinion of Blayney J. no court would consider it fair to increase the burden on H. to make further provision for the plaintiff. He also thought that the settlement between H. and the two other children came within the category of other circumstances which the court may consider to be of assistance in arriving at a decision referred to in section 117 (2) and was entitled to take them into account and cited the judgment of Barron J. in *In the Goods of J.H.: M.F.H. v. W.B.H.*[56] in support of his doing so. Accordingly he had no doubt that it would not be fair to H. to impose a liability on him to pay out more than that which he already had to discharge and that the legacy left to the plaintiff should not be increased. The plaintiff had not discharged the high onus of proof placed on an applicant under section 117 to establish a positive failure on the part of the testator in his moral duty to make proper provision for him. Blayney J. concluded that if the plaintiff had been a farmer he might have had a justifiable complaint in not being given any land.

9–18   Thus, when deciding on the quantum of proper provision the court must take into consideration the provisions of section 117(2) which prescribes the perspective from which the court must view such matter and the circumstances which must be taken into account which includes any pre-existing moral obligations which a testator may owe at the time of his death with a spirit of fairness to the applicant child and other children of the testator.

Summary

9–19   Where a testator has failed to fulfil his moral duty towards his children to make proper provision for them in accordance with his means they may apply to the court under section 117 to have proper provision made for them out of the estate. The court when considering whether a testator has failed to fulfil his moral duty will take many factors into account including the behav-

---

[55] Above, n.52 at 111.
[56] Above, n.14 at 607.

iour of a child towards the testator. While a testator may freely dispose of his property the way in which he disposes of it may be impugned after his death if he has failed to fulfil his moral duty towards his children. It is the relationship of testator and child which creates the moral duty but the kind of relationship between *child and testator* may also cause its demise or diminution, for instance, the misbehaviour of a child towards the testator during his lifetime. However, where it is established that a testator has failed to fulfil his moral duty towards his children proper provision must be made for them out of the estate. Proper provision in this instance does not mean that all the children of the testator will be given equal shares. The court when determining the amount of the share will take the individual circumstances of each child into account and will strive to be fair to all without having to take into consideration the maxim equality is equity.

CHAPTER 10

An Alternative in Equity to Section 117

INTRODUCTION

10–01 Where a testator has failed in his moral duty to make proper provision for his children in accordance with his means by will or otherwise, all or any of them may apply to the court to have such provision made for them out of the estate.[1] The court assuming the role of a prudent and just parent will take into account the position of each of the children and any other circumstances which it may consider of assistance in arriving at a decision that will be as fair as possible to the child to whom the application relates and to the other children.[2] What constitutes proper provision for each child then will depend on his or her position in life and/or any other circumstances which have a bearing on that child's position. The court is not obliged to treat each of the testator's children on an equal basis; the maxim 'equality is equity' is not applicable to a section 117 application.[3] Where such an application is in contemplation it must be instituted within six months from the first taking out of a grant.[4]

10–02 However, a child of the testator may be afforded an alternative claim in equity depending on the circumstances and one which will not be subject to the time strictures laid down by section 117. It may happen, for instance, that the testator may have put one of his children into possession of land owned by him which may even be his sole asset for the purpose of building a house without any formal conveyance of the land and if that child subsequently builds a house on it at his own expense a right may be established in equity in the form of a proprietary estoppel and it may be relied on as a cause of action, or indeed, a defence, against all claimants to the land on which the house is built.[5] The same kind of equity may be established to the testator's own house where a child of the testator builds an extension or makes improvements to the house at his own expense on being promised that it will be left to him by the

---

[1] Succession Act 1965, s.117(1); See Chap. 9.
[2] Succession Act 1965, s.117(2).
[3] *E.B. v. S.S.* [1998] 2 I.L.R.M. 141.
[4] Succession Act 1965, s.117(6) as amended by the Family Law (Divorce) Act 1996, s.46.
[5] *Dillwyn v. Llewelyn* 4 De G. F. & J. 517; *Inwards v. Baker* [1965] 1 All E.R. 446.

testator in his will.[6] Thus the doctrine of proprietary estoppel can be used as a 'shield' as well as a 'sword' unlike the contractual doctrine of promissory estoppel which can be used as a 'shield' or defence only.[7] Although usually a monetary expenditure is required to establish the doctrine this may not necessarily be the only kind of expenditure recognised by the court as it was said, albeit *obiter*, in the Supreme Court in *McCarron v. McCarron*[8] that:

> "In principle I see no reason why the doctrine should be confined to the expenditure of money or the erection of premises on the land of another. In a suitable case it may well be argued that a plaintiff suffers as severe a loss or detriment by providing his own labours or services in relation to the lands of another and accordingly should equally qualify for recognition in equity. In practice, however, it might be difficult to determine the extent of the estate or interest in land for which a plaintiff might qualify as a result of his personal efforts. Perhaps a claim of that nature would be adequately compensated by a charge or lien on the lands for a sum equivalent to reasonable remuneration for the services rendered."

Thus if the doctrine of proprietary estoppel were developed in this way it might perhaps make it possible for a child of a testator who stays at home to look after elderly parents, and perhaps forfeit a career in the process, or a child who works the family farm or business, on being told that he would be left the house, farm or business, to rely on the doctrine, and if such were the case, such a child's equity would be protected against the claims of other children under section 117, even where the house, farm or business is the testator's sole asset.

10–03 It must be emphasised that, unlike section 117, the doctrine of proprietary estoppel is not confined in its scope to the relationship of testator and child although such a focus is maintained for the purpose of the present analysis. Even though there are recent English decisions dealing with proprietary estoppel these will not be discussed here because the parties were other than testator and child.[9] Another reason for not referring to these decisions for the purpose of the present analysis is that they were not at Court of Appeal level. When one looks at *Smith v. Halpin*[10] the leading Irish case on the matter references are made to older English decisions at Court of Appeal level and even though one such case, *Pascoe v. Turner*,[11] did not involve a testator and child it was a Court of Appeal decision. Besides, the Irish courts may decide to evolve the doctrine in a different way.

---

[6] *Smyth v. Halpin* [1997] 2 I.L.R.M. 38.
[7] *Combe v. Combe* [1951] 2 K.B. 215.
[8] Unreported, February 13, 1997, *per* Murphy J.
[9] *Taylor v. Dickens* [1998] 1 F.L.R. 806; *Gillet v. Holt* [1998] 3 All E.R. 917.
[10] Above, n.6.
[11] [1979] 2 All E.R. 945.

THE EXTENT OF THE EQUITY

10–04   The extent of the equity for the purposes of Irish law was considered
by Geoghegan J. in *Smyth v. Halpin*.[12] For this purpose he traced the development of the doctrine of proprietary estoppel from the decision of Lord Westbury
L.C. in *Dillwyn v. Llewelyn*.[13] In that case the testator who was the father of
the plaintiff by his will dated June 21, 1847, devised his real estate to the
plaintiff and defendant in trust for his wife for life and after her death in trust
for the plaintiff for life with remainder in trust for the son or sons of the plaintiff. In 1853 the testator, knowing that the plaintiff intended to build a house
for himself, offered him a farm on which to build the house. The plaintiff
accepted this offer and a memorandum was signed by the testator which stated
that the purpose of "presenting" the farm was to furnish "himself with a dwell-
ing-house." The plaintiff took possession of the farm and built a house at the
cost of £14,000. However, there was no formal conveyance of the legal estate
to the plaintiff. In August 1855 the testator died. Later the plaintiff sought a
declaration of the court to the effect that the equity acquired by him entitled
him to the fee simple estate. The Master of the Rolls who first heard the case
held that the plaintiff was entitled only to an equitable interest in the estate for
his life. On appeal, Lord Westbury L.C. granted the declaration sought stating
that:

> "About the rules of the Court there can be no controversy. A voluntary agree-
> ment will not be completed or assisted by a Court of Equity, in cases of mere
> gift. If anything be wanting to complete the title of the donee, a Court of Equity
> will not assist him in obtaining it; for a mere donee can have no right to claim
> more than he has received. But the subsequent acts of the donor may give the
> donee that right or ground of claim which he did not acquire from the original
> gift. Thus, if A. gives a house to B., but makes no formal conveyance, and the
> house is afterwards, on the marriage of B., included with the knowledge of A.,
> in the marriage settlement of B., A. would be bound to complete the title of the
> parties claiming under the settlement. So if A. puts B. in possession of a piece
> of land, and tells him, 'I give it to you that you may build a house on it', and B.
> on the strength of that promise, with the knowledge of A., expends a large sum
> of money in building a house accordingly, I cannot doubt that the donee ac-
> quires a right for the subsequent transaction to call on the donor to perform that
> contract and complete the imperfect donation which was made."[14]

He went on to say that:

> "The equity of the donee and the estate to be claimed by virtue of it depend on
> the transaction, that is, on the acts done, and not on the language of the memo-
> randum, except as that shews the purpose and intent of the gift. The estate was

---

[12] Above, n.6.
[13] Above, n.5.
[14] *ibid.* at 521-522.

> given as a site of a dwelling-house to be erected by the son. The ownership of the dwelling-house and the ownership of the estate must be considered as intended to be co-extensive and co-equal. No one builds a house for his own life only, and it is absurd to suppose that it was intended by either party that the house, at the death of the son, should become the property of the father."[15]

He was therefore of the opinion that the expenditure by the plaintiff together with the approbation of the testator supplied a valuable consideration originally wanting and the memorandum signed by the father and son must be thenceforth regarded as an agreement for the soil extending to the fee simple of the land. He thought that the only inquiry was whether the plaintiff's expenditure in furtherance of the memorandum supplied a valuable consideration and created a binding obligation and he had no doubt that it did.

10–05 Geoghegan J. then considered *Inwards v. Baker*[16] which was a Court of Appeal decision. In that case the defendant was contemplating the building of a bungalow for himself but the site on which he intended to build was too expensive for him. His father who owned some land suggested that the defendant build his bungalow on that land: "Why not put the bungalow on my land, and make the bungalow a little bigger ?" As a result the defendant built a bungalow on the land provided by his father. His father also contributed money towards the building of the bungalow some of which was repaid. He lived in the bungalow from 1931 and his father paid him a few occasional visits there. In 1951 his father died leaving a will which was made in 1922 and which pre-dated the purchase of the land by the father on which the bungalow was built. By his will the father appointed a Miss Inwards with whom he had been living for a number of years as the executrix and left nearly all his property to her and by whom he had two children and who were later appointed as trustees of the will by Miss Inwards. The defendant was left a legacy of £400. The trustees of the father's will did not attempt to have the defendant ejected from the bungalow until 1963, in fact up to that time they were on friendly terms with the defendant. The plaintiffs alleged that the defendant had only a licence to live in the bungalow, and as that it had been revoked he had no right to stay. Lord Denning, M.R., having referred to the decisions in *Dillwyn v. Llewelyn*[17] and *Plimmer v. Wellington Corpn.*,[18] went on to say:

> "It is quite plain from those authorities that, if the owner of land requests another, or indeed allows another, to expend money on the land under an expectation created or encouraged by the landlord that he will be able to remain there, that raises an equity in the licensee such as to entitle him to stay. He has a licence coupled with an equity."[19]

---

[15] *ibid.* at 522-523.
[16] Above, n.5.
[17] Above, n.5.
[18] 9 App. Cas. 699.
[19] Above, n.5 at 448.

It seemed to him from Plimmer's case in particular that the equity arising from the expenditure on land did not fail merely on the ground that the interest to be secured had not been expressly indicated. The court can look at the circumstances of the case and see whether there is an equity arising out of the expenditure of money.

10–06   In *Smyth v. Halpin*[20] the plaintiff intended to build a dwelling house for himself and his wife. He asked his father for a site to the build the dwelling house. His father replied, referring to the land and dwelling house owned by him, by saying: "This place is yours after your mother's day – what would you be doing with two places?" The father then suggested that the plaintiff build an extension to the family home. An architect was employed to design the extension with the view that the entire house would ultimately become the plaintiff's. To build the extension the plaintiff had to seek a loan from a building society but they required security for the loan. The father transferred a site to the plaintiff and this was given as security for the loan. The extension was then built and even though it was a self-contained part of the house it was not separate from the main building. The father made a number of wills, the earliest was dated April 20, 1966 which devised his cottage and farm to his wife for life and on her death to his son Ian Smyth absolutely subject to the rights of his other children to reside in the cottage until they attained the age of twenty-five years or married. The Ian Smyth referred to in the devise was a brother of the plaintiff. He made another will dated February 13, 1976 where he devised the same cottage and farm to his wife for life but this time left the remainder to the plaintiff absolutely subject to the same rights of residence. He made yet another will dated October 21, 1986 which post-dated the original conversation between the plaintiff and his father. Under that will he again left a life interest in the cottage and farm to his wife for life and thereafter to the plaintiff but subject to the right of his daughters, Ann and Regina, to have an option to choose a half-acre site each from his lands for the purpose of building a dwelling house. The option was to remain open for a period of four years from the date of his death. The next will was made on June 25, 1991 and by that will the farm was devised to the plaintiff's mother for life and on her death to the plaintiff absolutely. However, the cottage was left to the plaintiff's mother for life and on her death to his daughter Regina, the second-named defendant absolutely. Under his last will dated July 23, 1992 the testator appointed the first-named defendant as one of the executors of his will and again devised his farm to his wife for life and on her death to the plaintiff absolutely. He again devised the cottage to his wife for life and on her death to his daughter Regina absolutely. After leaving a number of legacies to his other children he devised

---

[20] Above, n.6.

to the plaintiff a right of way used by him for the benefit of his property over the lands surrounding the cottage. The plaintiff knew nothing of his father's testamentary arrangements and his change of mind in relation to the cottage until the will was read out after the father's death. The plaintiff then instituted proceedings seeking a declaration that he was entitled to the reversionary interest in the cottage after the death of his mother. He also sought an order directing the first-named defendant to transfer the interest to him.

10–07   The plaintiff based his claim to the reversionary interest on the doctrine of proprietary estoppel. Geoghegan J., in the course of his judgment, stated that:

> "The question I have had to consider therefore is whether in the light of the authorities on proprietary estoppel the facts of this case give rise to a proper recourse to that principle and if so, whether the application of the principle of proprietary estoppel in this case actually requires that this Court make an order directing a transfer of the reversionary interest. The granting of the latter remedy would effectively involve permitting the estoppel to be used as a sword and not merely a shield and would also be an exceptional inroad into the well established principle that equity will not complete an uncompleted gift."[21]

He went on to refer to *Dillwyn v. Llewelyn*[22] and *Inwards v. Baker*[23] to discover the kind and extent of the proprietary estoppel established in the case before him. He thought that the plaintiff had a clear expectation that he would have a fee simple in the entire cottage. He found it difficult to conceive that the plaintiff would ever have adopted the father's suggestion in relation to the extension to the cottage if it was not understood that he was to become the ultimate owner of the entire cottage.

10–08   However, once the extent of the equity is established in the form of a proprietary estoppel matters do not stop there, the next question to be addressed is how this equity can be satisfied. As was stated by Scarman L.J. in *Crabb v. Arun District Council*:[24]

> "But there can be no doubt that since *Ramsden v. Dyson*[25] the courts have acted on the basis that they have to determine not only the extent of the equity, but also the conditions necessary to satisfy it, and they have done so in many cases."

---

[21] *ibid*. at 42-43.
[22] Above, n.5.
[23] Above, n.5.
[24] [1975] 3 All E.R. 865.
[25] L.R. 1 H.L. 129 at 171.

SATISFYING THE EQUITY

10–09 "It is for the court to say in what way the equity can be satisfied."[26] In *Dillwyn v. Llewelyn*[27] Lord Westbury L.C. held that by virtue of the original gift made by the testator and the subsequent expenditure by the son with the approbation of the testator, and of the right and obligation arising therefrom, the son was entitled to have the whole fee simple conveyed to him. In *Inwards v. Baker*[28] Lord Denning, M.R. held that the son had an equity to remain in the bungalow for the rest of his life:

> "In this case, it is quite plain that the father had allowed an expectation to be created in the defendant's mind that this bungalow was to be his home. It was to be his home for his life or, at all events, his home as long as he wished it to remain his home. It seems to me that, in the light of that equity, the father could not in 1932 have turned to the defendant and said: 'You are to go. It is my land and my house'. Nor could he at any time thereafter so long as the defendant wanted it as his home."[29]

He was also of the view that any purchaser who took with notice would "clearly be bound by the equity." Accordingly, the plaintiffs as successors in title were also bound by this equity: "It is an equity well recognised in law." In *Smyth v. Halpin* Geoghegan J. held that the protection of the equity arising from the expenditure required that an order be made by the court directing a conveyance of the reversionary interest to the plaintiff. He stated that the same principle was enunciated in the judgment of Cumming-Bruce L.J. in *Pascoe v. Turner*:[30]

> "So the principle to be applied is that the court should consider all the circumstances and the counterclaimant having at law no perfected gift or licence other than a licence revocable at will, the court must decide what is the minimum equity to do justice to her, having regard to the way in which she changed her position for the worse, by reason of the acquiescence or encouragement of the legal owner. The defendant submits that the only appropriate way in which the equity can be satisfied is by perfecting the imperfect gift as was done in *Dillwyn v. Llewelyn*."

In *Pascoe v. Turner* the defendant lived as the wife of the plaintiff in the plaintiff's home since 1964. The defendant helped the plaintiff in business as well as doing the housekeeping. "She did all that a wife would have done." In 1965 the plaintiff bought a new house in which the plaintiff and defendant continued to live as man and wife. The plaintiff gave her the housekeeping money

---

[26] *Inwards v. Baker*, above, n.5 at 449 *per* Lord Denning M.R. and cited by Geoghegan J. in *Smyth v. Halpin*, aboe, n.6 at 43-44.

[27] Above, n.5.

[28] Above, n.5.

[29] Above, n.5 at 449.

[30] Above, n.11 at 950.

but she used her own money to buy her clothes and small items for the house. In 1973 "Cupid aimed his arrow" and struck the plaintiff who began an affair with another woman. The plaintiff declared on a number of occasions after he had left the defendant that "The house is yours and everything in it." However, he never conveyed the house to her or put anything in writing to the effect that the house and contents were hers. The defendant stayed on in the house and spent money on repairs and bought new furniture. The plaintiff lived nearby and paid her occasional visits. Then they had a quarrel and he decided to eject her from the house. In 1976 his solicitors wrote to her giving her two months' notice to determine her licence to occupy and demanded possession of the house. She refused to leave the house. Having established that the defendant had an equity the court went on to consider on how it might be satisfied. Cumming-Bruce L.J. was of the view that

> "the problem of remedy on the facts resolves itself into a choice between two alternatives; should the equity be satisfied by a licence to the defendant to occupy the house for her lifetime or should there be a transfer to her of the fee simple ?"[31]

He went on to say:

> "The main consideration pointing to a licence for her lifetime is that she did not by her case at the hearing seek to establish that she had spent more money or done more work on the house than she would have done had she believed that she had only a licence to live there for her lifetime. But the court must be cautious about drawing any inference from what she did not give in evidence as the hypothesis put is one that manifestly never occurred to her. Then it may be reasonably held that her expenditure and effort can hardly be regarded as comparable to the change of position of those who have constructed buildings on land over which they had no legal rights."[32]

But the court will look to all the circumstances of the case to see how the equity might be satisfied. Cumming-Bruce L.J. took the view that an equity cannot be satisfied without granting a remedy which ensured that the defendant had security of tenure, quiet enjoyment and freedom of action in respect of repairs and improvements without interference from the plaintiff. In furtherance of this view he directed that the estate in fee simple in the house should be vested in the defendant. Geoghegan J. thought that the plaintiff in *Smyth v. Halpin* fell within the principles laid down by Cumming-Bruce L.J. in *Pascoe v. Turner* and he went on to direct that the appropriate instrument be executed to effect the vesting of the remainder interest in the plaintiff.

10–10 *Pascoe v. Turner* differed from *Dillwyn v. Llewelyn* and *Inwards v.*

---

[31] *ibid*. at 951.
[32] *ibid*.

Baker in that it did not involve a will, it involved an inter vivos transaction. It may be observed however that although a will is required for basing a claim under section 117, the moral duty may be fulfilled *otherwise* than by will, therefore, if a child of a testator establishes an equity and has it satisfied by the court during the lifetime of the testator it may be taken into account by the court when deciding on the entitlement to shares by children in the estate. Moreover, while an order of the court under section 117 cannot affect the legal right of a surviving spouse, or if the spouse is the mother or father of the child any devise or legacy to the spouse or any share to which the spouse is entitled on intestacy,[33] the legal right of a spouse or a devise or legacy to a spouse or any share to which a spouse is entitled on intestacy cannot affect a pre-established equity in the form of a proprietary estoppel by a child of the testator.

PROPRIETARY ESTOPPEL AS AN ALTERNATIVE

10–11   One of the main advantages of establishing an equity rather than making a claim under section 117 is that once it is established it prevails even over the legal right of the spouse and the claims of other children of the testator to a share in the estate. Furthermore, even though a child may have a pre-established equity and as such it may be taken into account by the court where other children also apply under section 117, the court may, nevertheless, in the circumstances, give the child with the equity an additional share in the estate notwithstanding the unassailable equity established by that child to a definite part of the testator's estate. However, as can be seen from the decisions of the courts fairly cogent evidence must be adduced to establish the equity and there is always the risk that the courts may decide that no such equity exists, and further it is for the court to satisfy the equity in the way it deems fit. While the relationship of testator and child will create the moral duty under section 117, no such a relationship will create a moral duty in equity although it may prove to be a factor in favour of establishing the equity.

SUMMARY

10–12   Instead of, or in addition to, a section 117 application, a child of the testator may prefer to rely on a proprietary estoppel. Once the estoppel is established and satisfied by the court the property which composes it will not form part of the deceased's estate out of which provision may be made for other children, or indeed, cannot form part of the legal right share of the surviving spouse. The advantage of the equity over a section 117 application is

---

[33] Succession Act 1965, s.117(3).

that it is definite in subject matter and has the protection of equity and is not subject to the legal right share of a spouse or section 117 and the strict time limits for making applications under that section. Furthermore, it does not preclude a child from making an application under section 117 for further provision to be made although it may be viewed by the court as the fulfilment of the testator's moral duty towards that child by making provision for him otherwise than by will.

CHAPTER 11

The Power and Right to Appropriate

INTRODUCTION

11–01 Even though the testator is the only person who has the power to dispose of his property, and intestate estates must be distributed in accordance with the statutory rules of intestacy, personal representatives have a statutory power of appropriation over the estate of the deceased whether he died testate or intestate.[1] This power of appropriation is exercisable over the whole estate of the deceased thus making any part of it subject to appropriation in its "actual condition or state of investment in or towards the satisfaction of any share in the estate, whether settled or not, according to the respective rights of the persons interested in the estate."[2] "Share", in relation to the estate of a deceased person, includes any share or interest, whether arising under a will, on intestacy or as a legal right, and includes the right to the whole estate.[3] However, the power cannot be exercised in such a way as to affect prejudicially any specific devise or legacy except in the case where the personal representatives are required by the surviving spouse to appropriate to him or her the dwellinging and/or household chattels under section 56 of the Succession Act. As the definition of "share" in the deceased's estate includes the legal share of a surviving spouse, and as the legal right share has priority "over devises, bequests and shares of intestacy,"[4] and has the quality of an interest arising under a will,[5] it would seem that an appropriation by the personal representatives must also not prejudicially affect the legal right share of the surviving spouse notwithstanding the fact that a surviving spouse does not require an appropriation of the dwelling and/or household chattels in or towards the satisfaction of the legal right share under section 56.

11–02 Although the power of the personal representatives to appropriate the estate of the deceased is a discretionary power and they cannot be compelled to exercise it, a person entitled to a share in the estate may apply to the court to prohibit them from exercising it,[6] except in the case of an appropriation made

---

[1] Succession Act 1965, s.55.
[2] Succession Act 1965, s.55(1).
[3] Succession Act 1965, s.3(1).
[4] Succession Act 1965, s.112.
[5] See *In re Cummins: O'Dwyer v. Keegan* [1997] 2 I.L.R.M. 401 at 403.
[6] Succession Act 1965, s.55(3).

by them under section 56. However, it is for a spouse to require the personal representatives to make an appropriation under section 56 in the first place: they are not obliged to make an appropriation under section 56 unless they are required to do so by the surviving spouse. Therefore, although personal representatives have the power to appropriate under section 55 they have a *right* not to exercise the power except where they are required to do so under section 56, but should they do so otherwise than in furtherance of section 56 the intended appropriation may be prohibited by the court.[7]

11–03 The statutory power to appropriate by personal representatives and the statutory right of a surviving spouse to require an appropriation of the dwelling and/or household chattels are further examples of statutory inroads being made into the so-called testator's freedom of testation, particularly so as it would seem that a testator cannot exclude such power and right by a provision in his will.

THE DISCRETIONARY NATURE OF THE POWER UNDER SECTION 55

11–04 A personal representative may, subject to the provisions of section 55, appropriate any part of the estate of a deceased person in its actual condition or state of investment at the time of the appropriation in or towards satisfaction of any share in the estate, whether settled or not, according to the respective rights of the persons interested in the estate.[8] However, an appropriation by a personal representative must not be made so as to affect prejudicially any specific devise or legacy or bequest except in a case to which section 56 applies,[9] nor can it be made unless notice of the intended appropriation has been served on all parties entitled to a share in the estate and any one of which parties may within six weeks from the service of the notice on him apply to the court to prohibit the appropriation except, again, in a case to which section 56 applies.[10] The notice of the intended appropriation required to be served by a personal representative on those entitled to a share in the estate need not be served on persons who may come into existence after the time of the appropriation or who cannot after reasonable enquiry be found or ascertained at that time.[11] However, consent to an appropriation must be obtained from a person absolutely and beneficially entitled in possession, or when it is made in respect of any settled share, the consent of either a trustee, if any, who is other than the personal representative or the person who may for the time being be

---

[7] *H. v. O.* [1978] I.R. 194; *H. v. H.* [1978] I.R. 138.
[8] Succession Act 1965, s.55(1).
[9] Succession Act 1965, s.55(2).
[10] Succession Act 1965, s.55(3).
[11] *ibid.*

entitled to the income.[12] Where such consent is required from a minor or person of unsound mind it may be given on his behalf by his parents or parent, guardian, committee or receiver, or where in the case of a minor there is no parent or guardian, by the court on the application of his next friend.[13] No such consent will be required on behalf of a person who may come into existence after the time of appropriation, or who cannot after reasonable enquiry be found or ascertained at that time.[14] Any property duly appropriated under the powers conferred by section 55 will thereafter be treated as an authorised investment, and may be retained and dealt with accordingly.[15]

11–05 Before making an appropriation the personal representative may ascertain and fix the values of the respective parts of the estate and the liabilities of the deceased as he may think fit, and for this purpose employ a qualified valuer in any case where a valuation of the estate is required and he may thereafter may make any conveyance of estate which may be requisite for giving effect to the appropriation.[16] An appropriation made in pursuance of section 55 will bind all persons interested in the property of the deceased whose consent is not required unless the court otherwise directs arising out of an application to it under subsection (3). However, the personal representative in making the appropriation must have regard to the *rights* of any person who may thereafter come into existence, or who cannot after reasonable enquiry be found or ascertained at the time of appropriation, and of any person whose consent is not required by section 55. The personal representative may have additional powers of appropriation conferred on him by law or by the will of the deceased and these powers will not be prejudiced by the power of appropriation under section 55 and the power under section 55 will take effect with any extended powers conferred by the will, and where an appropriation is made under section 55 in respect of any settled share, the property appropriated will remain subject to all trusts for sale and powers of leasing, disposition and management or varying investments which would have applicable thereto or to the share in respect of which the appropriation is made.[17] A "settled share" for the purposes of the section includes any share to which a person is not absolutely entitled in possession at the date of the appropriation and also an annuity.[18] Where property has been appropriated under section 55 and if the person to whom the appropriation has been made disposes of it or any part of it in favour of a purchaser, the appropriation will be deemed to have been

---

[12] Succession Act 1965, s.55(4).
[13] Succession Act 1965, s.55(5).
[14] Succession Act 1965, s.55(6).
[15] Succession Act 1965, s.55(9).
[16] Succession Act 1965, s.55(10).
[17] Succession Act 1965, s.55(13).
[18] Succession Act 1965, s.55(15).

made in accordance with the requirements of the section and that all the requisite notices and consents have been given.[19] Section 55 applies whether the deceased died intestate or not, and whether before or after the commencement of the Succession Act, and extends to property over which a testator exercises a general power of appointment, and authorises the setting apart of a fund to answer an annuity by means of the income of that fund or otherwise.[20] The powers conferred by section 55 may also be exercised by the personal representative in his own favour.[21]

11–06 Section 55 is an enabling provision giving a personal representative a discretionary power to make an appropriation. As it is discretionary a personal representative cannot be compelled to exercise it by those entitled to a share in the estate. However, where he exercises the power to appropriate he must do so in compliance with the provisions of section 55 and must send such notices and seek such consents as are necessary to its proper exercise. Moreover, since a personal representative holds the estate under section 10(3) of the Succession Act as a trustee, "the exercise of the statutory discretion to appropriate must be viewed as an incident of trusteeship," so that it is the court's duty to prohibit the appropriation if it is calculated to operate unjustly or inequitably by unduly benefiting one beneficiary at the expense of another.[22] However, the court's function is "essentially supervisory and prohibitive" and it will not intervene unless it is established that the exercise of the power would be unjust and inequitable having regard to the rights of all persons who are or will become entitled to an interest in the estate, or that the intended appropriation would not be legally possible.[23]

11–07 The nature and extent of the personal representative's power to appropriate was considered by the Supreme Court in *H. v. O.*[24] In that case the plaintiff was also the plaintiff in *H. v. H.*[25] who having failed in her attempt as surviving spouse to have an appropriation made under section 56 immediately instituted proceedings to have an appropriation made under section 55. The testator left all of his property to the second defendant subject to the right of widow to reside in part of a dwelling which was situated on the devised property for her life. The property consisted of agricultural land. There were no children of the marriage. The widow, who was the plaintiff in the action, elected to take her legal right share pursuant to section 115 of the Succession Act

---

[19] Succession Act 1965, s.55(14).
[20] Succession Act 1965, s.55(16).
[21] Succession Act 1965, s.55(18).
[22] *H. v. O.*, above, n.7.
[23] *ibid.*
[24] *ibid.*
[25] Above, n.7.

instead of the life interest given to her in the will. She then applied to the High Court under section 56 for an order directing the personal representative to appropriate the dwelling to her in or towards legal right share in the estate. The second defendant objected to the appropriation on grounds that it would diminish the value of the agricultural land which was left to him. When the Supreme Court held against her in *H. v. H.* she instituted proceedings under section 55 and succeeded in her application in the High Court. However, the second and third defendants appealed the decision to the Supreme Court.

11–08 Henchy J., having first noted in the course of his judgment for the Supreme Court that in cases of appropriation under section 55 the court only acquired jurisdiction in the matter when a party, on being served with a notice of intended appropriation, applied within six weeks to the court to prohibit the appropriation and that the section was silent on the question of the jurisdiction of the court, stated that the court's function was essentially "supervisory and prohibitive". "So it must be assumed, having regard to the tenor, the scope and the purpose of the section, that the court should prohibit an intended appropriation only (a) when the conditions in the section have not been complied with; or (b) when, notwithstanding such compliance, it would not be just or equitable to allow the appropriation to take place, having regard to the rights of all persons who are or will become entitled to an interest in the estate; or (c) when, apart from the section, the appropriation would not be legally possible."[26] He went on to say that as a personal representative holds the estate under section 10(3) of the Succession Act for the persons entitled to a share in the estate, the exercise of the discretionary power to appropriate must be viewed as "an incident of trusteeship" and that it was the court's duty to prohibit an appropriation if it was calculated to operate unjustly or inequitably by unduly benefiting one beneficiary over another. "But otherwise, where the conditions of the section have been observed and the personal representatives have made a bona fide decision to appropriate, the exercise of their discretion to appropriate should not be interferred with unless for some reason unrelated to the terms of the section the appropriation would be legally unacceptable, e.g., if it would amount to a sub-division prohibited by law."[27]

11–09 Turning to the circumstances of the case Henchy J. found that the land left by the testator consisted of approximately 112 acres. Of that 112 acres, 12 acres stood some short distance apart from the remainder. The remainder was bisected by the Ennis-Limerick road. The dwelling and 52 acres were situated on the west side of that road. The remaining 48 were situated on the east side. The dwelling and 52 acres were therefore easily identifiable as a

---

[26] Above, n.7 at 206–207.
[27] *ibid.*

"severable block." The proposed appropriation meant that the first defendant, as personal representative, would convey to the plaintiff the 52 acres in or towards the satisfaction of the half share of the estate to which she was entitled. The plaintiff accepted that appropriation. It was opposed, however, by the second defendant, who was entitled to the balance of the estate, which was subject to five legacies amounting to £2,200 and to an annuity of £150 and the rights of residence and support in favour of the third defendant.

11–10   The second defendant sought to prohibit the appropriation on two grounds. The first ground was that to allow the appropriation was contrary to the testator's primary intention that the lands should pass in their entirety to him and that any appropriation contrary to that intention should be prohibited by the court. The second ground was that the proposed appropriation was unfair in that the plaintiff would benefit at his expense by making the unappropriated part of the lands worth appreciably less than a half share in the proceeds of the lands if they were sold as a single unit. In relation to the first ground, Henchy J. considered that the intention of the testator had no part to play in the operation of section 55 in the circumstances of the case. As the legislature had specifically allowed the testator's intention to be set aside by enabling the plaintiff as his widow to have the will "amended" so as to give her a half share of the estate in place of the benefits given to her by the testator in his will, the testator's intention as to the devolution of his estate on his death must be not be taken into account. Furthermore, as section 112 of the Succession Act stipulates that the half share to which the plaintiff became entitled as her legal right shall have priority over devises and bequests, even though the plaintiff and second defendant are each entitled to a half share, the plaintiff's half share being a legal right takes priority over the defendant's half share which derives from the will.[28] In relation to the second ground, Henchy J. thought it necessary to consider the financial consequences of the intended appropriation as compared with those of a sale of the lands as a single unit. Three valuers gave evidence in the High Court, two for the plaintiff and one for the second defendant. One of the plaintiff's valuer's assessed the market value of the dwelling and all the lands as a single residential farm at £112,000 and the other valued the same at £110,200. The defendant's valuer gave a valuation of £109,600 by reference to the three component parts. Henchy J. thought it was a common case therefore that a half share of the proceeds of a sale of the dwelling and all the lands as one unit free of the interest of the third defendant, who was 82 years, amounted to approximately £55,000. One of the plaintiff's valuers valued the dwelling and 52 acres at £58,000 if sold separately, and the plaintiff's other valuer gave a valuation for the same at £59,000. The defendant's valuer gave a valuation of £52,000. The corresponding

---

[28] *ibid.* at 208.

valuations of the valuers for a sale of the rest of the lands were £56,000, £51,000 and £57,000 respectively. Therefore, the evidence of the valuers showed that the intended appropriation of the dwelling and 52 acres benefited the plaintiff to the extent of about £55,000, and if the rest of the land went to the second defendant it represented a financial benefit to him of about the same amount. As a result Henchy J. was of the opinion that the second defendant had not substantiated his claim that the intended appropriation should be prohibited and also that the intended appropriation "would eminently accord with the merits of the case." He concluded by saying that the appropriation would ensure that the plaintiff, who was widowed and without children, would not be condemned to the harsh fate of having to leave the dwelling and seek a new home.

THE RIGHT TO REQUIRE AN APPROPRIATION UNDER SECTION 56

11–11   Where the estate of a deceased person includes a dwelling in which at the time of the deceased's death the surviving spouse was ordinarily resident, the surviving spouse may require the personal representative in writing to appropriate the dwelling in or towards the satisfaction of any share of the surviving spouse.[29] The surviving spouse may also require the personal representative in writing to appropriate any household chattels in or towards the satisfaction of any share of that spouse.[30] Thus, it would appear that a surviving spouse may require the personal representative to appropriate either the dwelling or household chattels, or both the dwelling and household chattels, in or towards the satisfaction of any share to which such a spouse is entitled to in the estate of the deceased. The expression "any share of the surviving spouse" in relation to the estate of the deceased includes any share or interest, whether arising under a will, on intestacy or as a legal right.[31] "Dwelling" means "an estate or interest in a building occupied as a separate dwelling or a part, so occupied, of any building and includes any garden or portion of ground attached to and usually occupied with the dwelling or otherwise required for the amenity or convenience of the dwelling."[32] A field, for instance, has also been held to form part of a dwelling if it contains the well and septic tank which service the dwelling.[33] The expression "household chattels" means "furniture, linen, china, glass, books and other chattels of ordinary household use or ornament and also consumable stores, garden effects and domestic animals, but does not include any chattels used at the death of the deceased for business

[29] Succession Act 1965, s.56(1).
[30] Succession Act 1965, s.56(2).
[31] Succession Act 1965, s.3(1).
[32] Succession Act 1965, s.56(14).
[33] *In re Hamilton* [1984] I.L.R.M. 306 *per* O'Hanlon J.

or professional purposes or money or security for money."[34] It may also be mentioned that a surviving spouse may elect to take the legal right share under section 115 of the Succession Act instead of a gift in a will and, perhaps, as a result increase his or her share in the estate and may then proceed to require the personal representative to appropriate the dwelling and/or household chattels in or towards satisfaction of the share under section 56(1) and (2).

11–12 Where it transpires that the share of the surviving spouse is insufficient to enable an appropriation to be made of the dwelling or household chattels, as the case may be, the right of appropriation may also be exercised in relation to the share of any infant for whom the surviving spouse is a trustee.[35] It will be observed that the exercise of the right of appropriation where an infant's share is also involved is based on a trustee/ beneficiary relationship between the spouse and children and is not based on a guardian/minor relationship although the two kinds of relationship may coincide. However, where the share is insufficient a surviving spouse may still require an appropriation partly in satisfaction of a share in the deceased's estate and partly in return for a payment of money by the surviving spouse on the spouse's own behalf and also on behalf of any infant for whom the spouse is a trustee.[36] It is the duty of the personal representative to notify the surviving spouse of the rights conferred by section 56.[37]

11–13 The time period within which the right of appropriation must be exercised is six months from the receipt of the notice by the personal representative or one year from the first taking out a grant of representation of the deceased's estate, whichever is the later.[38]

11–14 However, there are limits placed on the exercise of the right of appropriation in relation to the dwelling. Where the dwelling forms part of a building, and an estate or interest in the whole building forms part of the estate; or where the dwelling is held with agricultural land an estate or interest in which forms part of the estate; or where the whole or part of the dwelling was, at the time of the death, used as an hotel, guest house or boarding house; or where the part of the dwelling was at the time of the death of the deceased used for purposes other than domestic purposes, the right of appropriation in relation to the dwelling will not be exercisable unless the court, on application made by the personal representative or the surviving spouse, is satisfied that the exercise of the right of appropriation in relation to the dwelling is unlikely to

---

[34] Succession Act 1965, s.56(14).
[35] Succession Act 1965, s.56(3).
[36] Succession Act 1965, s.59(9).
[37] Succession Act 1965, s.56(4).
[38] Succession Act 1965, s.56(5)(a).

diminish the value of the assets of the deceased, other than the dwelling, or to make it more difficult to dispose of them in due course of administration and authorises its exercise.[39] So long as the right to require an appropriation under section 56 continues to be exercisable, the personal representative other than where the surviving spouse is also personal representative, must not sell or otherwise dispose of the dwelling or household chattels without the written consent of the surviving spouse or the leave of the court given on the refusal of an application under section 56(5)(b) except in the course of administration owing to the want of other assets.[40] However, nothing in section 56(8)(a) and (b) will confer any right on the surviving spouse against a purchaser from the personal representative.[41]

11–15   A surviving spouse so long as the right continues to be exercisable may apply to the court for appropriation on his or her own behalf and also on behalf of any infant for whom the spouse is a trustee under section 57 or otherwise.[42] Where such an application is made the court may order that appropriation to the spouse be made without the payment of money provided for in section 56 (9), or subject to the payment of such amount as the court considers reasonable, if owing to the special circumstances of the case hardship would otherwise be caused to the surviving spouse or to such a spouse and any infant.[43] The court may make such further orders in relation to the administration of the estate as may appear to be just and equitable having regard to the provisions of the Act and to all the circumstances.[44] However, the court will not make an order in relation to a dwelling unless it is satisfied that the order would be unlikely to diminish the value of the assets, other than the dwelling, or to make it difficult to dispose of them in due course of administration.[45] Where a surviving spouse is of unsound mind a requirement or consent under section 56 may, if there is a committee of that spouse's estate, be made or given on behalf of the spouse by the committee by leave of the court which has appointed the committee, or if there is no committee, be given or made by the High Court or by the Circuit Court in relation to case coming within the jurisdiction of the Circuit Court.[46] Although all proceedings in relation to section 56 are required to be heard in chambers this does not mean that the judgment in such proceedings in chambers may not be published.[47]

---

[39] Succession Act 1965, ss.56(5)(b) and 56(6)(a), (b), (c) and (d); *H. v. H.*, above, n.7.

[40] Succession Act 1965, s.56(8)(a) and (b).

[41] Succession act 1965, s.56(8)(c).

[42] Succession Act 1965, s.56(10).

[43] Succession Act 1965, s.56(10)(b).

[44] Succession Act 1965, s.56(10)(c).

[45] Succession act 1965, s.56(10)(d); See s.56(6).

[46] Succession Act 1965, s.56(12).

[47] Succession Act 1965, s.56(11); *H.v. H.*, above, n.7 at 149 *per* Parke J. citing Lord Denning M.R. in *Wallersteiner v. Moir* [1974] 1 W.L.R. 991 at 1003.

11–16   On any application to the court under section 56(5)(b) by the surviving spouse or the personal representative the onus of proof rests on him to
satisfy the court that the exercise of the right of appropriation is unlikely to
diminish the value of the assets of the deceased, other than the dwelling, or to
make it more difficult to dispose of them in due course of administration.[48]
The words "the value of the assets of the deceased other than the dwelling"
have been construed to refer to all the assets of the deceased other than the
dwelling.[49] Thus where a spouse has elected to take the legal right share, the
words cannot be construed to mean the value of the assets of the deceased,
other than the dwelling and those assets passing to the spouse, as such a construction would not be in conformity with the words used in section 56(5)(b).
The words plainly refer to all the assets of the deceased other than the dwelling. It was stated by Parke J. in *H. v. H.*[50] that as the dwelling is the only
exclusion all doubt is removed as to the comprehensiveness of the word "all."
Furthermore, any construction of section 56 (5) (b) which makes a distinction
in value between a residential agricultural holding and a non-residential agricultural holding in the belief that a residential holding is more valuable than a
non-residential holding would be an incorrect one. The words required that all
the assets be taken into account other than the dwelling.[51]

11–17   The wording of section 56(5)(b) not only provides that the court must
not only be satisfied that the exercise of the right of appropriation is unlikely
to diminish the value of the assets of the deceased, other than the dwelling, but
goes on to provide that "or" it must not make it more difficult to dispose of the
assets in due course of administration. A question arose in *H. v. H.* whether
the effect of the "or" between the two expressions was disjunctive, and if such
were the case, whether the onus of proof on an application under section
56(5)(b) could be discharged by establishing one or other of the two. Where,
for instance, no sale of the assets was contemplated the question of whether
the exercise of the right of appropriation would diminish the assets would
then become irrelevant as there would be no imposition placed on a personal
representative when distributing the assets in due course of administration.
The word "them" used in the expression "or to make it more difficult to dispose of them" could be interpreted as meaning the assets of the deceased other
than the dwelling, and the word "dispose" as including a voluntary distribution among the beneficiaries in specie. However, no matter how plausible the
latter interpretation of section 56(5)(b) may seem it was not enough to satisfy
Parke J. in *H. v. H.* as he was of the opinion that any reading of section 56(5)(b)

---

[48] *H. v. H.*, above, n.7 at 147.
[49] *ibid.*
[50] *ibid.*
[51] *H. v. H.*, above, n.7 at 147–148.

requires the court to be satisfied that *neither* of the specified circumstances is likely to happen.[52]

11–18   The facts of *H. v. H.* were substantially the same as those in *H. v. O.* except that an application was made under section 55 in *H. v. O.* However, it would be appropriate to reiterate them here because of the separate application under section 56. In *H. v. H.*[53] the testator left all of his property to the second defendant subject to the right of his widow to reside in part of a dwelling which was situated on the devised property for her life. The property consisted of agricultural land. There were no children of the marriage. The widow, who was the plaintiff in the action, elected to take her legal right share pursuant to section 115 of the Succession Act instead of the life interest given to her in the will. She then applied to the High Court under section 56 of the Succession Act for an order directing the personal representative to appropriate the dwelling to her in satisfaction of legal right share in the estate. The second defendant objected to this appropriation on the grounds that it would diminish the value of the agricultural land which was left to him. Parke J. in his judgment for the Supreme Court held that the plaintiff had failed to establish that the proposed appropriation of the dwelling was unlikely to diminish the value of the assets other than the dwelling, or to make it more difficult to dispose of them in due course of administration of the estate.

11–19   Thus, under section 56, a surviving spouse has a statutory right to require an appropriation of a dwelling and/or household chattels in or towards the satisfaction of any share under a will, or on intestacy or a legal right. However, the right of appropriation may not be exercisable in relation to a dwelling unless it is proved to the satisfaction of the court by either the personal representative or surviving spouse that the exercise of the right is unlikely to diminish the value of the assets of the deceased, other than the dwelling, or to make it more difficult to dispose of all the assets in due course of administration and authorises its exercise. The onus of proof rests on the applicants personal representative or surviving spouse to show that an intended appropriation is unlikely to diminish the value of the assets of the deceased other than the dwelling or to make it more difficult to dispose of them.

Summary

11–20   Where a person, other than a surviving spouse, is entitled to a share under a will or on an intestacy, the personal representative may by exercising the statutory power under section 55 appropriate any part of the estate of the

---

[52] *ibid.* at 148.
[53] Above, n.7.

deceased, other than the dwelling and/or household chattels, in or towards the satisfaction of such share. Where the surviving spouse becomes entitled to a share in the estate either under a will or on intestacy, that spouse may require the appropriation of the dwelling and/or house hold chattels in or towards the satisfaction of such share. It may be noted that the right to require such an appropriation is also given where a spouse exercises the right of election in favour of the legal right share under section 115 of the Succession Act. Although the personal representative's power is made subject to the surviving spouse's right to require an appropriation of the dwelling and/or household chattels under section 56, the spouse's right is not exercisable in relation to a dwelling if it is likely to diminish the value of the assets of the deceased, other than the dwelling, or to make it more difficult to dispose of them in due course of administration. Even though the personal representative's right to appropriate is made subject to the spouse's right under 56, a spouse cannot compel a personal representative to exercise his power in relation to the assets of the deceased other than the dwelling and/or household chattels.[54] Furthermore, where the court finds that the spouse's right to require an appropriation of the dwelling is likely to diminish the value of the assets or make it more difficult to dispose of them in due course of administration, it would appear that the personal representative's discretionary power to appropriate may extend over the dwelling as well, but in such an event there is nothing to prevent a spouse from making an application to the court under section 55(3) to prohibit such an appropriation.[55]

11–21 Under section 55(3) any person who is entitled to a share in the estate may apply to the court to prohibit an appropriation by a personal representative subject only to the provisions of section 56. It has been already said that the role of the court when entertaining applications under section 55(3) is primarily supervisory and prohibitive and thus it may only restrain appropriations where the conditions of section 55 have not been complied with, or that an appropriation would be unjust or inequitable in the circumstances, or that an appropriation would not be legally possible.[56]

11–22 Under section 56(5) the right of a surviving spouse to require an appropriation will not become exercisable unless the court is satisfied that its exercise would be unlikely to diminish the value of the assets of the deceased, other than the dwelling, or to make it more difficult to dispose of them in due course of administration and authorises its exercise. The onus of proof rests on the applicant (be it the personal representative or the surviving spouse) under section 56(5) to satisfy the court that the intended appropriation is un-

---

[54] *H. v. H.*, above, n.7.
[55] *H. v. O.*, above, n.7.
[56] *H. v. O.*, above, n.7 at 206–207.

likely to have such effect. The words "the value of the assets of the deceased" have been construed by Parke J. in *H. v. H.*[57] to mean *all* the assets of the deceased, other than the dwelling, and that the word "or" between the two eventualities is not to be viewed as a disjunctive, thus placing the onus on the applicant to establish that neither eventuality is likely to happen.[58] Thus it would seem that the role of the court for the purposes of section 56 is also supervisory and prohibitive to ensure that the statutory conditions have been complied with. The right of a surviving spouse may be based on a will, an intestacy, or on the cumulative effect of the exercise of the right of election under section 115. The surviving spouse must exercise the right under section 56 within six months of notification from the personal representative or one year from the first taking out of a grant of representation of the deceased's estate, which ever is the later.[59]

11–23 The court when determining whether to prohibit an appropriation under section 55 need not consider the intention of a testator. Its main concern will be to ascertain whether the statutory provisions have been complied with and not to ascertain and give effect to the testator's intention as in a construction suit. The effect of section 55 is to give a personal representative a discretionary power allowing him to override the provisions of a will altogether when making an appropriation and such an act will be valid when done in compliance with section 55. Thus an appropriation made by a personal representative under section 55 will be effective even though it may be contrary to the testator's intention as "the testator's intention as to the devolution of his estate on his death must be cast aside."[60] In fact, Henchy J. in *H. v. O.*[61] considered that the intention of the testator had no part in the operation of section 55 in the circumstances of the case. As section 55 prevails over any testamentary disposition it would seem to follow that any provision in a will which tends to exclude or curtail the personal representative's power to appropriate will be ineffective. The same can be said where an appropriation is made under section 56.

---

[57] Above, n.7.
[58] *H. v. H.*, above, n.7 at 148.
[59] Succession Act 1965, s.56(5)(a).
[60] *H. v. O.*, above, n.7 at 208.
[61] Above, n.7 at 208.

CHAPTER 12

Assents by Personal Representatives

INTRODUCTION

12–01 For an estate to vest in beneficiaries an assent must be executed by a personal representative. The form of assent will depend on the nature of the property: where personal property is concerned an oral assent will suffice; where real property is involved an assent must be executed in writing. An assent is required because the whole estate of a deceased person vests in his personal representative from the date of death in the case of an executor, and from the date of the grant in the case of an administrator. However, before a grant of letters of administration with the will annexed or intestate is made the estate vests in the President of the High Court and he will be treated as a corporation sole for this purpose.[1] The President will be entitled to the estate as 'true owner' until an administrator is appointed[2] and even though the President is recognised as 'true owner' he does not act as administrator and has no statutory power to assent to the vesting of property in beneficiaries.

12–02 A personal representative owes two basic duties to the estate of the deceased. The first duty is to discharge all expenses, debts and liabilities due by the estate. The second duty is to distribute what remains among the beneficiaries. The performance of these duties will, of course, depend on the degree of solvency of the estate. Where the estate is solvent it will first be applicable "towards the discharge of the funeral, testamentary and administration expenses, debts and liabilities and any legal right in the order mentioned in Part II of the First Schedule" to the Succession Act 1965.[3] Furthermore, although a creditor's right to payment can be facilitated by the provisions of a will it cannot be restricted by it.[4] The nature of a creditor's right to the payment of his debt takes the form of a chose in action. It is worth noting that a chose in action is "a known legal expression used to describe all personal rights in property which can be claimed or enforced by action and not by taking physical possession."[5] Thus a creditor can enforce his right to payment by taking

---

[1] Succession Act 1965, s.13.
[2] *Gleeson v. Feehan* [1997] 1 I.L.R.M. 522.
[3] s.46.
[4] Succession Act 1965, s.46(3) and (4); *Re Tankard: Tankard v. Midland Bank Executor and Trustee Co.* [1942] Ch. 69; [1941] 3 All E.R. 458.
[5] *Torkington v. Magee* [1927] 2 K.B. 427 at 430 *per* Channel J.

action against the personal representative once a grant has issued, or indeed, he may apply for a grant himself.[6] The legal right of a surviving spouse was described by Walsh J. in *In Re Urquhart, Deceased: The Revenue Commissioners v. Allied Irish Banks Ltd.*[7] as having the same effect as a debt due by the estate thus in effect making a surviving spouse a creditor of the estate and rendering it enforceable in the same way as any other debt due by the estate. However, in a later Supreme Court decision it was held by Barron J. as having the same quality as a testamentary interest.[8] The distinction is of importance because if it has the effect of a debt due by the estate it will become enforceable against the personal representative immediately a grant has been issued, but if it is viewed as having the quality of a testamentary interest the vesting of it may have to await the assent of the personal representative. In furtherance of the latter view no interest will vest in the surviving spouse until the personal representative has assented as the whole estate vests in him.[9] As a further consequence of the latter view the legal right share does not become ascertainable until the expenses, debts and liabilities of the deceased have first been discharged and until such time as it becomes ascertained it may, perhaps, be treated as chose in action in the same way as a unascertained residuary estate,[10] bearing in mind that the legal right share has priority over testamentary gifts.[11] Thus, it may be said, that the legal right share of a surviving spouse, although it has the quality of a testamentary interest, takes the form of a chose in action which becomes enforceable against the estate after the expenses, debts and liabilities of the estate have been discharged. It may also be said that the legal right share does not possess the true quality of a debt in the normal sense, because the legal right is dependent on a spouse surviving the testator, while in the case of an ordinary creditor his predecease will not preclude his personal representative from claiming the debt due by the estate. It would seem therefore that the personal representative must assent to the vesting of the legal right share in the surviving spouse once it is ascertained. The personal representative's second duty is to distribute the estate remaining after the discharge of expenses, debts and liabilities among the beneficiaries under the will or in accordance with the intestacy rules.

12–03 When distributing the estate among the beneficiaries and where land is concerned section 52(2) provides that the personal representative may at any time after the death of the deceased execute an assent vesting any estate or

---

[6] Rules of the Superior Courts, Ord. 79, r.5; See also *Bank of Ireland v. King* [1991] I.L.R.M. 796.

[7] [1974] I.R. 197; See Chap. 8.

[8] *In re Cummins: O'Dwyer v. Keegan* [1997] 2 I.L.R.M. 401; See Chap. 8.

[9] *Mohan v. Roche* [1991] 1 I.R. 560.

[10] See *Mohan v. Roche*, above, n.9.

[11] Succession Act 1965, s.112.

interest in any such land in the person entitled thereto. A "person entitled" includes, in relation to any estate or interest in land, the person including the personal representative of the deceased who whether by devise, bequest, devolution or otherwise may be beneficially entitled to that estate or interest.[12] Thus it would seem that in the case of the legal right share and where the deceased's estate consists wholly of land the need for an assent will depend on what view the court will take of the quality of the legal right share: if it is viewed as a debt no assent is required; if it is treated as having the quality of a testamentary interest an assent will be required. Generally, a personal representative owes a duty to beneficiaries to act diligently in the distribution of the estate among them "for the ultimate object of administration of an estate is to place the beneficiaries in possession of their interest, and that cannot be achieved unless all debts are satisfied."[13] The legal right share aside, where a beneficiary is entitled to a specific share in the deceased's estate that share will become vested in the beneficiary following the assent by the personal representative and where the share consists of an estate or interest in land the assent must be in writing, in all other cases an oral assent will suffice.[14] Before the assent is executed the nature of the interest which such beneficiary has in the estate has been described as an inchoate right capable of transmission on the death of the testator.[15] Where a beneficiary is left the residual estate the amount of which is not immediately ascertainable an assent cannot be executed until the amount of such estate has been ascertained; the same applies to shares on intestacies where the amount of such shares cannot be ascertained until after the payment of debts and liabilities of the deceased. The nature of such interests arising out of an unascertained estate or shares on intestacy take the form of choses in action.[16] However, where the personal representative is also a beneficiary it appears that no assent to the vesting of the property in himself is necessary as the whole estate, both legal and equitable, vests in him by virtue of his office.[17] Although where land is involved, it may be "desirable that a personal representative should sign an assent in writing in circumstances such as the present but that is far from saying that it is a necessary link in the title."[18]

12–04   The form of assent where land is concerned will further depend on whether it is unregistered or registered. An assent by a personal representative

---

[12] Succession Act 1965, s.51(1)(b); See *Bank of Ireland v. King*, above, n.6, where a judgment mortgagee was held not to be a "person entitled.
[13] *Re Tankard: Tankard v. Midland Bank Executor and Trustee Co.*, above, n.4 at 463 *per* Uthwatt J.
[14] See Succession Act 1965, ss.52(5) and 54(1).
[15] *Re Parsons: Parsons v. Attorney General* [1942] 2 All E.R. 496.
[16] *Mohan v. Roche* [1991] 1 I.R. 560.
[17] Above, n.12.
[18] Above, n.12 at 567.

to the vesting of unregistered land must comply with the provisions of section 53 of the Succession Act, while an assent involving registered land must be executed in the form prescribed by section 54 of the same Act which amends section 61(3) of the Registration of Title Act 1964.

THE NATURE OF A BENEFICIARY'S INTEREST

12–05   Section 10(2) and (3) of the 1965 Act provide that a deceased's personal representatives shall be deemed for time being to be his heirs and assigns within the meaning of all trusts and powers, and that they hold the estate as trustees for the persons entitled to it by law. But what is the nature of the interest of the beneficiaries, if any? Keane J. (as he then was) in *Mohan v. Roche*[19] stated that if one employs the terminology of 'legal' estate and the 'equitable' estate the position in law is that both estates are vested in the personal representative from the date of the grant. When the whole of the property is vested in one person, as it is in a personal representative, there is no need to make a distinction between the legal and equitable interest in that property, in the same way as no such distinction is required to be made in the case of a person who has full beneficial ownership of property.[20] If the personal representative is not the person to whom land has been had been devised or bequeathed he must execute an assent in writing in order to vest the legal estate in the beneficiaries entitled under the will. Keane J. in the course of his judgment in *Gleeson v. Feehan*[21] expressed the view, that in the case of an intestacy, the next-of-kin of the intestate owner of property had at least an 'interest' in ensuring that the administration of his property was carried out in accordance with law by the administrator. They had a right, in the nature of a chose in action, to payment after the debts had been discharged and enforceable against the personal representative. Whatever the nature of the estate vested in an executor or administrator however, he does not hold the property for his own benefit rather he is to be regarded as a trustee who must perform the duties of his office, not in his own interests, but in the interests of those who are ultimately entitled to the deceased's property. If the personal representative is not the person entitled to land on a distribution on intestacy he must give his assent in writing in order to vest the land in the person or persons entitled. In the case of persons entitled to the residuary estate in a will they also will not be treated as owners in equity of specific items forming part of the residue until such time as the extent of the balance has been ascertained

---

[19]   Above, n.12 at 566.

[20]   *Commissioner of Stamp Duties (Queensland) v. Livingston* [1965] A.C. 694 at 712 *per* Viscount Radcliffe cited by Keane J. (as he then was) in *Mohan v. Roche*, above, n.12 at 567 and in *Glesson v. Feehan*, above, n.2 at 537.

[21]   Above, n.2 at 537.

and the executor is in a position either to assent to the vesting of the proceeds of sale of the property comprised in the residue in those entitled or, where appropriate, to vest individual property *in specie* in an individual residuary beneficiary.[22] Until such time as the extent of the residue available to the beneficiaries is ascertained, there is no basis in law for treating them as entitled in equity to any specific item forming part of the estate. Once the residue is ascertained the personal representative may then assent to the vesting of the property in the persons entitled.

12–06 Before the decision of the Supreme Court in *Gleeson v. Feehan* there was some doubt as to the nature of a beneficiary's interest in the estate before the personal representative gave his assent to a vesting as a result of the House of Lords decision *in Cooper v. Cooper*,[23] particularly in the light of the speech of Lord Cairns, and also because *Cooper v. Cooper* was followed by the Irish Court of Appeal in *Gilsenan v. Tevlin*.[24] Lords Cairns had no doubt that the right of a next-of-kin was a right which could be asserted by calling on the administrator to perform his duty, and that the performance of the administrator's duty might require the conversion of the estate into money for the purpose of paying debts and legacies. But he thought that the rule of law which required the conversion of an intestate's estate into money was a rule introduced for the benefit of creditors and for the facility of the next-of-kin, but as regards "substantial proprietorship the right of the next-of-kin remains clear to every item forming the personal estate of the intestate, subject to those paramount claims of creditors."[25] In *Gilsenan v. Tevlin* O'Brien L.C.J. and Fitzgibbon L.J. considered themselves bound by *Cooper v. Cooper* and held that the next-of-kin of an owner of land who died intestate had a clear and tangible interest in the land from the date of death. However, Viscount Radcliffe in giving the advice of the Judicial Committee of the Privy Council in *Commissioner of Stamp Duties (Queensland) v. Livingston*[26] stated that Lord Cairns's speech in *Cooper v. Cooper*

> "cannot possibly be recognised today as containing an authoritative statement of the rights of next-of-kin or residuary legatee in an unadministered estate."

He was of the view that as the whole estate devolved on and vested in the personal representative there was no need to distinguish between the legal and equitable interest in the estate, "any more than there is for the property of a beneficial owner." Keane J. in his judgment for the Supreme Court in *Gleeson v. Feehan* stated that the decision of the Irish Court of Appeal in *Gilsenan v.*

---

[22] *ibid.*
[23] 7 H.L. 53.
[24] [1902] 1 I.R. 514.
[25] *Cooper v. Cooper*, above, n.23 at 64-66.
[26] Above, n.20.

Telvin cannot now be regarded as correctly stating the law in Ireland and over-ruled it and went on to adopt the reasoning of Viscount Radcliffe in *Commissioner of Stamp Duties (Queensland) v. Livingston* as being the correct statement of law on the matter.

ASSENTS WHERE THE PERSONAL REPRESENTATIVE IS A BENEFICIARY

12–07   Section 52(2) of the Succession Act provides that the personal representative may at any time after the death of the deceased execute an assent vesting any estate or interest in land in the person entitled thereto. Where land is concerned an assent "not in writing shall not be effectual to pass any estate or interest in land."[27] The written assent must be signed by the personal representative and will be deemed for the purposes of the Registration of Deeds Act 1707, with respect to priorities, to be a conveyance of that estate or interest from the personal representative to the person entitled.[28] It will also operate to vest the estate or interest in the person entitled subject to such charges and encumbrances as may be specified in the assent and as may otherwise affect that estate or interest.[29] In *Mohan v. Roche*[30] it was observed by Keane J. that there was nothing in the language used in either section 52 or section 53 to suggest "that the draughtsman considered it essential that the personal representative should also execute an assent where he himself was the person entitled to the property, either by reason of bequest or devise in the will or because of the distribution of the estate on intestacy."

12–08   The question as to whether a personal representative who is also a beneficiary must assent to the vesting of property in himself as beneficiary may be answered perhaps by considering why an assent is required for vesting property in a beneficiary in the first place? The main reason why a personal representative must assent to the vesting of property in a beneficiary is because the whole estate of a deceased vests in his personal representative *qua* personal representative and in order for a share in the estate to vest in a beneficiary *qua* beneficiary an assent must be given by the personal representative. It was formerly thought that because the legal interest vested in the personal representative immediately and the beneficial or equitable interest only vested in a beneficiary that an assent was required to vest the legal estate also in the beneficiary. A personal representative by virtue of his capacity acquires rights, powers and duties *qua* capacity to administer and distribute the whole estate of a deceased. One such duty is to pay the lawful debts of the deceased with due diligence having regard to the assets in his hands which are properly

---

[27] Succession Act 1965, s.52(5).
[28] Succession Act 1965, s.53(1).
[29] Succession Act 1965, s.53(1)(d).
[30] Above, n.9 at 565.

applicable for that purpose.[31] A duty of diligence is owed not only to the creditors of the deceased, but also to the beneficiaries, "for the ultimate object of administration of an estate is to place the beneficiaries in possession of their interest, and that cannot be fully achieved unless all debts are satisfied."[32] As the estate of a deceased includes all of his assets and is subject to the payment of debts owing and due by the deceased it would seem that a personal representative who is also a beneficiary cannot claim that such of the assets as were left to him by the deceased are to be excluded from liability for payment of the debts. The overall duty of a personal representative is to administer the whole estate of the deceased in a diligent manner and that where he fails in his duty to the whole estate he may be liable for a *devastavit* by the beneficiaries where he excludes such of the assets as are left to him for payment of the debts of the deceased on the grounds that such assets vested in him without the need to assent to their vesting in himself and therefore not subject to the payment of such debts. However, where all the debts are satisfied the next task for a personal representative is "to place the beneficiaries in possession of their interest" and this is the time when the question of assent arises. In order to the place the beneficiaries in possession of their interests the personal representative must give his assent to the vesting of the interests and the form of assent will depend on the nature of the assets: if the estate or interest is personal property an oral assent will suffice to vest such in a beneficiary, however, if the estate or interest is real property a written assent is required. Thus, it would seem, that the time for giving an assent to the vesting property in the beneficiaries is after a personal representative has carried out what might be called his administrative functions and when it comes to distributing the estate among the beneficiaries. This would also seem to be the moment in time when the question of whether a personal representative who is also a beneficiary must assent to the vesting in himself of the property to which he is entitled as beneficiary.

12–09 The matter was considered by Pennycuick J. in *In Re King's Will Trusts*[33] in relation to the effect of section 36 of the U.K. Administration of Estates Act 1925 which contains provisions similar to the Irish statutory provisions. In the course of his judgment he stated that section 36 presented no difficulty where the person entitled to an interest was someone other than a personal representative. He also mentioned that it was suggested by counsel for the plaintiff that where the personal representative is also entitled in some other capacity, for instance, as trustee of the will, or as beneficiary, "he may come to hold the estate or interest in that other capacity without any written consent."[34] Having reviewed the text of section 36(4) he said that it

---

[31] *Re Tankard: Tankard v. Midland Bank Executor and Trustee Co.*, above, n.4 at 463.
[32] *ibid*.
[33] [1964] Ch. 542.
[34] Above, n.34 at 547–548.

"contemplates that for this purpose a person may by assent vest in himself in another capacity, necessarily implies he is divesting himself of the estate in his original capacity. It seems to me impossible to regard the same operation as lying outside the negative provision contained in the second sentence of the subsection. To do so involves making a distinction between the operation of divesting and vesting the legal estate and that of passing the legal estate. I do not think that this highly artificial distinction is legitimate. On the contrary, the second sentence appears to me to be intended as an exact counterpart to the first."

Keane J. in *Mohan v. Roche*[35] thought that this reasoning was fallacious because it assumed that an assent was necessary to vest the interest in the personal representative so that he may enjoy it in another capacity. When applying the terminology of the "legal" estate and the "beneficial" estate, the position in law, was that both estates were vested in the personal representative from the date of the grant. "Manifestly, if he is not the person to whom the land had been bequeathed or devised by will or he is not entitled to it on a distribution on intestacy, he must execute an assent in writing in order to vest the legal estate in the persons entitled. If he is the person so entitled, then he need never execute an assent, since both the legal and beneficial estates remain vested in him at all times."[36] He went on to say that on the basis of this analysis section 52(5) of the Succession Act never became relevant,

"because it is necessary to 'pass any estate or interest in land' to the person beneficially entitled thereto: the estate or interest is already vested in him."

In *Mohan v. Roche* there was only one personal representative, however, if there is more than one it would seem that the other personal representatives would have to assent to the vesting of the estate or interest in one of their number who is also a beneficiary as they would in the case of other beneficiaries.[37]

12–10   In relation to the distinction made between the "legal" estate vesting in the personal representative and the "beneficial" estate vesting in a beneficiary, Keane J. thought that confusion arose in this area because of an erroneous assumption

"that the law requires the existence at all times of separate legal and equitable interests in property."[38]

He found support for this view in the advice of the Judicial Committee of the Privy Council given by Viscount Radcliffe in *Commissioner of Stamp Duties*

---

[35] Above, n.9 at 566.
[36] *ibid.*
[37] See Succession Act 1965, s.20(1).
[38] Above, n.9 at 566.

(Queensland) v. Livingston[39] when he said it was a mistake to assume that for the purposes

> "and at every moment of time the law requires the separate existence of two different kinds of estate or interest in property, the legal and the equitable. There is no need to make this assumption. When the whole right of property is in a person, as it is in an executor, there is no need to distinguish between the legal and equitable interest in that property, any more than there is for the property of a beneficial owner. What matters is that the court will control the executor in the use of his rights over assets that come to him in that capacity; but it will do it by the enforcement of remedies which do not involve the admission of recognition of equitable rights of property in those assets. Equity in fact calls into existence and protects equitable rights and interests in property only where their recognition has been found to be required in order to give effect to its doctrines."

According to Viscount Radcliffe there is no need to distinguish between the legal and equitable interest because the court will be in a position to control the personal representative in the exercise of his rights over assets that come to him in that capacity and it may do so by the enforcement of remedies without recognising any equitable rights of property in those assets. Keane J. adopting the view of Viscount Radcliffe was of the opinion that the legal estate and the beneficial estate vested in a personal representative from the date of the grant, and although it may be desirable that a personal representative who is also a beneficiary should sign an assent in writing "but that is far from saying that it is a necessary link in title."[40] A personal representative who is also a beneficiary is not required to execute an assent since both the legal and equitable estates remain vested in him at all times. However, Viscount Radcliffe also stated that the court may control the executor in the exercise of his rights over the assets that come to him in that capacity by the enforcement of remedies without recognising any equitable rights of property and this would seem to suggest that although both estates vest in him from the date of the grant, his interest will still be counted as an asset of the estate and used as such for the payment of the debts of the deceased, and indeed, any legal right of a surviving spouse and dependent upon the solvency or insolvency of the estate of the deceased.[41]

12–11 In *Mohan v. Roche*[42] the plaintiff agreed to buy a house from the vendor who was selling as personal representative of Mary Roche who was the widow of Michael Roche to whom the house was conveyed in 1959. Michael Roche died intestate in 1967 and letters of administration intestate were granted to his widow in 1968. By deed of family arrangement in 1969 made between

---

[39] Above, n.20.
[40] Above, n.9 at 567.
[41] See Succession Act 1965, ss.45 and 46.
[42] Above, n.9.

the nine children of Michael Roche and his widow, the nine children "granted released and conveyed" to the widow for natural love and affection their interest in the house. The widow died in 1989 leaving a will appointing the defendant as one of her executors. Probate of the will was granted to the defendant in 1990. The objections and requisitions raised by the purchaser's solicitors included one which stated: "Furnish a written assent registered in the Land Registry of Deeds by the personal representative of any person on the title who died after May 31, 1959." The reply stated: "vendor is selling as personal representative." The purchaser's solicitors assumed that an assent in writing by Mary Roche as personal representative to the vesting of the house in those beneficially entitled, including herself as she was also a beneficiary, would be furnished prior to completion of the sale. However, no such assent had been executed and as a result the purchaser's solicitors refused to close the sale unless title to the house was perfected by obtaining a grant of letters of administration de bonis non to the estate of Michael Roche followed by the execution and registration of the assent in the Registry of Deeds. The vendor's solicitors claimed that no such assent was required. The purchaser sought an order of the court to resolve the matter. The main question to be addressed was whether the fact that no assent was executed by the widow meant that the vendor could not convey the interest in the house. In answer to the question Keane J. held that: "In the present case, once the deed of family arrangement had been executed, there was no other than the widow who could have been entitled to this house. Consequently, there was no need to posit the existence of two different estates, legal and equitable, the first of which could only be vested in the widow by the execution of an assent in writing to satisfy the requirements of subsection 5."[43] He went on to say that it may well be desirable that a personal representative should sign an assent in writing in circumstances similar to those before him but that was far from saying that it was a necessary link in title. Accordingly, he refused to make the declaration sought by the purchaser. Towards the conclusion of his judgment however he emphasised the fact that there was nothing in the language used in the deed of family arrangement to suggest that it was intended "to do any more than vest whatever interest the children were entitled to in the widow." In other words, in no sense could the deed of family arrangement be read as an express or implied assent to the vesting of any interest in the property in the widow.

WHERE REGISTERED LAND IS THE SUBJECT MATTER

12–12   Any assent made by a personal representative in respect of registered land must be in the form required under section 61(3) of the Registration of

---

[43] Above, n.9 at 566–567.

Title Act 1964 as inserted by section 54(1) of the Succession Act. For this purpose an application for registration made by a person who claims by law to be entitled to the land of a deceased registered full owner, must be accompanied by an assent or transfer by the personal representative in the prescribed form, and this will then authorise the Registrar to register such person as full or limited owner of the land, as the case may be.[44] On the determination of the estate or interest of an owner who is registered as limited owner of land pursuant to such assent or transfer, the assent or transfer will, on application being made in the prescribed manner, authorise the Registrar to register, as full or limited owner, as the case may be, the person in whose favour the assent or transfer was made, or the successor in title of that person, as may be appropriate.[45] There is no duty on the Registrar to require information as to why any assent or transfer is or was made and he must assume that the personal representative is or was acting in relation to the application, assent or transfer correctly and *intra vires*.[46]

SUMMARY

12–13   As the whole of the estate of the deceased vests in his personal representative no interest in the estate either legal or equitable vests in the beneficiaries before the personal representative assents to such a vesting. However, where a personal representative is also a beneficiary it is unnecessary for him to assent to the vesting of the interest to which he is entitled as a beneficiary. The form of assent will depend on the nature of the property to which a beneficiary is entitled. Where personal estate is involved an oral assent will be sufficient. However, where land is involved a distinction is made between unregistered and registered land and such a distinction will also determine the form of assent which must be executed. In the case of unregistered land, the assent must be in writing. Where registered land is involved the assent must not only be in writing but it must also be in the form required by section 61(3) of the Registration of Title Act 1964 as inserted by section 54(1) of the Succession Act. As regards the legal right share of the surviving spouse, apparently the need for an assent and the form in which it must be executed will depend on whether the quality of the right will be treated as having the effect of a debt due by the estate or whether it will be viewed as possessing the quality of a testamentary interest: in the case of the former no assent will be required, and in the case of the latter, an assent will be required although the form in which it must be executed will depend on whether the legal right share consists of land or personal estate. It may also be observed that although the

---

[44] Registration of Title Act 1964, s.61(3)(a) as inserted by the Succession Act 1965, s.54.
[45] Registration of Title Act 1964, s.61(3)(b) as inserted by the Succession Act 1965, s.54.
[46] Registration of Title Act 1964, s.61(3)(c) as inserted by the Succession Act 1965, s.54

estate of a deceased may vest in the President of the High Court before a personal representative is appointed in the circumstances as laid down by section 13 of the Succession Act, the President is not empowered to assent to the vesting of estate in beneficiaries. The power of assent, if it may thus be called, is peculiar to the office of personal representative. On a final note, even though a personal representative who is also a beneficiary does not have to assent to the vesting of an interest in himself, this does not mean that his interest is not subject to the discharge of debts owing by the estate as expenses, debts and liabilities of the deceased must first of all be discharged out of the whole estate of the deceased.

CHAPTER 13

The Limitation of Actions in Succession Matters

INTRODUCTION

13–01　Where a person has a right to a share or interest in the estate of a deceased person under a will or on an intestacy, the right to claim such a share or interest will endure only for a specific period of time, and once the time period has elapsed the right to claim such a share or interest will cease to be actionable. The limitation of actions in relation to succession matters is governed mainly by section 126 of the Succession Act although such matters may continue to come within the provisions of the Statute of Limitations 1957 depending on the circumstances of the case which will be seen later. Section 126 provides that:

> "The Statute of Limitations, 1957, is hereby amended by the substitution of the following section for section 45:
>
> 45. (1) Subject to section 71, no action in respect of any claim to the estate of a deceased person or to any share or interest in such estate, whether under a will, on intestacy or under section 111 of the Succession Act, 1965, shall be brought after the expiration of six years from the date when the right to receive the share or interest accrued."

Similar to the other provisions of the Succession Act and in furtherance of the assimilation policy in the Act of real and personal estate, no distinction is made between real and personal estate both types of property comprising the estate of the deceased for the purposes of the limitation of actions. It will be seen also that the causes of action are specified in section 126 and are limited to claims arising under a will, on an intestacy and under section 111 of the Succession Act. It will be observed that the provisions of section 126 include the legal right of a spouse but exclude claims which may be made by the children of a testator under section 117 thus making the time period as specified by that section as amended as the only time period applicable to such claims.[1] Section 126 also excludes any actions based on section 56 of the Act in relation to a spouse's right to require an appropriation of the dwelling and/or household chattels thus the time period specified by section 56 will be the only applicable time for asserting the right of appropriation by a spouse. Sec-

---

[1]　Family Law (Divorce) Act 1996, s.46; See *M.P.D. v. M.D.* [1981] I.L.R.M. 179.

tion 126 is therefore exhaustive as regards the persons who may bring actions as beneficiaries against the estate.

13–02   By virtue of section 13 of the Succession Act where "a person dies intestate, or dies testate but leaving no executor surviving him, his real and personal estate, until administration is granted in respect thereof, shall vest in the President of the High Court who, for this purpose, shall be a corporation sole." Thus, before a grant has been issued in the circumstances laid down in section 13 the estate of the deceased vests in the President of the High Court as "owner" and as such the limitation period of twelve years as prescribed by section 13, of the Statute of Limitations 1957 will commence to run against the President from the date of death of the deceased.[2] However, as can be seen from the provisions of section 13 the estate of the deceased vests in the President only in the absence of an executor and this would appear to suggest that where the deceased leaves an executor surviving him the estate will vest in the executor on his death and thus making applicable to him also the limitation period of twelve years as prescribed by section 13 of the Statute of Limitations 1957.[3] One of the reasons, perhaps, why an executor is excluded from the provisions of section 13 of the 1965 Act is because the High Court has a degree of control over him even before a grant of probate is made as section 16 of the 1965 Act empowers the High Court "to summon any person named as executor in a will to prove or renounce probate." Even though an administrator may also rely on section 13 of the Statute of Limitations and the limitation period of twelve years if the period has run out against the President before a grant is made to him, it will also be deemed to have run out against him and the grant will not revive the limitation period.[4]

13–03   As the right to receive a share or interest in the estate accrues from the date of death of the deceased an action claiming any such share or interest must be brought within six years from the date of death of the deceased. The person against whom such action must be brought is the personal representative of the deceased which means the executor where one is appointed by the will or the person to whom a grant of administration has been made. Thus an action may be brought against an executor within six years of the date of death of the deceased, however, in the case of an administrator, beneficiaries must await the making of a grant to him, and even though his appointment commences from that time, the limitation period will still continue to run from the accrual date, *viz.* the date of death of the deceased. However, this does not mean that persons entitled to receive a share or interest in the estate must anxiously await the appointment of an administrator before moving to protect

---

[2]   *Gleeson v. Feehan* [1997] I.L.R.M. 522.
[3]   See Succession Act 1965, s.10.
[4]   *Gleeson v. Feehan*, above, n.2.

their interests. If the person entitled to apply for a grant is tardy in applying for a grant those entitled to receive a share or interest in the estate may set in motion the citation procedure set out in Order 79, rules 52–58 of the Rules of the Superior Courts citing such person to apply for a grant and his failure to do so will be viewed as a renunciation by him. Where six years have elapsed however from the date of death of the deceased any claim to share or interest in the estate as mentioned in section 126 will be deemed statute-barred. This applies to actions brought *against* an estate. But what of actions brought *by* the estate. The only person entitled to bring an action on behalf of the estate is the personal representative as the whole estate of the deceased vests in him from the date of death in the case of an executor and from the date of the grant in the case of an administrator. It would also appear from the provisions of section 13 of the Succession Act that the President of the High Court may be entitled to bring actions on behalf of the estate as the whole estate vests in him until the appointment of an administrator.[5] However, as section 126 of the Succession Act is exhaustive as regards the persons who may rely on its provisions and it does not include personal representatives, or indeed, the President of the High Court, what limitation periods govern actions brought by personal representatives? This question was first considered by McMahon J. in *Drohan v. Drohan*[6] and he was of the opinion that personal representatives were entitled to rely on section 13 of the Statute of Limitations 1957 which prescribes a period of twelve years within which actions may be brought by personal representatives to recover the land of the deceased. This view was subsequently approved of by the Supreme Court in *Gleeson v. Feehan.*[7] However, as it is not uncommon for a personal representative to be also a beneficiary, a situation may arise where other beneficiaries, because they do not bring their actions within six years, thus rendering their claims statute-barred by section 126, yet the beneficiary who is also the personal representative and in whom the whole estate vests may recover the estate of the deceased after six years for himself as beneficiary also and yet may rely on section 126 to bar the claims of the other beneficiaries. A personal representative who is also a beneficiary will not in his capacity as personal representative be treated as a trustee for the purposes of the Statute of Limitations 1957 unless he is expressly appointed as such.[8]

13–04 Where the limitation period elapses for a personal representative to bring an action on behalf of the estate those in adverse possession of the property will acquire the property rights of the deceased to the land whether they be next-of-kin or strangers. Insofar as next-of-kin are concerned they will ac-

---

[5] See *Gleeson v. Feehan*, above, n.2.
[6] [1984] I.L.R.M. 179.
[7] [1991] I.L.R.M. 783.
[8] Succession Act 1965, s.123(1).

quire such property rights as joint tenants by virtue of section 125 of the Succession Act and any stranger who was also in possession with the next-kin will acquire such rights as joint tenant with the next-of-kin.[9] There was a time when it was doubtful whether next-of-kin in possession acquired a joint tenancy or a tenancy in common because of a distinction made between legal and equitable interests in the estate in relation to claims prior to the Succession Act. However, since the decision of the Supreme Court in *Gleeson v. Feehan*[10] such distinction no longer exists and those in possession will acquire title as joint tenants even in relation to matters arising before the enactment of the Succession Act.[11]

THE LIMITATION PERIOD FOR A BENEFICIARY

13–05   Whenever a limitation period for bringing an action is raised as a defence the facts of the case will determine the matter and a plaintiff who delays in bringing an action may be deprived of a remedy not on the merits of the case but by the simple effluxion of time and of the slow but sure acquisition of his property rights by the defendant. On the other hand, a defendant who relies on a limitation period must do more than simply plead that time is up, he must further show that his possession of the property was adverse to the possession of the plaintiff for the duration of the specified time. The onus of proof is on the defendant to establish that the limitation period has passed. If a defendant is successful he will acquire whatever rights of property the plaintiff had himself or whatever rights of succession he had to the estate of the deceased under a will or on an intestacy or under section 111 of the Succession Act.[12] Although various statutes may alter the time period for bringing an action, the applicability of a time period to a particular case may also depend on the capacity or character of a person relying on a time period, for instance, the time period specified in section 126(1) is limited to those mentioned in the section, and as personal representatives are not included in this amendment to the Statute of Limitations 1957, they may continue to rely on the limitation period of twelve years for the purpose of bringing actions to recover the assets of the deceased.[13] The time period fixed in section 126(1) is six years and those persons who must institute proceedings within that time are those entitled to a share or interest under a will, or on intestacy and spouses entitled to a legal right under section 111 of the Succession Act. However, as a beneficiary may also be a personal representative and because of this dual

---

[9]   *Gleeson v. Feehan*, above, n.2.
[10]   Above, n.2.
[11]   See *Maher v. Maher* [1987] I.L.R.M. 582 at 587–588.
[12]   Succession Act 1965, s.126 (1).
[13]   See Statute of Limitations 1957, s.13.

capacity or character such a person may be able to rely on the greater period of time under the Statute of Limitations to recover property in his capacity as personal representative while automatically recovering it for himself as ben-eficiary.[14] A notable omission from the provisions of section 126(1) are the children of a testator who may apply to the court under section 117 as a result of which the time period for making such applications must be strictly ad-hered to and as specified by section 117 as amended by section 46 of the Family Law (Divorce) Act 1996, *viz.* six months.[15]

13–06　*Rudd v. Rudd*[16] which was decided under a former statute of limita-tions illustrates how a claim of a beneficiary under a will may be dealt with by the court when a limitation period is raised. In that case the testator bequeathed the residue of his estate to trustees to sell his interest in certain lands and also to call in certain sums of money and to invest a sum of £1,800 out of which each of his six daughters was to be paid an equal portion on their marriage or who may require to be paid their share for the purposes of advancement in life. One of the daughters went to Dublin and assisted a friend to carry on a business as a milliner. In 1876, this daughter, who was the plaintiff in the action, wished to acquire her friend's business and instructed her solicitor to demand her share of the sum of £1,800. The share was not paid. In 1885, she "took" a house in Gardiner Street in Dublin and supported herself by taking in lodgers. In 1891, she purchased the house for a sum of £240 which she bor-rowed from friends. She then instituted proceedings claiming her share of the £1,800. Walker C. thought that the pivotal question to be addressed was – Did the plaintiff in 1876 require her portion for the purpose of advancing herself in life? The plaintiff contended that the first time she required her portion for such purpose was in 1891, having then bought the house and borrowed the purchase money. It was further contended that the limitation period did not run from 1876 because a complete contract for the purchase of the business had not been made and the matter was at negotiation stage only, and as a logical consequence, if she had brought her action in 1876, stating the facts and alleging she required her portion to advance herself in life, the action would have been dismissed. Walker C. did not accept this contention and held that she claimed the portion in 1876 because it was then that she instructed her solicitor to demand her share as "the occasion and good opportunity had arisen." He thought that on the facts the right to receive the portion arose in 1876 and the statute began to run from that year, and consequently, the plaintiff's claim was statute-barred.

---

[14] See *Mohan v. Roche* [1991] 1 I.R. 560.
[15] See *M.P.D. v. M.D.*, above, n.1.
[16] [1895] 1 I.R. 15.

13-07 A recent Supreme Court decision illustrates how the courts should approach actions involving intestacies and limitation periods prior to the Succession Act where a number of persons were in adverse possession of land and claimed title to the shares of those who did not lay claim to them within the limitation period. The case was *Gleeson v. Feehan*.[17] In that case one James Dwyer was the registered owner of lands in Co. Tipperary. He died intestate in 1937 leaving a wife and six children surviving. Edmond Dwyer, one of the sons, took possession of the land following the death of his father. The other children left the land either before the intestate's death or shortly afterwards. Edmond Dwyer died a bachelor and without children in 1971. Following his death, Jimmy Dwyer, the illegitimate son of Edmond Dwyer's sister, remained in possession of the land. The land was comprised in Folios No. 11057, No. 3371 and No. 28973 of the Register of Freeholders. Edmond Dwyer was registered as owner in Folio No. 28973 pursuant to a fiat of the Irish Land Commission in 1953. In 1978 Jimmy Dwyer agreed to sell the lands comprised in Folios No. 11057, No. 3371 and No. 28973 to Patrick Purcell. Also in 1978 he agreed to sell the land comprised in Folio No. 28973 to Donal Feehan. The plaintiff was granted letters of administration intestate to the estate of Edmond Dwyer and Jimmy Dwyer in 1983. The plaintiff in his capacity as administrator of the estates of Edmond Dwyer and Jimmy Dwyer instituted ejectment proceedings against Francis Purcell, the son of Patrick Purcell, and Donal Feehan in the Circuit Court. The defendants pleaded in their defence that the plaintiff's claim was statute-barred. In an earlier judgment delivered by the Supreme Court it was held that the plaintiff's claim was not statute-barred.[18] The case was remitted to the Circuit Court where an order was made granting the plaintiff possession of the lands. The defendants, however, appealed to the High Court to determine whether Jimmy Dwyer was entitled to be registered as owner of the lands comprised in the folios to the exclusion of Edmond Dwyer's next-of-kin. All of the parties to the action accepted that Jimmy Dwyer was illegitimate and that he could not have inherited a distributive share in the estates of James Dwyer and Edmond Dwyer. Morris P., by way of case stated, posed the following questions for the Supreme Court:

1. (a) Where, prior to the Succession Act 1965, several next-of-kin in actual occupation of lands of a deceased person acquired title to those lands by adverse possession against the personal representative was the title so acquired the title to which they would have been beneficially entitled on due administration?

    (b) Where such next-of-kin acquired title by adverse possession against

---

[17] Above, n.2.
[18] [1991] I.L.R.M. 783; [1993] 2 I.R. 113.

other persons other than next-of-kin not in occupation, was such title acquired to joint tenants ?

2. Where such next-of-kin in actual occupation shared such occupation with persons other than next-of-kin, was the possession of such other persons adverse against (a) the personal representatives or (b) next-of-kin in occupation ?

3. If the answer to 1(a) is yes, was such title acquired jointly with next-of-kin in occupation as (a) joint tenants or (b) tenants in common ?

13–08   Keane J. (as he then was) in his judgment for the Supreme Court stated that Morris P. in the case stated identified the central issue clearly. It was accepted that had Jimmy Dwyer been in sole possession of the lands for the period of twelve years prior to January 1978, he would clearly have been entitled to be registered as owner of the lands to the exclusion of the next-of-kin of Edmond Dwyer.

13–09   However, it was contended on behalf of the plaintiff, that on the death intestate of the owner of the lands, the beneficial interest vested immediately in the next-of-kin and that any of them who remained on in possession were equitable tenants in common of the land. It was also contended that the land had vested in the six children of James Dwyer to the exclusion of anyone else, whether in possession or otherwise, and because the claims of the other five children were statute-barred, Edmond Dwyer was the sole owner of the l ands at the time of his death and it thereupon devolved on his next-of-kin which did not include Jimmy Dwyer.

13–10   On behalf of the defendants it was submitted that on the death of James Dwyer the lands became vested in the President of the High Court before a grant of letters of administration intestate issued. The next-of-kin acquired no legal or equitable interest on the death of James Dwyer in any particular asset which happened to form part of the estate. In those circumstances, it was urged that the occupation by Edmond Dwyer, or anyone else, was unlawful and could have been restrained by the legal owner, i.e. the President of the High Court. Since Edmond and Jimmy Dwyer had acquired title as disseisors, it followed that they acquired title as joint tenants and on the death of Edmond in 1971, Jimmy Dwyer, as surviving joint tenant, became entitled to the land.

13–11   The question which had first to be addressed was whether the lands comprised in Folios 11057 and 3371 of the Register of Freeholders, County Tipperary, of which James Dwyer was the registered owner, vested in the six children of James Dwyer as equitable tenants in common, and entitled them to one undivided sixth share each, after the deaths of James Dwyer and his wife.

When considering the nature of the interest, if any, of the next-of-kin of James Dwyer in these lands after his death, it did not seem to Keane J.

> "axiomatic that the existence of a beneficial interest in the property, if such was the case, ipso facto carried with it a right to possession of the land."[19]

Keane J. identified the rights of next-of-kin as taking the form of a chose in action for the payment to them of the balance of the estate after the debts of the deceased have been discharged, and that these rights were enforceable against the personal representative. However, it was contrary to elementary legal principles to treat next-of-kin as being the owners in equity of specific items forming part of the estate until such time as the extent of the balance of the estate had been ascertained and the personal representative was in a position to vest the proceeds of sale of the property comprised in the estate in the next-of-kin or, where appropriate, to vest individual property in specie in an individual member of the next-of-kin. Until the estate was ascertained after the discharge of debts and liabilities there was no basis in law for treating them as entitled in equity to any specific item forming part of the estate. He went on to consider the authorities on the matter but seemed most impressed by the decision of Viscount Radcliffe in *Commissioner of Stamp Duties (Queensland) v. Livingston*[20] where it was pointed out that it would be a mistaken assumption

> "that for all purposes and at every moment of time the law requires the separate existence of two different kinds of estate or interest in property, the legal and equitable There is no need to make this assumption. When the whole right of property is in a person, as it is in an executor, there is no need to distinguish between the legal and equitable interest in that property, any more than there is for the property of the full beneficial owner. What matters is that the court will control the executor in the use of his rights over assets that come to him in that capacity; but it will do it by the enforcement of remedies which do not involve the admission or recognition of equitable rights of property in those assets. Equity in fact calls into existence and protects equitable rights and interests in property only where their recognition has been found to be required in order to give effect to its doctrines."

He also referred to the judgment of O'Hanlon J. in *Maher v. Maher*[21] in relation to the kind of interest acquired by those who remained in adverse possession of land when the limitation period expired. O'Hanlon J. stated that:

> "From the death of an intestate the next-of-kin have no right to take possession of any part of the assets until they come to be vested in them by the personal representative. Under section 13 of the Administration of Estates Act 1959 it was provided that where a person died intestate his real and personal estate until

---

[19] Above, n.2 at 529.
[20] [1965] A.C. 694.
[21] [1987] I.L.R.M. 582 at 587-588.

administration was granted in respect thereof, should vest in the President of the High Court in the same manner and to the same extent as formerly in the case of personal estate it vested in the Ordinary. Under section 22 of the same Act it was provided that on the death of a sole registered owner of land the personal representatives of the deceased owner should alone be recognised by the registering authority as having any rights in respect of the land, until an assent in the prescribed form was made available by the personal representative for the purpose of securing the registration of the person named in such assent, as owner. It appears to me that if some of the next-of-kin take possession or remain on in possession of lands of an intestate to the exclusion of others, their possession of the entire interest in the lands is adverse to the claims of the personal representative and of the other next-of-kin and that they should not be regarded as occupying the lands in a different character as to the shares claimed by them in their capacity as next-of-kin and as to the shares of the other next-of-kin and the entitlement of the personal representative which they are in the process of extinguishing. I consider that their occupation was as joint tenants in the entire lands and every interest therein."

O'Hanlon J. was also of the view that the Succession Act 1965 was giving effect to what should always have been the true construction of the situation which arose in the circumstances which have already been referred to. The possession of Edmond Dwyer and Jimmy Dwyer after the deaths of James and Mary Dwyer was adverse to the title of the true owner, *i.e.* the President of the High Court. It was conceded that on behalf of the plaintiff that in the event of Edmond and Jimmy Dwyer being regarded in adverse possession during the limitation period they would have acquired title to the lands as joint tenants and not as tenants in common and that, accordingly, the interest of Edmond Dwyer in the lands would have devolved by survivorship on his death on Jimmy Dwyer. It was clear that at the end of the limitation period no persons other than Edmond and Jimmy Dwyer were entitled to an interest in the lands. As a result no estate or interest in the lands could thereafter be vested in the next-of-kin whether in or out of possession, by anyone.

13–12   Thus, whether before or after the commencement of the Succession Act, in the case of an intestacy where a number of persons are in possession adverse to next-of-kin not in possession, they will become entitled to the land as joint tenants after the limitation period has run out against the President of the High Court, and such persons in adverse possession will acquire the whole estate as joint tenants without any distinction being made between the legal estate and the equitable estate and the later appointment of a personal representative will not revive the title to the land.

THE LIMITATION PERIOD FOR A PERSONAL REPRESENTATIVE

13–13   It will be observed from the text of section 126(1) that, although an action in respect of any claim to the estate of a deceased person or to any share or interest in such estate, whether under a will, on intestacy or under section 111 of the Succession Act, cannot be brought after the expiration of six years from the date when the right to receive the share or interest accrued, it does not mention that the same period is applicable to the personal representative of a deceased who may also institute proceedings to recover the estate of the deceased held adversely either by a beneficiary or by a stranger to the estate. The time period within which a personal representative must institute proceedings, especially in relation to land, is that as specified by section 13(2)(a) of the Statute of Limitations 1957. Section 13(2)(a) of the 1957 Act provides that:

> "no action shall be brought after the expiration of twelve years from the date on which the right of action accrued to the person bringing it or, if it first accrued to some person through whom he claims to that person."

Among such persons who may rely on the twelve year period in section 13(2)(a) is the personal representative of a deceased person.[22]

13-14   The question as to whether the personal representative of a deceased was entitled to rely on the twelve year period in section 13(2)(a) of the 1957 Act for actions to recover the estate of a deceased was first considered by McMahon J. in *Drohan v. Drohan*.[23] In that case the deceased was the registered owner of freehold land. He died intestate and a grant of letters of administration intestate was made to his son, the plaintiff in the action. The defendant was the widow of another of the deceased's sons who was in possession of the land. The plaintiff issued a civil bill in the Circuit Court claiming to be entitled as personal representative to recover possession of the land from the defendant. The defendant pleaded that the plaintiff's action was statute-barred under section 126(1) of the Succession Act 1965 which prescribed that an action must be brought within a period of six years. The plaintiff, however, placed reliance on section 13(2)(a) of the Statute of Limitations 1957 which allowed for a twelve-year period to elapse before an action became statute-barred. McMahon J., in the course of his judgment, was of the view that section 126 (1) of the Succession Act which amended section 45(1) of the Statute of Limitations 1957 was not applicable to the plaintiff's claim and for support referred to a similar English provision found in section 20 of the Limitation Act 1939 and an interpretation of that provision by the Court of Appeal in *Diplock v. Wintle*[24] and which was affirmed by the House of Lords *sub nomine Ministry of Health v. Simpson*.[25] In section 45(1) as inserted by section 126(1)

---

[22] *Drohan v. Drohan*, above, n.6; *Gleeson v. Feehan*, above, n.7.
[23] Above, n.6.
[24] [1948] Ch. 465 at 509 *et seq.*
[25] [1951] A.C. 251.

and section 20 of the Limitation Act 1939 the claims barred were those in respect of a share or interest in the estate of the deceased whether under a will or on intestacy. It was held in Diplock v. Wintle that the words of section 20 of the 1939 Act had the effect of also including a claim by an unpaid beneficiary against one who has been overpaid or wrongly paid, and not only against an executor or administrator for the payment of a legacy or a share in the estate. However, actions instituted *by* a personal representative on behalf of the estate were not governed by the provision. Approving of *Diplock v. Wintle* McMahon J. was also of the view that section 45(1) as inserted by section 126(1) did not apply to an action brought *by* a personal representative to recover assets of the deceased from a person who was either a beneficiary or a stranger holding land adversely to the estate. Accordingly, he found that the plaintiff as personal representative of the estate of the deceased was entitled to rely on section 13(2)(a) and the limitation period of twelve years within which to recover the land and his claim against defendant was therefore not statute-barred.

13–15 A similar question in relation to the applicable limitation period also arose on appeal to the Supreme Court in *Gleeson v. Feehan*.[26] The facts of that case were the same as those in *Gleeson v. Feehan* decided by the Supreme Court in 1997[27] but involving different issues. In the 1997 case the Supreme Court was asked to determine whether Jimmy Dwyer was entitled to registered as owner of the lands comprised in the folios; in the 1991 case the Supreme Court was asked to determine the correct limitation period which was applicable. In the 1991 case the plaintiff was the personal representative of James Dwyer who died intestate on November 27, 1937. The deceased was the registered owner of freehold lands comprised in Folios 11057 and 3371 of the Register of Freeholders for Co. Tipperary. The plaintiff was also the personal representative of the deceased's son, Edmond Dwyer, who died intestate on October 22, 1971 and who was the registered of freehold lands comprised in Folio 28973 of the Register of Freeholders for the same county. Edmond Dwyer was the only member of the James Dwyer's immediate family to be in possession of the lands comprised in the folios. Jimmy Dwyer, an illegitimate child of one Edmond Dwyer's sisters, also went into possession of the lands with him. Jimmy Dwyer remained on in possession of the lands after the death of Edmond Dwyer and subsequently sold the lands comprised in Folios 11057 and 3371 to the predecessor in title of the second-named defendant in 1975 and sold the lands comprised in Folio 28973 to the first-named defendant in 1978. The plaintiff, as personal representative of James Dwyer and Edmond Dwyer, instituted ejectment proceedings against the defendants in 1983 in the

---

[26] Above, n.7.
[27] Above, n.2.

Circuit Court. The Circuit Court held that the plaintiff's claim was statute-barred and on appeal to the High Court a case was stated by Barron J. for the opinion of the Supreme Court pursuant to section 38(3) of the Courts of Justice Act 1936. The question raised in the case stated was whether section 45(1) of the Statute of Limitations as inserted by section 126(1) of the Succession Act 1965 which provided for a limitation period of six years barred the plaintiff's action taken in his capacity as personal representative from recovering the lands from the defendant.

13–16 The defendants submitted that if the plaintiff was allowed to rely on the twelve-year limitation period prescribed by section 13(2)(a) of the Statute of Limitations 1957 it would create a major anomaly and work an injustice. The anomaly and injustice arose because the next-of-kin of James and Edmond Dwyer were clearly statute-barred in their claims against the personal representative six years after their deaths, and although the personal representative had a discretion which allowed him to admit their claims, he was not bound to do so. It was on this basis that it would be unjust and open in other cases to abuse, to revive artificially a claim in respect of these lands which the next-of-kin could not assert by obtaining a grant of administration. They also submitted that the decision of McMahon J. in *Drohan v. Drohan*[28] allowing a personal representative to rely on the twelve-year limitation period under section 13(2)(a) when bringing an action to recover an estate was *obiter* only.

13–17 The plaintiff submitted that the provisions of section 45(1) of the Statute of Limitations 1957 as inserted by section 126(1) of the Succession Act 1965 did not apply to a claim by a personal representative in succession to a deceased owner of land for the recovery of possession of the land from a stranger. A claim by a person representative in such circumstances was governed by section 13(2)(a) of the 1957 Act. It was also submitted that the decision of McMahon J. in *Drohan v. Drohan* was not *obiter* but correct in point of law.

13–18 Finlay C.J. in the course of his judgment thought it was first necessary to classify the type of action which arose in the case. He classified it as an action to recover land and the title relied on was the title of the personal representative of a deceased registered owner claiming to be entitled to recover the lands of the deceased. Having thus classified it he was satisfied that it was a type of action that could be brought under section 45(1) of the Statute of Limitations 1957 as inserted by section 126(1) of the Succession Act 1965 and that the "plain and ordinary" meaning of section meant that those beneficially entitled could call upon a personal representative to give them their beneficial

---

[28] Above, n.6.

share or interest in the estate. The section does not, however, apply to an action taken by a personal representative against a stranger. In his view the decision of McMahon J. in *Drohan v. Drohan* was correct. He also considered that *Diplock v. Wintle sub nomine Ministry of Health v. Simpson*[29] which was referred to by McMahon J. in *Drohan v. Drohan* did not cover a claim brought by a personal representative of a deceased owner against a stranger in adverse possession of a deceased owner's lands. Any consideration of the provisions of section 13(2)(a) of the Statute of Limitations 1957 showed that they fitted precisely the form of action which was in question in the case before him. It was an action brought not by a person to whom it first accrued but rather by a person who claimed through the person to whom the action first accrued. Finlay C.J. was also satisfied

> "that no anomaly which could be said to occur could justify the interpretation of the sections otherwise than to make applicable to this cause of action s.13 (2) of the Act of 1957."[30]

He therefore answered the case stated by Barron J. in the negative. McCarthy J. in his judgment, while adopting the observations of Finlay C.J., went on to state that he did not understand *Drohan v. Drohan* to hold that section 45(1) of the Statute of Limitations as inserted by section 126(1) of the Succession Act 1965 included a claim by a personal representative against a stranger in wrongful possession. He found that the view expressed by Professor Brady in his *Succession Law in Ireland* at para. 10.23.2 summed up correctly the effect of the section when he said that the section in neither its original form nor amended form had any application to an action by a personal representative to recover assets of a deceased person from a person holding adversely to the estate, and was confined in its application only to actions against a personal representative by those entitled to share in the estate.[31] O'Flaherty J. rested his judgment on the basis that section 13 of the 1957 Act was clearly applicable to the case. He found that the language of section 45 as inserted by section 126 was inappropriate to bar claims *by* personal representatives to the estates of deceased persons. Egan J. was of the view that the decision of McMahon J. in *Drohan v. Drohan* was not "truly" *obiter*. He also considered the effect of the decision in *Diplock v. Wintle sub nomine Ministry of Health v. Simpson* more fully than McMahon J. did in *Drohan v. Drohan* and thought that it was really an authority "for the proposition that the section is not solely applicable to claims against a personal representative."[32] It is applicable to a claim by a beneficiary directly against a person who had wrongly been paid or wrongly received that to which the claimant was entitled.

---

[29] Above, nn.24 and 25.
[30] Above, n.18 at 789.
[31] See above, n.18 at 790.
[32] See above, n.18 at 796.

"Subject to this and having regard to the words 'whether under a will, on intestacy or under s.111 of the Succession Act 1965' it seems to me that section 45 of the Statute of Limitations 1957 (as amended) only applies to claims against a personal representative and has no application to a claim by a personal representative. The limitation which applies in the present case is the period of twelve years provided by section 13(2) of the Act of 1957 for claims for the recovery of land."[33]

Egan J. also answered the case stated by Barron J. in the negative.

THE INTEREST OF NEXT-OF-KIN IN POSSESSION

13–19   The interest of the next-of-kin in possession of land before a grant of administration has been issued was considered in-depth by Keane J. in his judgment for the Supreme Court in *Gleeson v. Purcell*.[34] The rationale underlying his judgment was based on the assumption that the deceased's whole estate vested in the personal representative after the issuing of a grant of administration. Consequently, no distinction between the legal and equitable interest was necessary, or indeed possible, as the whole estate, both legal and equitable, became vested in the personal representative. Thus no interest, either legal or equitable, vested in the next-of-kin before distribution by the personal representative. Before a grant issued to the personal representative, and as to allow no gap in the seisen, the whole estate of the deceased vested in the President of the High Court, as owner.[35] Therefore, if next-of-kin were either in possession of the estate already or subsequently went into possession, before the issuing of the grant, the limitation period began to run from the date of death of the deceased and against the President of the High Court. If those in possession held the property for twelve years from the date of death they would have acquired whatever title the deceased had to the property, as joint tenants. However, there were conflicting lines of authority concerning the nature of the interest which arose upon the death of the deceased. Earlier Irish decisions followed the House of Lords decision in *Cooper v. Cooper*,[36] while the English courts tended to follow the later House of Lords decisions in *Lord Sudeley v. Attorney General*[37] and *Dr. Barnardo's Homes v. Special Income Tax Commissioners*.[38] *Cooper v. Cooper* decided that the next-of-kin acquired a defined and tangible interest in specified property, and this decision was followed by the Irish Court of Appeal in *Gilsenan v. Tevlin*[39] and

---

[33] Above, n.18 at 796.
[34] Above, n.2.
[35] See Succession Act 1965, s.13.
[36] 7 H.L. 53.
[37] [1897] A.C. 11.
[38] [1921] 2 A.C. 1.
[39] [1902] 1 I.R. 514.

Palles C.B. in *Martin v. Kearney*.[40] Palles C.B. in *Martin v. Kearney* was of the view that next-of-kin in possession before the grant acquired rights as equitable tenants in common. *Lord Sudeley* and *Dr. Barnardo* decided that no beneficial interest in any item of property real or personal vested in them at the date of death of the deceased. Viscount Radcliffe in *Commissioner of Stamp Duties (Queensland) v. Livingston*[41] followed *Lord Sudeley v. Attorney General* and *Dr. Barnardo's Homes v. Special Income Tax Commissioners* and held that no property either legal or equitable vested in the next-of-kin from the date of death of the deceased. Keane J. approved of and followed the reasoning of Viscount Radcliffe and went on to hold that as no interest either legal or equitable vested in the next-of-kin those next-of-kin who were in adverse possession of the property for twelve years acquired title to it as joint tenants. O'Hanlon J. in an earlier High Court decision[42] came to the same conclusion without however relying on *Livingston* for support, and even though conscious of the fact that he was going against the weight of earlier authority on the matter in holding that next-of-kin held as joint tenants, and not as tenants in common, remarked that any doubts on the matter were ultimately resolved for the future by the provisions of section 125(1) of the Succession Act which provided that such persons held the property as joint tenants.

13–20 Before considering the authorities on the matter Keane J. made two preliminary observations. First, he thought it incongruous for a child who stays in possession of the family home when every other member of the family has left to be treated as a trespasser notwithstanding that in strict legal theory a person who occupies land adversely to another is viewed as a trespasser. Secondly, the nature of the interest of next-of-kin in the estate after the death of an intestate even if it took the form of a beneficial interest did not ipso facto carry with it a right to possession of land. The first authority he considered was *Martin v. Kearney*[43] which he described as the "sheet anchor" of the plaintiff's case. In that case, the plaintiff was one of four children who were in possession of a farm after their father's death, the other three children having died before the proceedings were instituted. The plaintiff claimed to be entitled to the entire farm as a surviving joint tenant. The defendant was his sister who had left the farm on her marriage before the father's death and had returned to it with her son at the request of the plaintiff's brother shortly before his death. Palles C.B. held that the plaintiff was entitled to no more than a one-fourth share in the farm as tenant in common, even though he could have followed a decision by Ross J. in *Coyle v. McFadden*[44] who held that next-of-

---

[40] 36 I.L.T.R. 117.
[41] Above, n.20.
[42] *Maher v. Maher*, above, n.11.
[43] Above, n.40.
[44] [1901] 1 I.R. 298.

kin in possession in such circumstances acquired a possessory title as joint tenants. Palles C.B. was of the view that next-of-kin remaining in possession before a grant intestate issued were equitable tenants in common under a good equitable title, and were not trespassers, and that when the limitation period ran out their equitable tenancy in common became a legal estate in common; he formed this view based on a decision of the House of Lords in *Cooper v. Cooper*.[45] In that case the testator left property called Pain's Hill in Surrey, together with personal property to trustees on trust after the death of his widow to sell and to hold the proceeds with his other property in trust for any one of his children in such form and manner as his widow, before a certain fixed period, should appoint. He died leaving three sons, W.H., R.E. and F.J. Before the expiration of the fixed period the widow executed a deed by which, after disposing of the other property, she directed the proceeds of Pain's Hill to be divided equally among the three sons. The deed reserved to her a power of revocation. She afterwards made a will, apparently under the impression that she still had power to dispose of Pain's Hill, under which she gave the property to W.H., the eldest son, and then by different successive codicils, gave benefits to the other two sons and a special legacy to each of the two children of R.E. (the only one of the three sons of the original testator who had married). R.E. died intestate before his mother. On his mother's death a suit was instituted in which it was declared that, so far as the estate of Pain's Hill was concerned, her will was inoperative, since it could only speak from the date of her death and therefore purportedly came into operation long after the expiration of the period fixed for the making of the appointment. The eldest son, W.H., then filed a bill to compel the two children of R.E. and his youngest brother, F.J., to elect between their claims under the deed of appointment and under the will and codicils. F.J. submitted; the two children of R.E. resisted. In the course of his speech the interest acquired by the next-of-kin in the estate of an intestate was described by Lord Cairns as a defined and tangible interest in specified property and this view was not dissented from by any of the other law lords. He said:

> "My Lords, it was very much pressed on your Lordships in the extremely able argument we heard at the bar from the counsel for the appellants, that the interest of a next-of-kin in the estate of an intestate is undefined and intangible interest, that it is a right merely to have the estate converted into money and to receive a payment in money after the debts and expenses have been discharged. My Lords, no doubt the right of a next-of-kin is a right, which can only be asserted by calling upon the administrator to perform his duty, and the performance of the duty of the administrator may require the conversion of the estate into money for the purpose of paying debts and legatees. But I apprehend that the rule of law, or the rule laid down by statute, which requires conversion of an intestate's estate into money, is a rule introduced simply for the benefit of credi-

---

[45] Above, n.36.

tors, and for the facility of division among the next-of-kin, the estate is to be turned into money, but as regards substantial proprietorship the right of the next-of-kin remains clear to every item forming the personal estate of the intestate, subject only to those paramount claims of creditors."[46]

13–21 However, in a later decision of the House of Lords, *Lord Sudeley v. Attorney General*,[47] it was held unanimously that a widow had no right to claim a share of any particular assets of the estate in specie and that she could only call on the executors to administer in due course and claim her share of the residue when finally ascertained. In that case the issue was as to whether probate duty was payable on the value of mortgages of property in New Zealand. The testator left one quarter of his residuary estate to his widow but did not specifically dispose of the mortgages in the will. The widow died domiciled in England before the administration of her husband's estate had been completed. It was claimed by her executors that the value of these mortgages should not be taken into account for the purpose of ascertaining the duty. Lord Herschell in the course of his speech said:

> "I do not think that they (the executors) have any estate, right, or interest, legal or equitable in these New Zealand mortgages so as to make them an asset to her estate."

The decision in *Lord Sudeley v. Attorney General* was followed by the House of Lords in *Doctor Barnardo's Home v. Special Income Tax Commissioners*.[48] In *Vanneck v. Benham*[49] Younger J. in the course of his judgment found it difficult to arrive at a distinction between *Cooper v. Cooper* and *Lord Sudeley* which he thought at first sight seemed to be in conflict. However, the distinction, as it appeared to him, was that an interest in an intestate's estate was sufficiently specific to raise a case of election representing as that interest does all the money's worth of the property comprised therein, but that such interest was not sufficiently specific apart from agreement of the next-of-kin to enable any one of the next-of-kin to say to the administrator 'This or that thing is mine. Hand it over to me.' This resolution of the conflict between the two decisions was later approved of by Evershed M.R. in *In Re Cunliffe-Owen*.[50]

13–22 In *Commissioner of Stamp Duties (Queensland) v. Livingston*[51] Viscount Radcliffe, when giving the advice of the Judicial Committee of the Privy Council, referred to Lord Cairns' speech in *Cooper v. Cooper* and stated that it:

---

[46] Above, n.36 at 64–66.
[47] Above, n.37.
[48] Above, n.38.
[49] [1917] 1 Ch. 60.
[50] [1953] 1 Ch. 545.
[51] Above, n.20.

> "cannot possibly be recognised today as containing an authoritative statement
> of the rights of next-of-kin or residuary legatee in an unadministered estate. His
> language is picturesque but inexact; and while it was no doubt sufficient to
> enforce the point with which he was concerned to deal, a beneficiary's right or
> duty of election, and the decision of the case remains an authority on that point,
> it would be idle to try to set it up as an exposition of the general law in opposi-
> tion to what was said and laid down in the *Sudeley* and *Barnardo* cases."

In that case the testator who died domiciled in New South Wales left his real
estate and the residue of his personal estate to his executors and trustees, of
whom his widow was one, on trust as to one-third for his widow absolutely.
His assets consisted of real and personal estate in both New South Wales and
Queensland. The widow died intestate, domiciled and resident in New South
Wales. The testator's estate was at the date of her death still in the course of
administration, no clear residue had been ascertained, and consequently no
final balance payable or attributable to the shares of residuary beneficiaries
had been determined. On a claim by the appellant, the Commissioner of Stamp
Duties (Queensland), under the relevant revenue legislation, that the respondent as administrator of the estate of the widow, or alternatively, as one of the
next-of-kin, was liable to pay duty in respect of her share of the Queensland
assets on the ground that her death conferred a succession on those becoming
entitled to her estate, it was held that no beneficial interest in any item of the
testator's property in Queensland, real or personal, belonged to his widow at
the date of her death and duty was therefore not exigible. In that case Viscount
Radcliffe pointed out that it was no answer to say that the beneficial interest in
the property must reside somewhere during the course of administration and
that, since the administrator is not beneficially entitled it must reside in the
next-of-kin. He thought that the dilemma was founded on a fallacy,

> "for it assumes mistakenly that for all purposes and at every moment of time the
> law requires the separate existence of two different kinds of estate or interest in
> property, the legal and equitable. There is no need to make this assumption.
> Where the whole right of property is in a person, as it is in an executor, there is
> no need to distinguish between the legal and equitable interest in that property,
> any more than there is for property of the full beneficial owner. What matters is
> that the court will control the executor in the use of his rights over assets that
> come to him in that capacity; but it will do it by the enforcement of remedies
> which do not involve the admission or recognition of equitable rights of prop-
> erty in those assets."

Keane J. was of the opinion that it could not plausibly be contended that the
Succession Act had brought about a wholly different result in Ireland from
that arrived at by the English decisions in *Lord Sudeley v. Attorney General*,[52]
Dr. Barnardo's Homes v. Special Income Tax Commissioners[53] and *Commis-*

---

[52] Above, n.37.
[53] Above, n.38.

sioner of Stamp Duties (Queensland) v. Livingston.[54] He also approved of the approach adopted by O'Hanlon J. in *Maher v. Maher*[55] even though Livingston was not cited in that case. He then went on to overrule the earlier Irish decisions on the matter. Therefore, prior to the Succession Act, next-of-kin in adverse possession of property against a personal representative did not acquire the title to which they would have been beneficially entitled in due course of administration, *viz.* as tenants in common. Where the next-of-kin shared occupation with other persons, the possession of such other persons would also be adverse to the personal representative though not against the next-of-kin who do not go into possession, and upon the expiration of the limitation period the next-of-kin and such other persons in occupation with them acquired title as joint tenants and not as tenants in common.

THE ROLE OF THE PRESIDENT OF THE HIGH COURT

13–23 Section 13 of the Succession Act provides that where a person dies intestate, or dies testate but leaving no executor surviving him, his real and personal estate, until administration is granted in respect thereof, shall vest in the President of the High Court who, for this purpose, shall be a corporation sole. Under section 13 of the Administration of Estates Act 1959 it was provided that where a person died intestate his real and personal estate until administration was granted in respect thereof, should vest in the President of the High Court in the same manner and to the same extent as formerly in the case of personal estate it vested in the Ordinary. Thus under section 13 of the 1959 Act the President of the High Court acquired a role only in the case of an intestacy, while under section 13 of the 1965 Act he acquired a role not only in the case of an intestacy but also in the case of a person who dies leaving a will but leaves no executor surviving him. Under section 13 of the 1965 Act the President will be treated as a corporation sole for this purpose and as such might be viewed as occupying a similar position to an Ordinary before the 1959 Act and as Ordinary meaning a bishop and *qua* bishop a corporation sole. His role only endures under both Acts until administration is granted. However, until that time the whole estate of a deceased becomes vested in him and as such he has a right to bring an action to recover the property of the deceased. If the property is real estate he has twelve years within which to institute proceedings and if he fails to do so those persons who are in possession of it may acquire whatever title the deceased had to the land. It may happen that when the limitation period has commenced to run a grant may be made to the person entitled under the Rules of the Superior Courts and where such is the case the land then becomes vested in the person to whom the grant

---

[54] Above, n.20.
[55] Above, n.11.

is made and who may as personal representative bring an action to eject those in possession of the land within the specified period of limitation. However, if the limitation period has run out against the President, the issuing of a grant will not revive any statute-barred claim. In other words, if the limitation period has expired against the President, it will also be deemed to have expired against a personal representative.[56] The President cannot be treated as a personal representative as a grant of administration would be required to make him so, however, the estate of a deceased still vests in him and gives him rights of ownership which may require protection, and accordingly, the section in the 1959 Act and the 1965 Act would seem to confer on him an active role where the property rights of the estate require protection, otherwise his position would be merely *otium cum dignitate.*

SUMMARY

13–24 By section 126 of the Succession Act which amends section 45 of the Statute of Limitations 1957 no action in respect of any claim to the estate of the deceased or to any share or interest in such estate, whether under a will, on intestacy or in relation to the legal right share of a spouse, may be brought after the expiration of six years from the date when the right to receive the share or interest accrued. It can be seen that notable exclusions from section 126 are the children of a testator making section 117 applications, the personal representative of the deceased and the President of the High Court who may all be involved one way or the other in the estate of a deceased person. Therefore, children making applications under section 117 must do so within the strict time limits prescribed for making such applications, personal representatives by virtue of their exclusion from section 126 will continue to be governed by the Statute of Limitations and will have twelve years within which to recover the estate of the deceased, and while that the President of the High Court might be thought an unlikely subject for section 126 the role of 'owner' of the estate given to him by section 13 until the appointment of a personal representative renders him also subject to the limitation of actions and thus placing a time limit of twelve years within which action must be taken to recover estate and upon the effluxion of twelve years title will be lost regardless of the fact that a personal representative is subsequently appointed.

13–25 As the whole of the estate of the deceased vests in the personal representative no distinction will be made between the legal and equitable estate for the purposes of the limitation of actions and where time has run out against the President of the High Court or the personal representative those in adverse

---

[56] Above, n.2 at 540.

possession will become entitled to the estate as joint tenants, and not as tenants in common, whether before or after the enactment of the Succession Act. Furthermore, right or interests arising on intestacy or arising out of the residuary estate in the case of a will will not become ascertainable until the expenses, debts and liabilities of the deceased have been discharged and until that time such rights or interests will be treated as choses in action enforceable against the personal representative.

CHAPTER 14

Settled Meanings?

INTRODUCTION

14–01 Where certain everyday words are used in wills, for instance, like the word 'money', the meaning attached to them by the court would seem to depend on the context in which they are used in the will and on whether or not the will was professionally prepared. Where a will is professionally prepared it will be presumed that, where words like 'money' are used, a strict legal meaning was intended unless the context indicates otherwise. On the other hand, where a will was prepared by the testator himself in the form of a holograph the court will not presume that a strict legal meaning was intended and may extend the meaning to include the popular meaning of the word and interpret the word in this way having regard to the context in which it is used and the surrounding circumstances of the case.[1] The meanings applied to words will be that which was intended by the testator in the context of his will and this will be sufficient to rebut the presumption of a strict legal meaning.

14–02 Where the word 'property' is used in a legal setting its meaning will depend on the nature of the property referred to. Where land is referred to it will be classified as 'real property' or 'realty' and all other property will be classified as 'personal property' or 'personalty'. Where real property is left in a will it will be known as a 'devise', and personal property will take the form of a 'legacy' or a 'bequest'. A further distinction is made between specific devises and legacies and residuary devises and legacies. Specific devises and legacies usually present no difficulty as to the subject matter intended and even though a legacy may be subject to accretion this will not affect its validity.[2] However, some difficulty may arise in the case of the residuary estate where a residuary legatee only is named and in ascertaining the extent of the property to which he is entitled. The use of the term residuary legatee only would appear to make a distinction between real and personal property and the *prima facie* meaning given to the term is that such a legatee will take only the residue of the personal property.[3] Any residual real property will then be distributed on a partial intestacy.

---

[1] *Re Jennings: Caldbeck v. Stafford and Lindemere* [1930] I.R. 196; *Re Moore: Taylor v. Sheering* [1947] I.R. 205.

[2] *Re Faris: Goodard v. Overend* [1911] 1 I.R. 165.

[3] *Singleton v. Tomlinson* 3 A.C. 404 at 417 *per* Lord Cairns; *Re Hogg* [1944] I.R. 244.

14–03 The use of the word 'issue' in a will, when not constrained by the context, comprehends objects of every degree, and includes children, grandchildren and even remoter issue, and anyone contending a narrower meaning by reference to the context must prove it.[4] 'Issue' may also be distinguished from 'children', 'issue' meaning all children, legitimate and, since the enactment of The Status of Children Act 1987, illegitimate children, and also, perhaps, adopted children because section 3 (2) (a) of the 1987 Act provides that an adopted person will be deemed from the date of the adoption order to be the child of the adopter or adopters and not the child of any other person or persons. Prior to the 1987 Act adopted children were not deemed issue.[5] Where the phrase 'dying without issue' is used in a will it will be taken to mean, unless a contrary intention appears, as a reference to the contingency of a person dying without issue during the lifetime of the testator, for otherwise it is not a contingency at all, but a certainty.[6]

14–04 Thus where certain words and phrases are used in a will the settled meanings will be applied to them especially in the case of a professionally prepared will as settled meanings will be presumed to have been intended by the testator. Where the will is prepared by the testator himself the court may apply the popular meaning of a phrase or word if the context of the will and circumstances of case indicates that such was intended by the testator. Although even where a will is professionally prepared the court may not apply a settled meaning if this would lead "to some absurdity or some repugnance or inconsistency with the rest of the will."[7]

THE MEANING OF "MONEY"

14–05 The meaning of the word 'money' when used in a will was very comprehensively considered by Meredith J. In *re Jennings: Caldbeck v. Stafford and Lindemere*.[8] In that case the testatrix's property consisted of cash in a current account and in a deposit account, money due to her in the form of a pension as the widow of an army officer, stocks and shares, leasehold and freehold properties. Her will provided as follows:

> "I wish my granddaughter, B.K.M.L., to have use of all my money for her lifetime. I now revoke all former wills."

---

[4] *Berry v. Fisher* [1903] 1 I.R. 484.

[5] *Re Stamp: Stamp v. Redmond* [1993] I.L.R.M. 383; *Re Patterson, Deceased: Dunlop v. Greer* [1899] 1 I.R. 324.

[6] *Mulhern v. Brennan*, unreported, High Court, May 26, 1998, McCracken J.; Succession Act 1965, s.95; See also *Re Stamp: Stamp v. Redmond*, above, n.5.

[7] *Re Jennings: Caldbeck v. Stafford and Lindemere*, above, n.1 at 204.

[8] Above, n.1.

14–06   A question arose as to the meaning of the word 'money' in the context of her will. It was argued on behalf of the next-of-kin that the word 'money' must, according to the long line of authorities, be construed in the strict legal sense of cash in hand or cash in a bank. On the other hand, it was argued on behalf of the granddaughter that there was sufficient context to show that the word should be interpreted in the extended or derivative sense. Before considering the authorities on the matter, Meredith J. thought that in a will in which legal phraseology is not adopted and that the word 'money' is not used in the strict legal sense, it would be illogical for the court to look for another technical legal distinction, such as that between real and personal property, and to suppose that the testator had that distinction in mind. "Money in the sense of personal estate is not money in a sense that is either legal or popular." Where a testator has not resorted to the strict legal sense, the logical course is to look for an ordinary popular sense in which the word may be presumed to have been used. The strict legal sense of the word 'money' will be viewed as the primary meaning of the word and the popular sense as an extended and well-recognised derivative sense. Meredith J. identified the primary sense by referring to the Oxford Dictionary as being

> "current coin: metal stamped in pieces in portable form as a medium of exchange and measure of value,"

and the derivative sense as being

> "coin considered In reference to its value or purchasing power; hence, property or possessions of any kind viewed as convertible into money or having value expressible in terms of money."

However, the contest between the primary and a well-recognised derivative sense of a word can hardly be said to be one between a right and a wrong use. Where a decision is one as to the sense in which a layman in a layman's will has used a common word it would be amiss if the interpretation put on the word by the court is one which laymen would view as sheer nonsense. Nevertheless, the reluctance of the courts in a number of cases to depart from the primary sense was due to the difficulty of putting precise limits on the extended or derivative sense of the word. It was said by Turner L.J. in *Lowe v. Thomas* [9] that:

> "If we deviate from the correct meaning of the words which the testatrix has used, we are immediately involved in the difficulty of deciding how far the deviation is to be carried."

However, the result of reconciling the authorities on the matter would seem to be:

> "The primary meaning of the word 'money' is the strict legal meaning in the

---

[9]   5 De G.M. & G. 315 at 318.

sense that it is the meaning adopted by lawyers in drafting legal documents, and it is the meaning in which the word must be taken to have been used in any document which the Court holds is a document that should be presumed to adopt legal language, unless such a construction leads 'to some absurdity or some repugnance or inconsistency with the rest of the instrument'. But in the case of a layman's will there is no presumption that the word "money" has been used in the clear and unambiguous sense in which it is used by lawyers, and the Court may look at once both to the context and to the surrounding circumstances without being compelled before doing so to find some pretext or justification in the context alone. If, however, the result of such a complete survey is entirely negative, then the Court, which must make a selection on some ground, can do nothing but decide in favour of the primary or legal meaning, and is at least a reason."[10]

In the case of *In re Cadogan: Cadogan v. Palagi*[11] it was observed by Kay J.

"that there should be no absolute technical meaning given to such a word 'money' in a will, but the meaning in every case must depend upon the context, if there is any, which can explain it, and upon those surrounding circumstances, which the Court is bound to take into consideration in determining the construction."[12]

Meredith J. in *In re Jennings* concluded that the authorities would suggest that the lawyer's dictionary is to be rigidly adhered to unless the context happens to provide an excuse for looking to a wider interpretation of the word.

14–07 Turning to the facts in *In re Jennings* the will obviously did not use the strict language of lawyers, and accordingly, Meredith J. considered himself "free and unfettered" from applying the strict legal sense of the word "money." The meaning of the word "money" was unaffected by its being in a bank account as that only affected its procurability. Although Gilbert C.B. in *Shelmer's Case* [13] said that:

"I am of opinion that the word 'money' . . . is a general word, but yet not so large and comprehensive as the word *pecunia* in the Roman tongue; for such word in that language would carry all the testator's substance, both real and personal, that can be converted into money; but the word 'money' in our language answers to the barbarian's Latin word *moneta*, and is a genus that comprehends two species, *viz.*, ready money and money due."

However, the response of Meredith J. to this observation (with the very greatest of respect) was "that one might as well say that the word "bird" is a genus that comprehends two species, *viz.*, birds in the hand and birds in the bush." The testatrix's property included a substantial War Loan and the largest item

---

[10] *In Re Jennings: Caldbeck v. Stafford and Lindemere*, above, n.1 at 203-204.
[11] 25 Ch. D. 154 at 157.
[12] See also *In re Finlay's Estate* 5 N.I.J.R. 166; *Prichard v. Prichard* L.R. 11 Eq. 232.
[13] Gilb. Rep. Eq. 200 at 202.

of property owned by her and on the question of whether this was 'money' it seemed to Meredith J. that as it was clearly a loan to the British Government it was money in the strict sense and it was hers in the sense that she was entitled to the interest on it pending redemption. Further, it seemed to Meredith J. that the distinction between the case of money secured on mortgage and money in War Loan, both referred to as "my money," was a question of degree,

> "not of kind, and of a degree which could hardly be conceived as of any material importance to the testatrix, who was giving the use of all her money for her life."

14–08   The expression "my money" was held to be comprehensive enough to pass the whole of what was unquestionably the testatrix's money, and the introduction of the word "all" was superfluous, and its presence suggested "qualitative, and not merely quantitative comprehensiveness – that is to say, that the words "my money" are being used in some wide sense." Meredith J. considered that the testatrix had intended the wide sense when referring to the word "money" and to the word "my", and to "all my money" in every sense.

14–09   A question arose In *re Moore: Taylor v. Sherring*[14] as to whether national savings certificates constituted 'money' and thereby forming part of a gift of money in a will. In that case the total value of the assets of the testatrix was approximately £1,800 comprising an English bank deposit account, a building society account and English National Savings Certificates. She bequeathed "any money on deposit in England" to the defendants. Gavan Duffy J. who was the trial judge thought that on a general note that the courts recognised

> "that the coercive ascription to a quite ordinary word of some 'primary' meaning with a sacrosanct value is out of date and that the right of a Court and its duty to construe the language of a will by the standard of the community are slowly, but decisively being accepted; see Wigmore (3rd ed., vol. IX), pars. 2460, 2463; and it is time; the wonder is that the public has so long endured the injustices produced by the vain logomachies of a bygone age. The difficulty now is, of course, that the standard is so flexible."[15]

He went on to refer to the "pungent and entertaining judgment" of Meredith J. in *In re Jennings: Calbeck v. Stafford and Lindemere*[16] for the purposes of seeking support for the view that the court is not bound to follow the primary meaning of the word "money" in a particular context, but that case was distinguishable from the case before him as it involved a home-made will, and the will before him, "if somewhat inartistic," was not home-made. He then re-

---

[14] Above, n.1.
[15] *Re Moore: Taylor v. Sheering*, above, n.1 at 210–211.
[16] Above, n.1.

ferred to the decision in *Perrin v. Morgan*,[17] and although it was not binding on the court, he thought that it "registers a signal victory for the candid, as against the rigid, approach to the construction of ordinary words in a will." In that case all the net personal estate was viewed in the context as "moneys." He also understood the case as having the double effect of rendering obsolete the old rule requiring a special context to justify any departure from the primary sense "judicially imposed on certain common words and dispelling any juristic presumption in favour of some more usual meaning for any word or expression in current use, so that the Court in England is now bound to pronounce for the most likely meaning open in all the circumstances of the particular will. A testator becomes a human being and his will ceases to be the lawyers' plaything." He knew of no reason why he should not welcome "a breath of fresh air from across the Channel." He also thought that "our jurisprudence is crying out for relief here." He concluded by holding that it was more probable than not that the testatrix's language "any money on deposit in England" was meant to include the National Savings Certificates."

14–10   Although Gavan Duffy J. was able to distinguish between the case before him and the case before Meredith J. *In re Jennings: Caldbeck v. Stafford and Lindemere* [18] by highlighting the fact that the will before him was not a home-made will, one feels from the tenor of his judgment that even if the will before him were a home-made will, he would have still preferred the views expressed in *Perrin v. Morgan*.[19] However, as Gavan Duffy J. observed the court was not bound by the decision in *Perrin v. Morgan*, and as his decision In *re Moore: Taylor v. Sherring* and the decision of Meredith J. in *In re Jennings: Caldbeck v. Stafford and Lindemere* were both of equal authority, it remains to be seen which view will be the preferred one if ever the Supreme Court will be given an opportunity to determine the matter. It may be noted, however, that O'Keeffe P. in the course of his judgment in *In the Goods of Martin*[20] referred to both *Re Jennings: Caldbeck v. Stafford and Lindermere* and *Perrin v. Morgan,* but not *In re Moore: Taylor v. Sherring,* when considering the expression "all my money" used in a will.

14–11   The use of the expression "all my money" in a later will may also revoke by implication an earlier will where the later will contains no revocation clause and where the testator's estate consists of personal property only. This was the subject matter for consideration by the court in *In the Goods of Martin*.[21] In that case the testatrix was a widow who died without issue having

---

17 [1943] A.C. 399.
18 Above, n.1.
19 Above, n.17.
20 [1968] I.R. 1.
21 Above, n.20.

made two wills. The second will contained no revocation clause and consisted of a legacy of "all my money" and a bequest of personal belongings. The estate of the testatrix consisted of stocks and shares, moneys in deposit and current accounts in two banks, and moneys in Irish and English Post Office Savings Banks. An application was made to the court for a grant of letters of administration with the second will annexed, or both the first and second will annexed. O'Keeffe P. considered it well settled that although the primary meaning of the word "money" is cash, the word when used in a will covered much more, so that a gift of "all my money" may be equivalent of "all my personal estate."[22] He came to the conclusion that the words "all my money" in the later will covered the entire personal estate of the deceased other than her personal belongings which were specifically disposed of, and that the earlier will was "impliedly" revoked.

THE MEANING OF "PROPERTY"

14–12 Although the use of the word "property" in a general legal sense means both real and personal property, when property is disposed of by will the distinction between real and personal is given an added refinement: a gift of real property is known as a 'devise', and a gift of personal property is known as a 'legacy or bequest' depending on the nature of the personal property so disposed. Where a certain parcel of land is left to a beneficiary this is known as a 'specific devise', and where personal property is left to a beneficiary this known as a 'specific legacy or bequest'. A 'legacy' so described in a will may have increased in value at the time of the testator's death and a question may arise as to whether a legatee is entitled to the increase in value also. This question arose in *In re Faris: Goddard v. Overend.*[23] In that case at the date when the testatrix made her will she had a sum of £170 ordinary stock of Guinness & Co. registered in her name, and of which she was the beneficial owner. She bequeathed her stock to certain beneficiaries. As a result of a resolution passed by the shareholders of Guinness & Co. the value of the testatrix's stock at the time of her death was increased to £340. The question was whether the legatees were entitled to this new value of stock as representing the original value of £170. The Master of the Rolls referred to the decisions in *Oakes v. v. Oakes,*[24] *Slater v. Slater*[25] and *The Carron Company v. Hunter*[26] and found that they all

---

[22] *Re Jennings: Caldbeck v. Stafford and Lindemere*, above, n.1; *Perrin v. Morgan*, above, n.17.

[23] Above, n.2.

[24] 9 Hare 666.

[25] [1907] 1 Ch. 665 at 672.

[26] L.R. 1 H.L. Sc. 362.

confirmed the view that when a testator gives shares, he gives all rights arising out of the possession and ownership of his shares. He went on to say:

> "This lady, in common with the other shareholders, was entitled to all the benefits of the reserve fund. It was for the shareholders themselves to settle the method in which their rights In regard to the reserve fund should be dealt with; and, in my judgment, it was not intended that, in acceding to the resolution, they should change the nature of their property, but only that they should alter the accidents and incidents of their holding in the company."

Accordingly, the £340 represented the £170 bequeathed by the will.

14–13   Where the residue of real property is left to a beneficiary he is known as a 'residuary devisee', and where the residue of personal property is left to a beneficiary he is known as a 'residuary legatee'; where the residue of both real and personal property is left to a beneficiary he is known as a 'residuary devisee and legatee'. Although it is clear that a 'residuary devisee' will receive all the residue of the real property remaining after the specific devisees have been dealt with, it becomes more problematical when a residuary legatee only is named in relation to the extent of the residuary estate to which he becomes entitled. The term 'residuary legatee' "is not of an invariable nature, and must be fashioned and moulded by the context of the will."[27] In *Singleton v. Tomlinson* [28] Lord Cairns pointed out that:

> "There is no doubt that if you found the term 'residuary legatee' standing alone, above all, if you found it in a will which appeared to make a distinction between real property and personal property, the *prima facie* meaning of 'residuary legatee' would be the person taking what the law calls the residue of the personal property."

In *Fetherston-Haugh-Whitney's Estate*[29] on appeal to the Irish Court of Appeal (Irish Free State) Molony C.J. was asked to construe the word "property" used in the residuary clause of the testatrix's will. The clause provided as follows:

> "I leave all the residue and remainder of my property after payment of my debts, legacies, and funeral and testamentary expenses to the said Rev. Thomas Fetherston and my stepdaughter, Mary Westby, to be equally divided between them, share and share alike, and I appoint them my residuary legatees and executor and executrix of my will."

14–14   Molony C.J. observed that the framework of the will made a clear distinction between the real and personal property of the testatrix. Having

---

[27] *Fetherston-Haugh-Whitney's Estate* [1924] 1 I.R. 153 at 160; See also *Singleton v. Tomlinson*, above. n.3.

[28] Above, n.3 at 417.

[29] Above, n.27.

made a complete disposition of her lands she went to deal with her personal estate. The draughtsman of the will was careful in the use of words. He always used "give and devise" in connection with the freehold estates and "leave" where pecuniary legacies were the subject matter. Then came the residuary clause which disposed of the remainder of her "property." Molony C.J. thought that the testatrix by using the word "property" in the residuary clause meant only personal property,

> "because at the commencement of the portion of her will dealing with personal estate she specifically directs her executors to pay her debts out of her personal estate, and the legacies out of her personal estate, and when she uses the words: 'I leave all the residue and remainder of my property after payment of my debts, legacies, and funeral and testamentary expenses', it is, I think, clear that she attached to the words 'personal estate' at the commencement of the portion of the will dealing with such personal estate."[30]

There was a specific and complete devise of the testatrix's real estate and for the purposes of deciding whether this had any repercussions in relation to the residuary estate he referred to the case of *In re Gibbs: Martin v. Harding* [31] where it was held by Joyce J., in considering whether the naming of a residuary legatee constituted a residuary devise, the fact that at the date of the will the testatrix possessed no real estate other than that specifically and completely disposed of must be borne in mind, although this was not conclusive on the point.[32] However, where part only of the real estate is specifically devised, the appointment of a residuary legatee may carry the undisposed of real estate.[33] But even this principle will only become applicable where the residuary legatee is one of the specific devisees.[34] Molony C.J. went on to hold that the residuary clause did not carry the real estate because, first, the will showed a clear distinction between real and personal property and used appropriate words exclusively in the gifts of each, secondly, the testatrix had no real estate other than that of which the will contained specific and complete dispositions, and thirdly, that the will itself, from the context, showed the word "property" used in connection with the residuary clause was limited to the personal estate.

14–15 In *re Hogg*[35] the testator left both real and personal estate but did not specifically devise his real estate. He left his residuary personal estate to his sister and in the event of her predeceasing him he appointed her children as residuary legatees and devisees. The testator's sister survived him. A question

---

[30] *Fetherston-Haugh-Whitney's Estate*, above, n.27 at 161.

[31] [1907] 1 Ch. 465.

[32] See *In re Stephen: Stephen v. Stephen* [1913] W.N. 210.

[33] *Hughes v. Pritchard* 6 Ch. D. 24; See also *In re Metheun and Blore's Contract* 16 Ch. D. 24.

[34] *Hillas v. Hillas* 10 Ir. Eq. R. 134; *In re Morris: Morris v. Atherton* 71 L.T. 179.

[35] Above, n.3.

arose as to whether the residuary personalty to his sister was sufficient to carry also the testator's real estate. Gavan Duffy J. in the High Court first observed that the will contained no specific devise of real estate. The residuary estate comprised a leasehold house which the testator *devised* and bequeathed. Yet he gave that to the residuary *legatee* in the first instance which showed that he meant that legatee to take land which he purported to devise and bequeath, and that he was not using the words "devise" and "legatee" in their proper relation to one another. Using the will as its own dictionary, Gavan Duffy J. was able to infer that the residuary legatee was intended by the testator to take the whole of his chattels real, but the dictionary did not allow for anything more. Just because the will showed on its face that the residuary legatee was meant to take any residuary leaseholds fell short of saying that residuary legacy included real property. On appeal to the Supreme Court, O'Byrne J. came to the same conclusion as Gavan Duffy J. did in the High Court. However, he went on to mention two canons of construction which appeared to him to be well established:

1. Where a testator uses technical words, he is presumed to employ them in their legal signification, unless the context clearly indicates to the contrary.

2. The expression "residuary legatee" in a will is properly applicable to personalty only, and should be so construed, unless there is something in the context (including in that term the entire will) that the testator used it in a wider and more general sense.

14–16 Although various cases were referred to by counsel for the appellant O'Byrne J. was of the opinion that the cases referred to did not establish any general rule of construction but rather that they were all cases in the which the court found in the particular will clear indications that the testator had meant to dispose of his real estate, and had used the expression "residuary legatee" or some other similar term applicable to personal property only, in a sense as to include it. The decision in *Singleton v. Tomlinson* [36] was singled out and referred to and which involved an appeal from the Court of Appeal in Ireland to the House of Lords. In that case a question arose as to whether the concluding words of a will – "I constitute the said T.T. my residuary legatee" – carried the proceeds of a sale of real estate. The Irish Court of Appeal found that the determining factor was that the executors were directed to sell the entire real estate, and accordingly, that they held the proceeds in the form of money. This view was affirmed by the House of Lords. Lord Cairns in the course of his speech,[37] having stated that the expression residuary legatee "must be fashioned and moulded by the context, went on to say "and if you have a context in

---

[36] Above, n.3.
[37] Above, n.3 at 417–418.

which the testator is found looking at his landed property, not as land, but, as something which is all to be sold and turned into money, then the term 'residuary legatee' becomes a term applicable to the proceeds of the landed property as it would have been in the first instance to personal property." Lord Blackburn in the course of his speech stated that:

> "The testator shows an intention to turn the land into money out and out, he shows an intention that the residue, when the executors have paid the different things that they have to pay out of the fund, should go to Thomas Tomlinson."[38]

Loftus v. Stoney[39] was also referred to and in that case the testator, having disposed of all his real and personal property, left the residue of his "properties" to be divided among his then surviving children equally as residuary legatees. It was held by the Master of the Rolls that a failed specific devise passed by that residuary clause. The material word in the clause was "properties." However, O'Byrne J. stated that these cases were merely illustrations of the application of general principles of construction to particular cases, and were of little assistance in the construction of the will before the court. He then went on to consider the will before the court and having regard to the words used by the testator to determine what he had intended. It seemed to him that "the contrast is too pointed as between Mrs. Trouton as "residuary legatee" and the children as "residuary legatees and devisees." If the expressions occurred in different portions of the will, some attempt might be made to explain the matter; but, in the setting in which I find them, no such explanation as has been suggested by the appellant seems to me possible. If words mean anything having regard to the structure of the clause, some meaning must be given to the word "devisees," and the testator must be presumed to have meant something by adding that word in the gift to the children and omitting it in the gift to Mrs. Trouton."[40] It may be of interest to note in that case as the Supreme Court was equally divided on appeal the judgment of Gavan Duffy J. in the High Court was accordingly affirmed.

THE MEANING OF "ISSUE"

14–17   It was said by the Vice-Chancellor in *Berry v. Fisher*[41] that: "It may still, I think, be regarded as settled that the word "issue," when not restrained by the context, comprehends objects of every degree. This, therefore, is *prima facie* the meaning of the word, and it lies on anyone contending for a narrower interpretation to maintain that the context had this effect." In that case an

---

[38] Above, n.3 at 427.
[39] 17 Ir. Ch. R. 178.
[40] Above, n.3 at 256.
[41] Above, n.4.

action was brought by the trustees of the testator's will for the purpose of determining whether a legacy of £600 was divisible among the issue of his daughter. The sum of £600 was bequeathed in trust to pay his daughter the income arising from it to be given for her separate use, and free from the control of her husband in case she should marry. In the event of her marrying and leaving lawful issue the £600 and any interest arising from it was then to go to such issue. The will went on to provide, *inter alia*, that in the case of the death of any of the daughter's children leaving lawful issue of their own, the share or shares of such children were to go to the lawful issue of such children. The testator's daughter married and had several children and at the time of her death she had even grandchildren. A question arose as to whether the £600 was distributable among the daughter's children only to the exclusion of the grandchildren. The Vice-Chancellor, relying on the settled use of the word "issue" in his judgment, stated that:

> "It seems unsafe to rely on a mere general and vague terms as showing a general intention, which are often of little better than conjectures."[42]

The will provided: "In case of the death of my said daughter leaving issue, said interest money to be paid and payable to such issue, share and share alike, for their support and maintenance; and on their attaining twenty-one years, such principal sum, and such other sum as they or their said mother may be entitled unto in this will, shall be divided among them, share and share alike." As the word "issue" was used in the technical meaning of the word the Vice-Chancellor held that the fund was divisible among all the children, grandchildren and remoter issue, if any, living at the period of distribution.

14–18 The question of whether adopted children were included in the settled meaning of "issue" was considered in *In re Stamp: Stamp v. Redmond*.[43] In that case the testator devised and bequeathed all his property to his executors and trustees on trust for his son Patrick Stamp 'provided always that if he shall die without leaving issue then upon trust for my grandson John Stamp.' The testator died in 1954. Patrick Stamp was unmarried when the testator made his will and also at the date of the testator's death. He married two years later. There were no children of the marriage but he and his wife adopted two daughters. The matter for the court to decide was whether the words 'die without leaving issue' used in creating the gift included not only blood relatives but also adopted children. It was submitted by the plaintiff that the use of the word "issue" in the will did not manifest an intention to exclude adopted children and in the absence of words showing an intention to exclude the court should lean in favour of the construction of the word "issue" as including adopted children. However, Lardner J. was of the view that the word "issue"

---

[42] Above, n.4 at 488–489.
[43] Above, n.5.

was "not so esoteric or so much a word used in some specialist field as to have no ordinary meaning in common usage. On the contrary, its ordinary meaning is issue of a marriage or descendents and it would be so understood by persons of ordinary education." When the will was made the settled meaning of a bequest to "issue" *prima facie* connoted descendents of every degree when not constrained by the context.[44] This was also recognised by the Supreme Court in *O'B. v. S.*.[45] It was also submitted by the plaintiff that the Adoption Act 1952 changed the scope and meaning of 'family' so as to include adopted as well as legitimate children, and that the policy of the law was to regard adopted children as equivalent to natural children and to confer the same status on them. The will however was made after the enactment of the Adoption Act 1952 and disclosed an intention to keep the residue in the testator's family. If there was no evidence to show that the testator considered the possibility of the plaintiff adopting a child the court should lean in favour of a construction which favours the inclusion of adopted children, and that this would be consistent with the policy of the Adoption Acts. Before considering this submission Lardner J. noted that section 26 of the Adoption Act 1952 was clearly concerned with the property rights of adopted children when a will is made after the making of an adoption order. In the present case the will preceded the two adoption orders by several years. Although the will clearly expressed an intention to benefit the plaintiff, he was unable to accept the argument that the plaintiff's two adopted daughters could be viewed as "issue" for the purposes of the will and the expression "die without leaving issue." The will was professionally prepared and Lardner J. thought it likely that the word "issue" was used in its well settled sense. He concluded that from a consideration of all its terms and of the context,

> "that was the sense in which the testator in this case used the words and his intention is to be found expressed in those words. I do not find that the terms of section 26 of the Adoption Act 1952, to which I have already referred, require me to reach a different conclusion."[46]

It should also be noted that although the Status of Children Act 1987 was referred to it did not affect the case. However, if the 1987 Act was relevant to the case in the context of time the case might have been decided differently as adopted children are deemed by that Act from the date of the adoption order to be the children of the adoptive parents and nobody else just as other "issue", and furthermore, illegitimate children under the 1987 Act will be viewed as "issue" and included in the connotation of descendents of every degree when not constrained by the context.[47] However, notwithstanding the changes intro-

---

[44] *Berry v. Fisher*, above, n.4.
[45] [1984] I.R. 316 at 330.
[46] *Re Stamp: Stamp v. Redmond*, above, n.5 at 386–387.
[47] See s.3.

duced by the 1987 Act, the well settled meaning of the word "issue" remains unaffected save that the marital status of parents will no longer be a relevant factor for the purposes of determining descendents of every degree.[48]

14–19 The expression "dying without issue" when used in a will was considered by McCracken J. in *Mulhern v. Brennan*.[49] In that case the testator, John O'Donoghue, died on April 8, 1915. By his will dated April 28, 1911 he provided In relation to the residue of his estate as follows:

> "All the rest residue and remainder of my estate and effects real and personal I will devise and bequeath to my four sons John Anthony O'Donoghue, James Frederick Caulfield O'Donoghue, David Geoffrey O'Donoghue and Peter Paul O'Donoghue share and share alike as tenants in common and in the event of any of my children dying without issue the surviving brothers or brother shall take his share original and accruing but in the event of his leaving issue such issue shall be entitled to the parent's share."

14–20 The court was asked to determine three issues arising on the construction of the residuary clause. They were as follows:

> Did the phrase "dying without issue" which appeared in the residuary clause mean:
>
> (i) Dying during the lifetime of the deceased to the effect, in the events which have happened, that each of the sons took absolutely a quarter share of the residue of the estate? or
> (ii) Dying at any time to the effect that on the death without issue of each son his share passed to the then surviving brother, or brothers, and ultimately, on the death of the last surviving brother (John Anthony O'Donoghue) without issue that an intestacy arose? or
> (iii) Dying at any time but to the effect that the defeasance provision in the clause only applied for so long as there was a surviving brother?

14–21 Although all four sons survived the testator, all four ultimately died without issue. The first point which McCracken J. had to consider was whether the expression "dying without issue" referred to the death of the beneficiary during the lifetime of the testator only, or whether it referred to his death without issue at anytime.[50] The relevant rule of construction to be applied was that "unless the contrary be clearly indicated, a reference in a will to the contingency of a person dying only refers to that person dying during the lifetime of the testator, for otherwise it is not a contingency at all, but a certainty."[51]

---

[48] See *Re Patterson, Deceased: Dunlop v. Greer*, above, n.5, where the question of 'blood relatives' was considered in relation to the exercise of a power of appointment.
[49] Above, n.6.
[50] See Succession Act 1965, ss.90 and 100.
[51] See *Re Hall* [1944] I.R. 54.

14–22 Two authorities on the matter were referred to by McCracken J. The first, *Woodroofe v. Woodroofe*[52] considered a residuary clause similar in effect to the one in the present case. The testator's residual estate was to be divided among his four sons subject to the proviso: "but if any of my said sons shall die without leaving lawful issue him surviving, my will is that the share of such son shall go and be divided between such of my other sons as shall be then living, in equal shares, the children of a deceased son to take the share to which their father would have been entitled." It was held by the Master of the Rolls that the share of each son was defeasible in the event of his dying at anytime without leaving issue. The following illuminating passage from the judgment of the Master of the Rolls[53] was cited by McCracken J.:

> "When death is spoken of by a testator as a contingent event, and if the words import no other contingency, then, since death is an event which must happen to all, the time of it alone being uncertain, the Courts have long treated the time of death as being the contingency contemplated, and for want of a reference to any other time, have construed the will as referring to death before the testator. Thus such common expressions as 'in the event of his dying' or 'if he should die' or 'in case of his dying' and the like, without more, have always been held to mean dying before the testator. This construction, however, is only adopted ex necessitate, and because the will treats a certain event as uncertain, thus introducing the uncertain element of time, and no other time than the death of the testator can be supposed to be in view. But whether this rule was originally sound or not there is plainly no reason for its application where some other contingency is in express terms connected with the event of death; as, for instance, where the event is not merely the death of A.B., but the event for instance of his dying before C.D., or dying under 21, or dying without leaving lawful issue him surviving; for these are all events to which language of contingency is strictly and properly applicable, and therefore there is no need to suppose, or imply, a reference to any other contingency than that which is expressed."

14–23 The second authority referred to was *Richardson's Trusts*.[54] In that case the will contained the provision that "in case both, or either of my sons, Albert or Alexander dying leaving their children fatherless, I leave to such children the sum of £500 sterling to be divided among them share and share alike." The court construed the provision as meaning that the gift took effect on the death of either of the testator's sons leaving children at anytime, and was not confined to death during the testator's lifetime. McCracken J. cited the following passage from the judgment of the Vice-Chancellor:[55]

> The next question arises on the words 'dying leaving their children fatherless.' At what period of time must this event happen? This is not a case in which the

---

[52] 1 Ch. D. 299.
[53] *ibid*. at 302
[54] 1 Ch. D. 295.
[55] *ibid*. at 300.

Court is compelled, in order to avoid a failure of intention, to confine the death to the period of the testator's life. That construction is not to be resorted to unless no other contingency is mentioned; and where a contingency is coupled with death there is no necessity for limiting it to the life of the testator. The contingency must be ascertained from the will itself, and in the present case it sufficiently appears that the contingency contemplated is the death of a son leaving his family without provision."

14–24   It appeared to McCracken J. that these decisions reflected the clear meaning of the words used. He went on to say:

"If it was intended to limit the contingency to the death of any of the testator's sons during his lifetime, it would have been very easy for the will to have said so. To hold that this is the meaning of the words as they in fact appear in the will would be to add the words *in my lifetime* to the gift, and a Court will only supply additional words of limitation in a will where that is necessary to give a rational construction."

Accordingly, he held that the true construction of the will is that the gifts over took effect on the death of any of the testator's sons without issue at any time, either before or after the death of the testator.

14–25   On the question where the contingency takes effect in relation to all the beneficiaries, McCracken J. stated that:

"quite clearly the entire estate became vested in the last surviving son of the testator, the stated contingency having occurred In relation to the other three sons."

The clause left open to two constructions: one, either the testator totally failed to make any provision for the event which happened, in which case an intestacy resulted, or two, there is a further contingency provided in the will to the effect that there must be a surviving brother or brothers to take the share, and as that contingency did not occur, the last surviving brother took absolutely. McCracken J. opted for the latter. He concluded by stating that in construing a will the court will presume that the testator did not intend to die intestate as to any part of his estate, "for otherwise he would not have made a will." He cited Lord Esher M.R. in *In re Harrison* [56] as saying:

"You ought, if possible, to read the will so as to lead to a testacy, not an intestacy. This is the golden rule. I do not deny that this will may be read in two ways, or that it requires a blank should be filled up. But it may be read in such a way as not to amount to a solemn farce."

---

[56] 30 Ch. D. 390 at 393.

SUMMARY

14–26   Although there are certain legal expressions used to describe gifts
left by wills, the property which comprises such gifts will be a matter for the
court to decide, and while this may be an easy matter in relation to gifts of real
estate, the same cannot be said for gifts of personal estate because of its vari-
able nature. The difficulty becomes more acute when determining the extent
of the property to which a residuary legatee becomes entitled. The court when
deciding what property is comprised in a gift will concentrate on the language
used by the testator and interpret that language with the assistance of well
established canons of construction. One canon provides that where a testator
uses technical words, he is presumed to employ them in their legal sense,
unless the context clearly indicates to the contrary.[57] There was a time when
ordinary words also carried a settled legal meaning, for instance, where the
word 'money' was used its meaning depended on whether or not the will was
prepared professionally and where it was professionally prepared a presumption arose that a strict legal meaning of the word was intended by the testator,[58] although this seems to be no longer the case.[59] Also where testamentary
expressions are used by a testator, for instance, 'residuary legatee', the expression will be construed to be applicable to the personal estate of a testator
only, unless there is something in the context of the clause or the whole will to
show that the testator used it in a wider and more general sense.[60] Words and
expressions like 'issue' and 'dying without issue', however, continue to bear
their legal meaning, unless a contrary intention appears in the will, although
their scope, but not effect, has been broadened by statute, especially by the
Status of Children Act 1987.[61]

14–27   Therefore, the language used by a testator will have primacy of place
when the court is called upon to interpret a will, and words and expressions
which carry a strict legal meaning will not be interpreted in their legal sense
where the context of the will shows that they were used to mean otherwise,
and the court may seek the assistance of well settled canons of construction
when attempting to ascertain what a testator intended by the language used in
the will.

---

[57] See *Re Hogg*, above, n.3 at 252–253.

[58] See *Re Jennings: Caldbeck v. Stafford and Lindemere*, above, n.1.

[59] See *Moore: Taylor v. Sheering*, above, n.1; *Perrin v. Morgan*, above, n.17; *In the Goods of Martin*, above, n.20.

[60] See *Hogg*, above, n.3; *Fetherston-Haugh-Whitney's Estate*, above, n.27.

[61] See *Berry v. Fisher*, above, n.4; *In re Stamp: Stamp v. Redmond*, above, n.5; *Mulhern v. Brennan*, above, n.6; *Re Patterson, Deceased: Dunlop v. Greer*, above, n.5.

CHAPTER 15

The Introduction of a Foreign Element

INTRODUCTION

15–01   Where a foreign element is required to be considered by a domestic court the principles of private international law may be resorted to by the court to deal with the matter. The principles which are applied by the Irish court are those which have been evolved by the common law and the provisions contained in Part VIII of the Succession Act 1965. A grant of probate or letters of administration made to an executor or administrator by an Irish court obliges such executor or administrator to administer the estate of the deceased in this country in accordance with Irish law and as such will have title to the estate notwithstanding the fact that a personal representative has been appointed by a foreign court and that the deceased died domiciled within the jurisdiction of that court.[1] A grant made by a foreign court authorises the personal representative to act within the jurisdiction of the foreign court only.[2] However, where the personal representative appointed by a foreign court brings assets of the deceased into this country, he will be regarded as legal owner of the assets, and will not require a domestic grant to establish his title to such assets.[3] The principle is that the administration of an estate will be regulated by the law of the country in which the grant is made and the law of the domicile will regulate succession rights to moveables.[4]

15–02   The law which regulates succession rights to property depends on the nature of the property left by the deceased. The personal estate of a deceased, i.e. his moveables, will be regulated by the law of his domicile at the date of his death; the real estate, *i.e.* his immoveables, will be regulated by the *lex situs*. A person acquires a domicile of origin at birth and this will continue to be his domicile unless he subsequently changes it. Any alleged change of domicile must satisfy two conditions: one, the *factum* which means that a person must acquire a residence in a place, and two, the *animus manendi* which means that he must intend to reside in that place permanently or indefinitely.[5] When an Irish court is asked to determine whether a person had acquired a domicile of choice it will be done so in accordance with the requirements of

---

[1]   *Preston v. Melville* 8 Cl. & F. 1.
[2]   *Re M'Sweeney: M'Sweeney v. Murphy* [1919] 1 I.R. 16.
[3]   *In re Walsh: O'Brien v. Phelan* [1931] I.R. 161.
[4]   *Preston v. Melville*, above, n.1.

Irish law irrespective of whether or not such a person had acquired such a domicile in a foreign country in the eyes of the law of that country.[6] Where immoveables are involved the applicable law will be the law of the place where the real estate is situated, i.e. the *lex situs.*[7]

15–03   The same principles are applicable to intestacies.[8] They are also applicable to cases involving the legal right of a spouse and claims by children where it is alleged that the testator had failed in his moral duty to make proper provision for them in accordance with his means under the Succession Act 1965.[9]

15–04   Where a will is required to be construed by the court concerning the deceased's moveables it will *prima facie* be construed in accordance with the law of the testator's domicile. This rule of construction, however, will not be applied by the court where it is shown that the testator made his will with reference to the laws of another country.[10] Once a person makes a will, however, any construction of it will be in accordance with the law of the domicile he had acquired at the time of making it and it will not be altered by reason of any change of the testator's domicile after the making of the will.[11] A will appointing or disposing of immoveables will be construed in accordance with the *lex situs.*[12]

15–05   While substantive issues raised in the course of a trial will be determined in accordance with the relevant foreign law, any issues of a procedural or evidential nature will be determined in accordance with the *lex fori.*[13]

GRANTS OF ADMINISTRATION INVOLVING A FOREIGN ELEMENT

15–06   A personal representative to whom a grant has been made in Ireland will take priority over a personal representative appointed by a foreign court in relation to the administration of the moveable estate of the deceased within the jurisdiction of the Irish courts. The Irish grant under which a personal representative acts,

---

[5]   *Re Silar: Hurley v. Wimbush* [1956] I.R. 344.
[6]   *Re Adams: Bank of Ireland Trustee Company Ltd. v. Adams* [1967] I.R. 424.
[7]   See Rules of the Superior Courts, Ord. 79, r.5(8); *Re Rea: Rea v. Rea* [1902] 2 I.R. 451.
[8]   *Pipon v. Pipon* 25 14 (Trin. 1744).
[9]   *In the Goods of G.M.: F.M. v. T.A.M.* 106 I.L.T.R. 82.
[10] *Re Silar: Hurley v. Wimbush*, above, n.5.
[11] See Succession Act 1965, s.107 (1).
[12] *In re Bonnet: Johnston v. Langfield & Ors.* [1983] I.L.R.M. 359; *Murray v. Champerowne* [1901] 2 I.R. 232.
[13] *In the Estate of Fuld (No. 3)* [1965] 3 All E.R. 776; See also *In the Estate of Fuld* [1965] 2 All E.R. 653 and *In the Estate of Fuld (No. 2)* [1965] 2 All E.R. 657.

"directs him to do, and he takes an oath that he will well and truly administer all and every one of the goods of the deceased, and pay his debts so far as the goods will extend, and exhibit a full and true account of his administration. That such are the duties of an executor and administrator acting under a probate or letters of administration in this country, is certain, although the testator or intestate may have been domiciled elsewhere. The domicile regulates the right of succession, but the administration must be in the country in which possession is taken and held, under lawful authority, of the property of the deceased."

The latter passage is taken from the speech of the Lord Chancellor in *Preston v. Melville*.[14] In that case the personal representatives and trustees of the deceased who died domiciled in Scotland declined to apply for a grant of probate. The deceased's next-of-kin in England, however, obtained a grant of letters of administration to administer his estate in England. The Court of Session in Scotland later appointed other persons as personal representatives and trustees in place of those who declined to act. The new personal representatives instituted proceedings against the personal representative appointed by the English courts in the Court of Session calling on her to transfer to them all the personal estate possessed by her under the English administration, and offering to release her from all liability as personal representative. In the House of Lords a declaration was sought by the Scottish personal representatives to the effect that all the funds and personal estate of the deceased in England and in the hands of the English administratrix belong or ought to be transferred to them as the personal representatives of the deceased. However, the Lord Chancellor stated that

"the person to whom administration is granted by the Ecclesiastical Court is by statute bound to administer the estate, and to pay the debts of the deceased."

Although the law of the domicile of the deceased regulates the right of succession, the law of the country in which the grant is made regulates the administration of the deceased's property in that country. The Lord Chancellor held that the personal representatives and trustees appointed by the Court of Session had no right to administer the estate in England as against the administratrix appointed for that purpose by the Ecclesiastical Court.

15–07 A grant made by a foreign court "clothes a person with the character of personal representative within the area of jurisdiction of the Court which makes the grant; the character is "local and territorial" only."[15] As a corollary, therefore, no proceedings may be instituted against a personal representative appointed by a foreign court in relation to the deceased's estate except only within the jurisdiction of the foreign court who appointed him as such as it is

---

[14] Above, n.1.
[15] *Re M'Sweeney: M'Sweeney v. Murphy*, above, n.2 at 21 *per* Ronan L.J.; See *Ewing v. Orr Ewing* 9 A.C. *per* Lord Selborne.

from that court he derives his authority.[16] In *In re M'Sweeney: M'Sweeney v. Murphy*[17] the deceased died intestate and the defendant obtained a grant of letters of administration in England. As administratrix she sold and realised the deceased's securities, but, notwithstanding several demands from the deceased's next-of-kin, neglected to distribute the assets among them. The plaintiff, as next-of-kin, sought an Irish grant of administration to the deceased's estate. On appeal to the Irish Court of Appeal Molony C.J., having referred to the decision in *Ewing v. Orr Ewing*,[18] thought that that decision clearly established, in the first place, that a grant of probate or its statutory equivalent was necessary to clothe a person with the character of executor or administrator in whatever part of the United Kingdom proceedings were brought against him; and secondly, that it in no way followed, that because the character acquired by such a grant is local and territorial, the administration must be local and territorial. It was said by Lord Selborne in *Ewing v. Orr Ewing*[19] that by taking out probate an executor who is also a trustee "accepts the trusts of the will, as well as the office of legal personal representative; and the acceptance of these trusts extends to the whole property which, under the terms of the will, is the subject of the trust, real as well as personal, although the real estate cannot be, and part of the personal estate may not be, within the jurisdiction of the Court of Probate." Ronan L.J. also referred to the speech of Lord Selborne for support and held that there was no legal personal representative before the court.

15–08 Thus in order for a person to be clothed with character of personal representative for the purpose of administering the estate of the deceased within the jurisdiction of the Irish courts he must first apply for a grant in this country. Order 79, rule 5(8) of the Rules of the Superior Courts provides that where it is established that the deceased died domiciled outside Ireland (on or after January 1, 1967) a grant of letters of administration intestate or with the will annexed of the moveable estate may be made to the person entrusted with the administration of the moveable estate by the court having jurisdiction at the place where the deceased died domiciled, or to the person entitled to administer the moveable estate by the place where the deceased died domiciled. A grant in relation to immoveable estate must be made in accordance with the law as though the deceased died domiciled in Ireland. Section 29 of the Succession Act also provides that the High Court shall have jurisdiction to make a grant of representation in respect of a deceased person even though no estate is left in the State, and to make a *de bonis non* or other form of grant of unadministered estate, even though there is no estate of the deceased in the State.

---

[16] *Re M'Sweeney: M'Sweeney v. Murphy*, above, n.2 at 20 *per* Molony C.J.
[17] Above, n.2.
[18] Above, n.15.
[19] Above, n.15.

15–09 However, where a person has already being appointed as personal representative by a foreign court and he brings assets belonging to the deceased's estate into this country he will be regarded, by virtue of the comity of courts, as the legal owner of such assets, and he does not require a grant of administration in this country to establish his title and can sue for such assets as if they were his own.[20] However, if such assets are within the jurisdiction of the Irish courts and the administration of which are not included in the foreign grant from which the personal representative derives title, the Irish courts can make a decree for administration of such assets to a creditor or beneficiary.[21] In *In re Walsh: O'Brien v. Phelan*[22] the deceased, who was domiciled in Ireland, died in Germany. He left a will and three codicils. He left a considerable amount of assets in England. The residuary legatee was granted letters of administration in England. As personal representative he sold railway stock belonging to the deceased's estate in England and transferred the proceeds to the Irish Free State where he resided. The personal representative died in Ireland having left a will appointing his wife as executrix and to whom probate was granted. She afterwards obtained a grant of administration *de bonis non* in England to the estate of the deceased for whom her husband was administrator. She then commenced an action in this country for administration of the deceased's estate naming a beneficiary in the will who resided in England as defendant. On appeal to the Supreme Court, Fitzgibbon J. held that in the case of a creditor or beneficiary the court has jurisdiction to make a grant of letters of administration in order that an action for administration may be properly constituted, and in such a case it might be desirable that the grant should be made to the foreign personal representative if willing to act. But a grant by the court is discretionary and as the applicant in her capacity as personal representative for her husband and for the deceased under an English *de bonis non* grant was having no difficulty in recovering moneys or securities in this country, and as her sole object in applying for a grant in this country was for the purpose of renewing an action here against the defendant who was resident in England, no grant in this country should issue to her.

THE LAW GOVERNING FOREIGN SUCCESSION RIGHTS, STATUTORY RIGHTS AND INTESTACIES

15–10 As was said by the Lord Chancellor in *Preston v. Melville*,[23] although the law of the country in which the grant is made regulates the administration of the deceased's property in that country, the law of the domicile regulates

---

[20] *In re Walsh: O'Brien v. Phelan*, above, n.3
[21] *ibid*.
[22] Above, n.3.
[23] Above, n.1.

the right of succession. Therefore, where a foreign will or intestacy is involved it first becomes necessary to ascertain the domicile of the deceased person in order to determine the succession rights of the beneficiaries. However, it must be emphasised, that the law of the domicile regulates succession rights to moveables only. It does not regulate the succession rights to immoveables, the *lex situs*, i.e. the law of the place where the immoveables are situated, regulates these rights. But what is meant by 'domicile' in the eyes of the law? "Domicile," says Lord Cranworth in *Whicker v. Hume*[24] "meant permanent home, and if that was not understood by itself no illustration would help to make it intelligible." Budd J. in *In re Silar: Hurley v. Wimbush*[25] said in relation to Lord Cranworth's meaning of 'domicile' that:

> "While many factors have to be considered in most cases relating to domicil, I cannot help feeling that at times, in the welter of argument and citations of case law, that simple elementary proposition is in danger of being forgotten."

All persons acquire a domicile of origin at birth and this will persist until it is shown that it has been abandoned by the acquisition of a domicile of choice, and although several domiciles of choice may be acquired and abandoned during the lifetime of a deceased person, the one that matters for succession purposes is the domicile which he had at the time of his death. It was said by Black J. in *In re Joyce: Corbet v. Fagan*[26], with whom Sullivan C.J. and Murnaghan J. agreed, that: "now, whatever difference of view may be possible on any aspect of the law of domicil, one principle at least is beyond doubt, namely, that the domicil of origin persists until it is proved to have been intentionally and voluntarily abandoned and supplanted by another." Where it is alleged that a domicile of choice has been acquired two things must be established: first, that a person acquired a residence in a place, *i.e.* the *factum*, and secondly, that he intended to reside in that place permanently or indefinitely, *i.e.* the *animus manendi*. As was said by Lord Westbury in *Udney v. Udney*:[27] "Domicil of choice is a conclusion or inference which the law derives from the fact of a man fixing voluntary his sole or chief residence in a particular place, with an intention of continuing to reside there for an unlimited time." Once it is shown that a person intended to reside permanently in a place the fact of domicile will be established. Although long residence in a particular place may be indicative of an intention to reside there permanently, but where it is shown that a person resided in a particular place with the ultimate intention of returning to his domicile of origin, long residence alone may not be sufficient to establish a domicile of choice. The "colour or characteristics" or

---

[24] 28 L.J. (Ch.) 396 at 400.
[25] Above, n.5 at 348-349.
[26] [1946] I.R. 277.
[27] L.R. 1 H.L. 441 at 458.

"quality" of residence may be taken into account when the *animus manendi* is being considered.[28]

15–11 However, Budd J. in *In re Silar: Hurley v. Wimbush*[29] thought that it was clearly

> "a question of fact to determine from a consideration of all the known circumstances in each case whether the proper inference is that the person in question has shown unmistakenly by his conduct, viewed against the background of the surrounding circumstances, that he had formed at some time the settled purpose of residing indefinitely in the alleged domicil of choice. Put in more homely language, that he had determined to make his permanent home in such place. That involves, needless to say, an intention to abandon his former domicil."

Budd J. was asked to ascertain the domicile of the deceased in *In re Silar: Hurley v. Wimbush*.[30] In that case the deceased was born in Shanghai on April 17, 1856, of English parents. In 1860 he went to England with his parents. He was educated in England and qualified there as an electrical engineer. He resided in England up to the year 1905. In that year he came to Ireland to assist in the management of the business of his brother-in-law. After the death of his brother-in-law in 1905 the deceased remained on in Ireland to look after the business at the request of his mother-in-law. He resided in rented accommodation in Dalkey, County Dublin, and continued to manage the business until it was sold in 1941. After that he continued to reside in Dublin until his death in 1953. During his lifetime he was a member of the Dublin Chamber of Commerce and of a social club in Dun Laoghaire. However, in the year 1942 he declared himself to be a domiciled Englishman and that he had never lost his English domicile and that he intended to return to England when circumstances permitted. In his will made in 1949 he described himself as an English subject, domiciled in England and resident in Ireland. He, however, obtained an Irish passport in 1931, and renewed it in 1941. He also held a British passport which was valid from 1946 to 1951. By his will he left his residuary estate to certain named nephews and nieces in equal shares, and provided that the share of any such nephew or niece who predeceased him should go to the child or children of such nephews or nieces living at his death. One of the nephews predeceased the testator without issue, but he had adopted a child in accordance with English law. Three matter arose for the court to decide: one, whether the deceased died domiciled in Ireland or England, two, whether his will should be construed in accordance with Irish or English law, and three, whether the words "child or children" applied to an adopted child. When ascertaining the domicile of a deceased person Budd J. was of the view that any declaration

---

[28] *Bowie v. Liverpool Royal Infirmary* [1930] A.C. 588.
[29] Above, n.5 at 355.
[30] Above, n.5.

made by him on the matter during his lifetime must be weighed with the rest of the evidence, and may be a determining factor, but will not be permitted to prevail against established facts indicating a contrary conclusion. Therefore, the declarations made by the deceased in his will were of considerable importance if taken at face value, and one of the phrases used by him "at present residing" suggested a temporary residence in Ireland. Also the description of himself as an English subject and domiciled in England, although important evidence, was by no means conclusive. Budd J. stated that: "Where a person is in fact physically resident in a place and the proper inference from all the known circumstances is that he had formed the intention of remaining indefinitely in that place, he cannot alter the fact that he has acquired a domicil of choice by stating something to the contrary."[31]

15–12   When an Irish court is asked to ascertain a deceased's domicile of choice, it will do so in accordance with the requirements of Irish law, irrespective of a ruling on the matter by a foreign court.[32] However, before a new domicile of choice can be acquired the former domicile of choice must be shown to have been abandoned by the person concerned ceasing to reside in the former domicile. In *Revenue Commissioners v. Matthews and Others* [33] it was said by Maguire C.J. that: "The process of abandoning a domicile is the converse of acquiring one – *Udny v. Udny* L.R. H.L. (Sc.) 441. It must be shown to have happened *animo et facto*." In *In re Adams: Bank of Ireland Trustee Company Ltd. v. Adams*[34] the court had to ascertain the domicile of the deceased at the time of his death. In that case the deceased testator, whose domicile of origin was Irish, later acquired a domicile of choice in England where he married and established his family home. In 1951, when he was 67 years old, he bought a house in France and went to live there with his wife. He continued to live there until his death. However, he spent a major portion of each year away from France and visited Ireland and England regularly. In 1948 he registered as an Irish citizen and he held an Irish passport from 1950 until his death. In 1959 he took a lease of a flat in London and stayed there on his visits to England. A few months before his death he sold his house in France subject to a life interest vested in him and reserved a right for his wife to reside in it for six months after his death. During his lifetime he made statements to the effect that he was not domiciled in France and evidence was adduced that he moved to France for health and fiscal reasons, and that he intended to return to England in the event of surviving his wife. By his will he

---

[31] Above, n.5 at 355.
[32] *Re Adams: Bank of Ireland Trustee Company Ltd v. Adams*, above, n.6; See *In re Annesley: Davidson v. Annesley* [1926] Ch. 692.
[33] 92 I.L.T.R. 44 at 52.
[34] Above, n.6.

left all his property to his wife, and by a codicil he left a legacy to the second defendant. The codicil provided that:

> "I bequeath any sum of money standing in my name in whatever currency and any script or securities held on my behalf with Lloyd's Bank . . . Geneva, Switzerland, to Miss Carol Hutchings. . . ."

It was submitted by the second defendant that the terms of the codicil covered all money standing in the name of the testator no matter where it was situated. The testator died in 1962 in London and was survived by his wife, the first defendant, his daughter, the third defendant, and by the second defendant. His estate consisted totally of moveables. The action was brought by the personal representatives to have the deceased's domicile determined by the court and to have the terms of the legacy contained in the codicil construed. Did the testator when he went to France in 1951 or at some time during the period of his living there, abandon his English domicile of choice and acquire a new domicile of choice in France? If so, did he later abandon that new domicile and re-acquire a domicile of choice in England? In answering these questions Budd J. looked at the evidence relative to the factum of residence and animus manendi. He stated that the evidence of domicile must be considered as a whole in order to arrive at a proper conclusion. He had no doubt that in the year 1951, or at some time between then and 1958, the testator acquired a domicile of choice in France. The facts revealed that the testator never during his lifetime ceased to reside in France. It remained at all material times his matrimonial home and place of residence. All his furniture and personal belongings were there. "His *lares et penates* were never removed therefrom." Applying the test laid down by the Supreme Court In *Revenue Commissioners v. Matthews and Others*[35] to the facts of the case before him it was clear that the deceased did not abandon either his residence or domicile in France. He went on to hold that the testator died domiciled in France.

15–13   It has been already stated that the question whether a person acquired a domicile of choice in a foreign country is to be determined in accordance with the laws of Ireland irrespective of whether he or she has not acquired a domicile of choice in a foreign country in the eyes of the law of that country.[36] This means that an Irish court must adopt this approach "uninfluenced" by a decision of a foreign court in relation to the matter.[37] This was also one of the factors considered by Costello J. in *In the Goods of Rowan*.[38] In that case the deceased was born in Ireland in 1914. He was an Irish citizen and his domicile of origin was Irish. But from 1949 until his death in 1984 he resided in France.

---

[35] Above, n.33.
[36] *Re Adams: Bank of Ireland Trustee Company Ltd. v. Adams*, above, n.6 at 434-435.
[37] *In the Goods of Rowan* [1988] I.L.R.M. 65.
[38] Above, n.37.

A question was raised by his brother, the plaintiff, who was also the executor of the will, as to whether the deceased had abandoned his domicile of origin and acquired a domicile of choice in France. The deceased's widow was one of the defendants. She obtained no benefit under the deceased's will, but if it were found that that the deceased died domiciled in Ireland she became entitled to a one-third share of the Irish assets under the Succession Act 1965. On the other hand, if, at his death, he had acquired a French domicile she would have no claim to his Irish assets. Notwithstanding this the deceased's widow submitted that the deceased had acquired a domicile of choice in France and conceded that if this were so she had no claim to a share in the deceased's assets under the Succession Act. The deceased's children who were also joined as defendants also submitted that their father had acquired a French domicile. The plaintiff however argued to the contrary and submitted that the deceased had never abandoned his Irish domicile of origin. A similar matter was litigated in France, where the deceased had bank accounts. The French courts held that the deceased had died domiciled in France. It was established in evidence that, although the deceased retained his Irish passport and driving licence, he never had an Irish residence. Moreover, the children of the deceased acquired French citizenship as a result of the deceased's insistence. Although he visited Ireland in search of medical treatment he later returned to Paris and underwent medical treatment there. However, the deceased made a will in Ireland and declared that he was domiciled in Ireland. He had also intended to spend his remaining years in Ireland and in furtherance of this transferred a sum of £100,000 from France to a bank account in Ireland, and had made arrangements for his burial in Ireland. Costello J., having stated that it was for Irish court to say whether or not the deceased acquired a domicile of choice irrespective of whether or not he had acquired a French domicile in accordance with French law, was of the opinion that the issue was whether the deceased had acquired a domicile of choice in France and had abandoned his Irish domicile of origin. The evidence showed that he had intended to reside permanently in France notwithstanding the declaration that he was domiciled in Ireland. He went on to hold that the deceased had died domiciled in France.

15–14   Where real estate or immoveable property is involved the applicable law will be the *lex situs*, *i.e.* the law of the place where the property is situated or "in accordance with the law which would have been applicable if the deceased had died domiciled in Ireland."[39] As was said by the Master of the Rolls in *In re Rea: Rea v. Rea*:[40]

"In the case of immoveable property of whatever tenure the *lex loci sitae* ap-

---

[39] See Rules of the Superior Courts, Ord. 79, r.5(8).
[40] Above, n.7 at 461; See also *Freke v. Lord Carbery* L.R. 16 Eq. 461 at 466 *per* Lord Selborne.

plies, instead of the *lex domicilii*, the reason being that immoveable property, that is land or things appurtenant to land, forms part of the actual territory controlled by the law at that place, and by international comity and for manifest convenience is deemed to be, for the purposes of descent and inheritance, regulated by the *lex loci*."

In that case the deceased died intestate and domiciled in Ireland. He was married but had no children and left a widow surviving him. He owned real and personal property in Ireland and also owned land in Victoria, Australia. The only creditors he had were Irish. The law of Victoria provided that land devolved on a personal representative as personal property. A grant of letters of administration was made to his widow in Ireland in relation to his Irish property, and an Australian grant was made to a person especially appointed for that purpose. The personal representative in Victoria sold the land there and forwarded the proceeds of the sale to the widow of the deceased. By the law of Victoria a widow in such circumstances was entitled to a first charge of £1,000 with the residue being divided up between her and the next-of-kin. The widow brought an action against the heir-at-law claiming that she was entitled to her share in the deceased's estate both in Ireland and in Australia after the payments of his debts. The Master of the Rolls referred to the decision in *Freke v. Lord Carbery* [41] where it was said by Lord Selborne that: "Domicil is allowed in this country to have the same influence as in other countries in determining the succession of moveable estate, but the maxim of the law of the civilised world is *mobilia sequntur personam*, and is founded on the nature of things. When '*mobilia*' are in places other than that of the person to whom they belong, their accidental *situs* is disregarded, and they are held to go with the person. But land, whether held for a chattel interest or held for a freehold interest, is in nature, as a matter of fact, immoveable and not moveable." He went on to say: "I think, therefore, that the doctrine, which appears to me to be clearly the true doctrine, is recognized by necessary implication in those passages to which reference has been made, and *Story* says, with regard to some things, such as fixtures, which may or may not be moveable or immoveable, which are ambiguous in their nature, if they are at all connected with immoveable property, then it belongs to the law of the country in which the property is situate, to determine whether they shall be deemed moveable or immoveable." The Master of the Rolls thought that the necessary result of these principles was that the land in Australia passed in the mode prescribed by the law of that "colony," and that when in fact sold the net proceeds should be treated as "pure personalty."

15–15 The same principles determine intestate succession to moveables and immoveables: the law of the domicile regulates the succession rights to move-

---

[41] Above, n.40.

ables and the *lex situs* is the applicable law in relation to immoveables. The question of intestate succession to moveables arose in *Pipon v. Pipon*,[42] and even though it is an old case it succinctly sets out the law which is still applicable. In that case the intestate died in Jersey and at the time of his death £500 was owing to him in London. The plaintiffs, as personal representatives of the deceased, brought a bill for the distribution of the £500 according to the Statute of Car. 2, and the question was whether it should be distributable according to the laws of England in which case the plaintiffs would be entitled to part, or whether it should be distributed according to the laws of Jersey, where the intestate resided at the time of his death, in which case the plaintiffs would not be entitled to any part of the £500. Lord Hardwicke C. in the course of his judgment stated that the personal estate

> "follows the person, and becomes distributable according to the law or custom of the place where the intestate lived. As to the usage of taking out administration, that is only to give the party power to sue within such a jurisdiction, and does not any way determine the equitable right which the party has to its effects: this argument holds the same as to foreign countries, in relation to this question."

The personal estate of the deceased was distributable according to the laws of the country where his domicile was at the time of his death. The place of his residence at that time is *prima facie* his domicile, yet that may be rebutted by circumstances.[43] Jersey was the place of the deceased's domicile.

15–16   Section 73(1) of the Succession Act 1965 provides that in default of any person taking the estate of an intestate, the State shall take the estate as ultimate intestate successor. While in a domestic situation this may create no difficulties if there is no other person to succeed to the estate of the deceased, it may be a different matter where the deceased left property in a foreign country. In order for the State to lay claim to the moveable property of a deceased intestate under section 73 of the Succession Act it must first be established that the deceased died domiciled in this country. It is a different matter where the deceased leaves immoveable property since succession to immoveable property is governed by the *lex situs*, and accordingly, the law of the country in which the immoveable property is situated will determine the succession rights to it. The approach of the English courts to cases involving a claim by a foreign State to moveable property of the deceased may be illustrated by *In re Maldonado (deceased): State of Spain v. Treasury Solicitor*.[44] In that case the deceased was a Spanish national who died intestate and domiciled in Spain.

---

[42] Above, n.8.
[43] *Bemped v. Johnson* 3 Ves. 198; *Somerville v. Lord Somerville* 5 Ves. 750; *Munroe v. Douglass* 5 Madd. 379.
[1953] 2 All E.R. 300.

She left personal estate in England to which the State of Spain laid claim under Spanish law which provided that the State became entitled to the estate of an intestate where no other heirs existed. Barnard J. came to the conclusion that the State of Spain was not making itself the owner of property in England, nor was it seeking in any way to exercise its authority in England. It was merely claiming property in England, as heir to the property by Spanish law, in the same way as one of the next-of-kin might claim as heir. He felt satisfied that there was nothing either contrary to English public policy or repugnant to English law in permitting a foreign State to take possession of the moveables of one of its subjects in England.

15–17   In cases involving the legal right of the testator's spouse and provision for children under Part IX of the Succession Act 1965, the principles that succession to moveable property is regulated by the law of the domicile of the deceased and that succession to immoveable property is regulated by the *lex situs* are applicable in the same way as they are to cases involving wills and intestacies.[45] This question was considered by Kenny J. in *In the Goods of G.M.: F.M. v. T.A.M..*[46] In that case the testator died domiciled in Ireland. An adopted child of the testator applied to the court under section 117 of the Succession Act claiming that the testator had failed to make proper provision for him in accordance with his means. Included among the assets of the testator was a farm in England, and a question arose as to whether this property should be taken into account by the court when calculating the amount to which the adopted child was entitled. It was conceded, however, on the basis of the principles referred to above that estate for the purposes of Part IX did not include the farm in England. The court in deciding whether a testator has discharged his duty to make proper provision for his children in accordance with his means may however take into account the immoveable property owned by the testator in a foreign country. Therefore, the court when deciding whether the moral duty has been fulfilled must take all the testator's property into account, including the farm in England,

> "but if it decides that the duty has not been discharged, the provision for the child is to be made out of the estate excluding the immoveable property."

Kenny J. considered one-half of the estate to be proper provision, excluding the farm in England.

---

[45] *In the Goods of G.M.: F.M. v. T.A.M.*, above, n.9.
[46] Above, n.9.

THE CONSTRUCTION OF FOREIGN WILLS

15–18   Where moveables are concerned, a will is *prima facie* to be construed in accordance with the law of the testator's domicile. But this rule of construction may be departed from where it is shown that the testator made his will with reference to the laws of another country. The intention of the testator will determine whether this should be the case and the court is bound to give effect to his intention.[47] Furthermore, once a person makes a testamentary disposition the construction of it will not be altered by reason of any change in the testator's domicile after the making of such disposition.[48] In *In re Silar: Hurley v. Wimbush*[49] the testator left his residuary estate to certain named nephews and nieces in equal shares, and further provided that the share of any such nephew or niece who predeceased him should go to any child or children of such nephews or nieces at his death. One of the nephews who predeceased the testator was survived by an adopted child. Among the issues which the court had to determine was whether the will should be construed in accordance with Irish law or English law and whether the words 'child or children' included an adopted child. It was held by Budd J. that since a will is *prima facie* to be construed in accordance with the law of the testator's domicile, and since the testator died domiciled in Ireland, his will should *prima facie* be construed according to Irish law.[50]

15–19   In *In re Adams: Bank of Ireland Trustee Company Ltd. v. Adams*[51] the testator bequeathed all his property to his wife and by a codicil he left a legacy to the second defendant in the following terms:

> "I bequeath any sum of money standing in my name in whatever currency and any script or securities held on my behalf with Lloyd's Bank . . . Geneva, Switzerland, to Miss Carol Hutchings. . . ."

The second defendant submitted that the legacy to her in the codicil was broad enough to cover all monies standing in the name of the deceased wheresoever situated. Among other matters the court was asked to construe the terms of the legacy in the codicil. Budd J. held that the codicil was to be interpreted in accordance with the law intended by the testator. He reiterated that this law will *prima facie* be presumed to be the law of his domicile at the time when the codicil was made, but this was a mere canon of construction which will not be adhered to when there is any reason, from the nature of the will or otherwise, to suppose that the testator made it with reference to the laws of

---

[47] *In re Silar: Hurley v. Wimbush*, above, n.5; *In re Price: Tomlin v. Latter* [1900] 1 Ch. 442.
[48] Succession Act 1965, s.107 (1).
[49] Above, n.5.
[50] Above, n.5 at 361.
[51] Above, n.6.

another country. However, he accepted the view that the proposition is subject to the rule that material validity of the will and codicil was governed by the law of the testator's domicile at the date of his death.[52] Proceeding then to interpret the codicil according to the law intended by the testator, the nature of the indications given by him were considered. The codicil was in the English language and in the form appropriate to an Irish will or codicil, in that executors were appointed and it was attested in the Irish form. The executors were Irish companies. It was not in holograph form as required by French law. "Apart from the testator's anxiety to have his estate administered in Ireland it would appear to me that are sufficient indications contained in the will itself for me to come to the conclusion that it was the testator's intention that his will should be interpreted, as regards matters of construction, in accordance with Irish law."[53]

15–20   In relation to immoveables, O'Hanlon J. in *In re Bonnet: Johnston v. Langfield & Ors.*[54] referred to Dicey and Morris's *Conflict of Laws* (10th ed. 1980 Vol. 2 at 629) for the following statement:

> "It is clear that the *lex situs* determines what is included in a general devise of an estate, for instance, whether it means the lands and buildings thereon only or includes livestock or other moveables necessary for the work of the estate. Further, the use of technical language of the *lex situs* may indicate the intention that its law should govern the construction of the will."[55]

In *In re Bonnet: Johnston v. Langfield & Ors.*[56] the deceased was a German national and was domiciled in Germany at the date of her death. She left a will and codicil written in German whereby she left a farm in Ireland to 'the Protestant Church in Ireland.' The deceased and her husband formed a company, Alfred Bonnet Central Agencies Ltd., for the purpose of buying a farm. This farm was the main asset of the company. At the date of her death the deceased held all the shares in the company. Her will was drafted by a German notary who had no knowledge of the deceased's legal title to the farm. Two questions arose for consideration by the court: one, whether the gift in the will was a gift of shares in the company, and two, whether the gift to 'the Protestant Church in Ireland' was a gift to the Lutheran Church in Ireland. O'Hanlon J. found that the clause to be construed referred to a disposition of a farm and appeared at first sight to be a disposition of immoveables. There was some debate in the course of the hearing as to the proper law to be applied in construing this part of the will. Having referred to Dicey and Morris's *Conflict of Laws* (10th ed., Vol. 2) for the statement that the *lex situs* determines what is to be included in

---

[52] *Whicker v. Hume* 7 H.L. Cas. 1124; *Re Annesley: Dividson v. Annesley*, above, n.32.
[53] Above, n.6 at 459.
[54] Above, n.12 at 361.
[55] See *Lushington v. Sewell* 1 Sim. 435; *Stewart v. Garnett* 3 Sim. 398.
[56] Above, n.12.

a general devise of an estate and to *Re Adams: Bank of Ireland Trustee Company Ltd. v. Adams*[57] where Budd J. construed a codicil dealing with money and securities in accordance with Irish law even though the testator was domiciled in France at the time of making the codicil after deducing that it was the testator's intention that it should be so construed from a number of circumstances, O'Hanlon J. did not feel obliged to choose between German law and Irish law in the construction of the will before him since he was satisfied from the evidence that the German legal code applied the same primary principle of construction, *viz.* a will is to be construed in accordance with the intention of the testator.

15–21   Where a will purports to exercise a power of appointment it will also be valid as regards form so far as it exercises a power of appointment, if its form complies with the law governing the essential validity of the power and will not be treated as invalid by reason only that its form is not in accordance with formal requirements contained in the instrument creating the power.[58] However, so far as the appointment of immoveables is concerned, it would appear that the formalities required by the *lex situs* must be complied with.[59] It was said by Andrews J., as far back as 1901, in *Murray v. Champernowne*[60] that:

> "It is settled law that the formalities required for the disposal by will, and the validity of a will, of immoveable property in Ireland, are governed by the testamentary law of Ireland (the *lex situs*) which, I think, must also apply to a testamentary appointment under a power."

In that case the deceased in 1853 vested real estate owned by him in Ireland and also a sum of money in the trustees of a marriage settlement to sell the real estate and to hold the proceeds of the sale and the sum of money on trust for such person or persons for such estates and interests and in such manner as the deceased should by deed or by his will appoint. In 1862, the deceased while domiciled in Scotland made a will in accordance with the Wills Act, but not in accordance with Scottish law, leaving all the rest of his real estate to his wife for life and also appointing her as residuary legatee. He died in 1865, and in 1866, his executor obtained a grant of probate of the will. His wife died in 1897 having made a will appointing her executor as residuary legatee. The deceased's real estate in Ireland remained unsold. An action was brought to revoke the grant of probate of the deceased's will on the grounds that his will was invalid by Scottish law and that the power made under it was not validly executed. Andrews J. was of the opinion that, if the lands in Ireland were to be

---

[57] Above, n.6.
[58] Succession Act 1965, s.104(1) and (2).
[59] Succession Act 1965, s.102(1)(e).
[60] Above, n.12 at 236.

regarded as immoveables, the will of 1862 was a valid testamentary appointment of the beneficial interest in those lands and in the case of a subsequent
sale under the trusts of 1853 the appointee would be entitled to the proceeds of
the sale.

ISSUES FOR THE *LEX FORI*

15–22   Where a foreign will containing foreign elements is brought before
the court any element of a substantive nature will be determined by reference
to the relevant foreign law and any element of a procedural or evidential character will be determined by the *lex fori*.[61] For instance, any question relating
to the testamentary capacity of a testator will be deemed to be a substantive
issue, while any question involving the onus of proof or the knowledge and
approval by a testator of the contents of his will will be deemed to be a procedural or evidential issue. Such issues were considered in *In the Estate of Fuld
(No. 3)*.[62] In that case the deceased was born in Germany in 1921. He went to
live in Canada and in 1946 he became a Canadian national. After 1946 he
resided in England. In July 1961, he made a will in England in accordance
with English law. In October 1961, he made the first codicil to his will in
Germany in a form recognised by both English and German law. In November
1961, he made a second codicil while in a nursing home in London but which
was not duly executed, and a third codicil in compliance with English law.
While in Germany he made a fourth codicil in February 1962. In March 1962,
he died in Germany. Proceedings were instituted challenging the validity of
the third and fourth codicils, and a question arose as to which law governed
their validity taking into account such matters as formal validity, testamentary
capacity, knowledge and approval and undue influence. The will and first codicil were not impugned. Scarman J. (as he then was) considered the question of
the formal validity of a will as one of substantive law and fell to be determined
by the law of the domicile. Although Scarman J. did remark that the testator
died too soon to take the benefit of the U.K. Wills Act 1963 which broadened
considerably the laws which may govern the formal validity of a will, similar
to Part VIII of the Succession Act 1965. In relation to the capacity of a testator, he stated that the general rule was clear that such an issue was for the law
of the domicile to determine.[63] He considered that the principle of knowledge
and approval to be evidential in character and to be viewed by the English
court as part of its *lex fori*, if the facts of the case are such as to call for its
application. On the question of undue influence, he thought that it required no
analysis "to support the assertion that the law which defines the nature and

---

[61] *In the Estate of Fuld (No.3)*, above, n.13.
[62] Above, n.13.
[63] *In the Goods of Maraver* 1 Hag. Ecc. 498.

consequence of undue influence is part of the substantive law of wills."[64] He was also of the opinion that where two systems of law differ as to the incidence of proof the domestic court must follow the *lex fori*. He concluded that: (i) formal validity was to be determined by German law, (ii) on a true comparison between English and German law each treated testamentary capacity as a substantive issue and attaches the same meaning to it, and (iii) on the question of proof, the *lex fori* must apply.

15–23 An issue raised during the course of a trial relating to a will containing a foreign element may be treated by the court as a discretionary matter. For instance, where a litigant party speaks a foreign language only, the court may have to decide whether he should be facilitated by having the testimony of witnesses translated into his language as it is given, or whether he should have the assistance of an interpreter only. This matter was considered by Scarman J. in *In the Estate of Fuld*.[65] In that case one of the parties to the action who was suspected of fraud was unable to speak or understand English. He was a German. He was initially allowed legal aid but this was subsequently withdrawn. As a result he could not afford legal representation or the costs of an interpreter. He sought leave of the court to have the evidence translated into German during the course of the proceedings. Scarman J. thought that matter was entirely one of discretion although it should be balanced against the rights of other parties to the proceedings to have the proceedings concluded as expeditiously as possible. However, although the court had the discretion for this to be done, he "would hesitate long before exercising it, particularly in the present case." He decided that the evidence should not be translated as it was given. The rights of natural justice having been accorded to the applicant by being allowed to have an interpreter in court who would make it possible for him to follow the evidence.

15–24 A question peculiar to domestic law may also be raised during the course of a trial involving a will containing a foreign element and as such must be decided in accordance with domestic law. For instance, where a question of privilege is raised concerning the production of a document in evidence which contains evidence of the circumstances surrounding the due execution of a will or codicil, the court may not regard such document as truly privileged and may treat the information contained in it as being necessary to the court when deciding whether a testamentary instrument has been duly executed.[66] In *In the Estate of Fuld* (No. 2)[67] the executor of a will and a codicil,

---

[64] Above, n.13 at 781.

[65] Above, n.13.

[66] *In the Estate of Fuld (No. 2)*, above, n.13; See also Crawford and *Hogan v. Tracy, Lovegrove and O'Mahony*, unreported, High Court, November 4, 1998, O'Sullivan J.

[67] Above, n.13.

who was one of the defendants, claimed privilege for three documents. Under the general law the documents were within legal professional privilege, being statements of a witness made at the request of the executor's solicitors for the purpose of the action. The witness had in his possession at the hearing copies of two of the three documents. An objection was made to the production of the documents. The witness's evidence was in relation to the execution of the codicil. Scarman J. observed that in a probate action there appeared to be a conflict between the right of the court to know everything that its witness knows about execution, and the right of a litigant party to claim privilege in respect of communications passing between the witness and him or his solicitor for the purpose of collecting evidence with a view to a trial. However, where such a conflict arose it had to be resolved in favour of the court, although in reality there should be no such conflict because the court in its inquisitorial capacity is seeking the truth as to execution. The litigant parties concerning the issue of execution will be viewed as assisting the court in its search for the truth. Therefore, it was held by Scarman J., that "if the court comes to the conclusion that the truth can be discovered only by asking a witness to produce earlier statements that he may have made in writing concerning execution, the court is entitled to insist on seeing those statements, and I so rule."[68] The judgment of Scarman J. was referred to by Sullivan J. in the course of his judgment in *Crawford and Hogan v. Tracy, Lovegrove and O'Mahony*[69] a case involving a claim of privilege by the executors of the deceased for certain documents.

SUMMARY

15–25   Where a grant is made by a foreign court the administration of the deceased's estate must be conducted in accordance with the law of the foreign country in which the grant was made for such estate of the deceased as is situated in the foreign country. Where the deceased has left property in Ireland a grant may be made to his foreign personal representative in compliance with Order 79, rule 5(8) of the Rules of the Superior Courts to administer the deceased's Irish estate and the same must be undertaken in accordance with Irish law. However, where a grant is made to an Irish personal representative in relation to the deceased's estate in Ireland the right of the Irish personal representative to such estate will prevail over the right of the deceased's foreign personal representative who derives his authority from a foreign court. But where a foreign personal representative brings assets of the deceased into this country his title to such assets will be recognised by the Irish court.

---

[68] Above, n.13 at 659.
[69] Above, n.66.

15–26   Although the making of an Irish grant will require the estate of the deceased to be administered in accordance with Irish law in relation to property left by him in this country, the succession rights to his moveables will be regulated by the law of the domicile at the time of his death. The succession rights to immoveables left by him in Ireland will be regulated by Irish law as the *lex situs*. Where a grant is sought to the immoveable estate of the deceased situated in Ireland it may be made by the probate officer in accordance with the law which would have been applicable if the deceased had died domiciled in Ireland.[70]

15–27   Where the Irish court is asked to determine the domicile of the deceased at the date of his death it will do so in accordance with the requirements of Irish law notwithstanding any decision on the matter by a foreign court. Furthermore, the way by which succession rights are acquired whether by will, on an intestacy or by statute, will not affect the law which regulates such rights as it is the nature of the property which determines the law which regulates such rights and not the way by which such rights are acquired.

15–28   Where a will containing a foreign element is required to be construed by the Irish court, *prima facie*, it will be construed in accordance with the law of the deceased's domicile at the time when he made his will subject only to a contrary intention appearing in his will. Where a deceased testator intended that his moveables be regulated by the law of a country other than that of domicile, his intention that this should be so will prevail and his will will be construed accordingly. However, a will disposing of immoveables will continue to be construed in accordance with the *lex situs*.

15–29   In any legal proceedings involving the estate of a deceased and containing a foreign element, substantive matters will be determined by reference to the relevant foreign law and procedural or evidential matters will be determined by the *lex fori*.

---

[70] See Rules of the Superior Courts, Ord. 79, r.5(8)(b).

Index